Defending Taiwan

Defending Taiwan

Essays on Deterrence, Alliances, and War

Edited by
Kori Schake
Allison Schwartz

AEI PRESS

Publisher for the American Enterprise Institute
WASHINGTON, DC

ISBN-13: 978-0-8447-5058-3 (Paperback)
ISBN-13: 978-0-8447-5059-0 (eBook)

Library of Congress Cataloging in Publication data have been applied for.

Cover image: AP Photo/Daniel Ceng

AEI PRESS

Publisher for
**American Enterprise Institute
for Public Policy Research**
1789 Massachusetts Avenue, NW
Washington DC, 20036
www.aei.org

Printed in the United States of America

Contents

Foreword

KORI SCHAKE

This book grew out of the American Enterprise Institute (AEI) Foreign and Defense Policy team's weekly conversations on issues of the day. In the fall of 2021, those conversations centered on comments by President Joe Biden that seemed to recast the American policy of ambiguity about Taiwanese independence and, further, state that the US was committed to the defense of Taiwan.[1]

As a community of scholars devoted to the principles of defending human dignity, expanding economic opportunity, and making the world a freer and safer place, we at AEI believe US policy rightly belongs on the side of people seeking freedom. We were concerned, however, that the president appeared not to know the fundamentals of his own administration's policy, nor did he seem cognizant of his statements' potential to unsettle the issue in ways that might endanger Taiwan. Moreover, in the aftermath of President Biden's abandonment of Afghanistan, we worried he was provoking China without being genuinely committed to protecting Taiwan.

The White House quickly released a statement to walk back the president's comments: "The president was not announcing any change in our policy and there is no change in our policy"; this statement was reaffirmed by the secretary of defense and the State Department.[2] We regret that no one in the administration took the opportunity to build public understanding on the issue of China's threats to Taiwan and why Taiwan deserves America's support and protection. That context will be essential for ensuring America has the diplomatic, economic, and military capability for preventing China from attacking Taiwan, rallying international support for Taiwan's safety and autonomy, and defending Taiwan should deterrence fail.

The vocation and great fun of think tank work is providing explanations and policy recommendations that shape public attitudes and administration policies. The chapters in this book have been written to do what the president has not: explain to Americans why the US should care about Taiwan's sovereignty, what it means for the international order that has made us safe and prosperous if we do not defend the principles on which that order relies, and what it would take to successfully protect Taiwan from Chinese predation—either an outright attack or subversions that might collapse its ability to defend itself.

The scholars of AEI's Foreign and Defense Policy team disagree on some important issues regarding Taiwan, such as whether the threat of Chinese invasion is more acute in the near term or the Chinese Communist Party's reticence to attempt and fail at taking control of Taiwan makes the threat longer term. Nevertheless, the chapters all reflect a commitment to our values of defending human dignity and building a freer and safer world—in this instance, as it relates to Taiwan.

The chapters in this book are designed to identify major questions about Taiwan's security and provide trenchant analysis and data to inform American and allied national security policies. In this second edition of the book, we've added two new chapters, important work that has been undertaken since the original publication: Dan Blumenthal and Frederick W. Kagan's assessment of China's campaign to regain Taiwan and Blake Herzinger's analysis of the worrisome divergence of operational planning by Taiwan and the US. We intend for this book's chapters to inform policy development and deliberation—to help policymakers determine how to hedge against the uncertainty of China's intentions and timetable; build the military capabilities necessary to deter and, if needed, defeat a Chinese attack on Taiwan; and develop the alliance relationships that facilitate peace and stability in Asia.

In the first chapter, Michael Rubin explores the history of China's claim to control over Taiwan, concluding that "the historical reality is that the 'One China' concept is a lie." He traces the linguistic roots of Taiwan (or "Formosa," as it was known), the ethnic identity of Taiwan's earliest inhabitants, and the political mythmaking of a constructed Sino-centric history that excludes Portuguese, Spanish, Dutch, and Japanese involvement. He also deconstructs the legal case for Chinese control of Taiwan, concluding,

> Beijing may dispute Taiwan's sovereignty and the legitimacy of its government, but two facts remain: First, periods in which governance in Taiwan is distinct from the mainland are greater than the time the two have had united authority. And second, the People's Republic has never had sovereignty in Taiwan.

Giselle Donnelly tracks changing American evaluations of China since 2000 in the history of the Pentagon's China military report. She laments that "the larger intent—to frame America's defense investments—has not been realized" and concludes that the Pentagon report has been a trailing indicator of Chinese capabilities, slow to acknowledge the nature of Chinese strategy and its force structure advances: "The China report has produced a conventional-wisdom consensus about the dark side of China's rise, but that has yet to translate into appreciable action."

Blumenthal and Kagan's chapter is the beginning of a larger project assessing China's campaign for regaining control of Taiwan, outlining three roads to success for China: persuasion, coercion, and compellence. Blumenthal and Kagan assess that China prefers to regain control of Taiwan by persuasion and coercion, targeting the will of Taiwan, the US, and America's allies to support and defend the island. They caution that

> the increasingly myopic focus on the supposedly imminent Chinese invasion threat can seriously hinder or prevent entirely the development and implementation of such a strategy. This outcome may be in part what China seeks.

Blumenthal and Kagan argue the US counterinvasion strategy needs to incorporate a counter-isolation strategy.

Elisabeth Braw evaluates the prospects for China winning over Taiwan without fighting, by effectively using gray-zone warfare. She catalogs Chinese politically motivated restrictions of market access to numerous countries and points out Taiwan's particular vulnerability, given the proportion of exports it sends to China and the openness of Taiwanese society. She concludes that aggression in the gray zone would be far more attractive to China than a military assault, primarily because China would incur minimal loss of blood or treasure. It would also be attractive because the Taiwanese government and public would struggle to determine whether a concerted gray-zone campaign against their country was taking place.

Michael Beckley, Zack Cooper, and Allison Schwartz explore how to deter China from attacking Taiwan. They identify trends making conflict more or less likely—with political dynamics and military imbalances making it more likely, while Taiwan's geography and technological innovation reduce the likelihood—and ask, "Can the United States use geographic and technological asymmetries to offset the Taiwan Strait's worsening political and military situations?" They posit and evaluate four different Chinese attacks, concluding, "Chinese leaders can only control Taiwan through an inherently risky full-scale invasion." They recommend, "The United States should shift to a denial strategy to prevent China from controlling waters and airspace along and within the first island chain," and they identify defense choices in readiness, modernization, force structure, and force posture needed to better deter China from attacking Taiwan.

Hal Brands and Beckley share concern that the US is anticipating a short, sharp, geographically localized war over Taiwan—but is preparing for the wrong kind of war:

> [The war] would expand and escalate as both countries look for paths to victory in a conflict they feel they cannot afford to lose. It would present severe war-termination dilemmas and involve far higher risks of going nuclear than many Americans realize. If Washington doesn't start preparing to wage, and then end, a protracted conflict now, it could face catastrophe once the shooting starts.

They assess how the Pentagon's planning revolves around a conflict of extended duration, especially since "in hegemonic wars—clashes for dominance between the world's strongest states—the stakes are high because the future of the international system is at issue, and the price of defeat may seem prohibitive." They describe the dangerous dynamics of great-power wars historically, the added complexity of great-power war in the nuclear age, and the difficulty of war termination. Brands and Beckley recommend amassing key weapons stockpiles to "win the race to reload," demonstrating through preparations the grit to endure losses, threatening retaliation, containing escalation, and being prepared for "defining victory down" to the status quo ante.

Donnelly's second chapter recommends widening the aperture of Taiwan's defense to introduce asymmetries beneficial to defending Taiwan. She reviews the literature about strategy, concluding that "the horizontal spaces—the boundaries of conflict, locations of targets and bases, elimination of sanctuaries, and even violations of neutrality—deserve more attention in the geostrategic competition with Beijing." This horizontal escalation would prevent China's proximate advantages from being determinative by expanding the geographic scope of any potential conflict. Donnelly reviews prospects for greater involvement by India, Japan, and South Korea in "uncertainty-creating and cost-imposing gambits," and she evaluates Beijing's attempts to sustain its strategic focus. She concludes that

> if Taiwan is to survive a savage opening salvo, it will be up to the United States to intervene rapidly, effectively, and directly.
>
> Yet were such a scenario to play out, it must be clear that these are the first shots in a long conflict and only part of an enduring great-power competition that will take decades to play out.

Olivia Garard mines her deep expertise on Carl von Clausewitz for her chapter on the inherently superior strength of defensive alliances. Clausewitz considered defensive allies *"essentially interested in maintaining* the integrity of the country"; Garard's insight is that "these allies are not accidental to the circumstances; these allies arise from the nature of the defensive form of war." Their preference is for the status quo. She connects this with Aristotle's typology of friendships, Rebecca Lissner and Mira Rapp-Hooper's writing on the importance of shared values in US alliances, Alexander Nehamas's work on the temporal element (that is, permanency) of friendship, and Jesse Glenn Gray's work on the necessity of military comradery, culminating with Clausewitz's observation that "people who complain about the ineffectiveness of coalitions do not know what they want; what better way is there to resist a stronger power?" And that, Garard concludes, makes Taiwan merit America's defending—and makes the shared values of the West the strongest basis for Taiwan's defense.

Cooper and Sheena Chestnut Greitens are skeptical the US could substantially increase allied and partner participation, worrying that "divergent expectations about allied involvement could not only threaten Washington's relationships with key allies but also undermine America's ability to deter a contingency with China in the first place." They explore four discrete scenarios, concluding that in contingencies involving a direct invasion, even the countries most likely to commit forces (Japan and Australia) would likely prefer defensive roles—to be shields rather than spears. Even allowing basing access for US forces is likely to be politically difficult, especially for the Philippines, Singapore, South Korea, and Thailand. The US should not expect force contributions beyond those partners, even from countries concerned about China, especially if the conflict proves protracted. Their policy recommendations include avoiding disputes over basing, seeking clarity with allies about nuclear posture, developing capabilities to survive a protracted blockade, and procuring smaller and more-survivable conventional systems.

Herzinger explains that Taipei and Washington have markedly divergent views on how to best defend Taiwan against a hypothetical Chinese invasion and that "differing opinions about how to prosecute the war will inhibit effective operations and hobble the war effort." Taiwan's strategy has focused on high-end platforms, but its "force structure is not one that will complement or enable US intervention." He concludes that

> Neutralizing the PLA's [People's Liberation Army's] center of gravity—the element without which it cannot successfully take Taiwan—should be the objective of Taiwan's defense strategy. Rather than promoting continued investment in tools to fight a battle on Taiwan's territory, the [Taiwanese Overall Defense Concept] correctly identified the crossing of the Taiwan Strait as the most precarious and vulnerable moment for the PLA

with naval, and specifically amphibious, forces as that center of gravity. A strategy that focuses on destroying those ships before the PLA's forces can hit the beach is the one that keeps Taiwan free.

That requires large numbers of more expendable systems. Recent US legislation allowing greater drawdown authority and Foreign Military Financing gives the means for bringing Taiwan's strategy back into alignment with the US. But like other AEI scholars, Herzinger cautions that "the US defense industrial base is perhaps the most glaring weakness in making this plan a reality."

Elaine McCusker and Emily Coletta review the readiness of the US military to defend Taiwan, identifying in detail four main barriers to success:

1. Defense is not a priority for the current administration, demonstrated by the fiscal year (FY) 2022 budget request and further emphasized with an FY23 budget proposal for defense that does not keep pace with rising inflation.

2. Delays in annual appropriations and authorizations reduce buying power, hinder readiness, and delay the pursuit of a competitive advantage.

3. The definition of defense has been expanded to allow for diversion of defense resources and diffusion of attention to nondefense priorities.

4. Institutional and statutory rules and processes do not promote speed and agility in testing, procuring, and integrating modern capabilities.

They recommend an evolutionary approach to modernization to begin breaking down these barriers and for the US to position itself to be capable of defending Taiwan.

Mackenzie Eaglen and John G. Ferrari also observe with concern the narrowing of American military advantages and recommend specific programmatic investments in conventional capabilities that would provide an edge in a range of Taiwan deterrence and conflict scenarios. Recommendations include:

1. Securing US Air Force air superiority across legacy and modernized systems, such as hypersonic missiles;

2. Increasing Army troop and funding levels, protecting both from budget sacrifices for the other services;

3. Expanding the US naval fleet and domestic production capacity; and

4. Ensuring Joint Force investments in regional posturing, air and missile defense, and intelligence, surveillance, and reconnaissance (ISR) are bolstered across services.

They also criticize the Biden administration's FY2023 defense budget request for largely ignoring the modernization needs relevant for near-term Taiwan contingencies.

Klon Kitchen's chapter addresses the role cyber operations could play in a Chinese attack on Taiwan. He assesses them as central to Chinese doctrine, "both 'a domain in which war occurs' and 'the central means to wage military conflict.'" He describes China's Strategic Support Force and its operational concepts as "a collection of ceaseless activities only varying in intensity based on political requirements." Taiwan should expect offensive cyberattacks in peacetime to "manipulate, disrupt, or destroy networks, infrastructure, and daily life," and in wartime to prevent communications networks and government services from functioning. The US should anticipate cyberattacks meant to impede US military responses. He concludes, "Taiwan is catastrophically vulnerable to Chinese cyber aggression," and he recommends engaging in more intensive joint cyberwar exercises, allowing US access to Taiwanese systems, and removing American companies' artificial intelligence research from China.

Paul Wolfowitz draws on the history of the Korean War for lessons on deterring Chinese aggression against Taiwan. In particular, he emphasizes how the unexpected consequences of that war strengthened the West: creation of NATO's integrated military command, increased US defense spending from $133 billion to $402 billion in four years, adoption of the more militarized containment recommended by NSC-68, and creation of the US-Taiwan mutual defense treaty of 1954. He concludes, "In the case of a [People's Republic of China] attack on Taiwan, one obvious concern would be that Japan or even South Korea might reconsider its nuclear nonproliferation commitments and reliance on the US to provide nuclear deterrence." For the US, the lesson should be that "the Korean War was preventable, if only the US had made clear beforehand that it would force-fully oppose North Korean aggression." He also draws on work by Blumenthal that recommends a strategic framework for US-Taiwanese relations.

We at AEI hope you find this book useful as you think your way through the demanding problems of defending Taiwan—and the consequences for American security if we should fail to do so.

Notes

1. Kevin Liptak, "Biden Says Taiwan's Independence Is Up to Taiwan After Discussing Matter with Xi," CNN, November 16, 2021, https://www.cnn.com/2021/11/16/politics/biden-china-taiwan/index.html; and David E. Sanger, "Biden Said the U.S. Would Protect Taiwan. But It's Not That Clear-Cut," *New York Times*, October 22, 2021, https://www.nytimes.com/2021/10/22/us/politics/biden-taiwan-defense-china.html.

2. Sanger, "Biden Said the U.S. Would Protect Taiwan."

Maps

Figure 1. The First and Second Island Chains

The first island chain is a string of islands central to America's Indo-Pacific defensive posture. The second island chain contains the US island territory of Guam.

Source: US Department of Defense, Office of the Secretary of Defense, *Annual Report to Congress: Military and Security Developments Involving the People's Republic of China, 2011*, 2011, 23, https:// dod.defense.gov/Portals/1/Documents/pubs/2011_CMPR_Final.pdf; and Terrence K. Kelly et al., *Employing Land-Based Anti-Ship Missiles in the Western Pacific*, RAND Corporation, 2013, xv, https:// www.rand.org/content/dam/rand/pubs/technical_reports/TR1300/TR1321/RAND_TR1321.sum.pdf.

Figure 2. US Indo-Pacific Command's Area of Responsibility

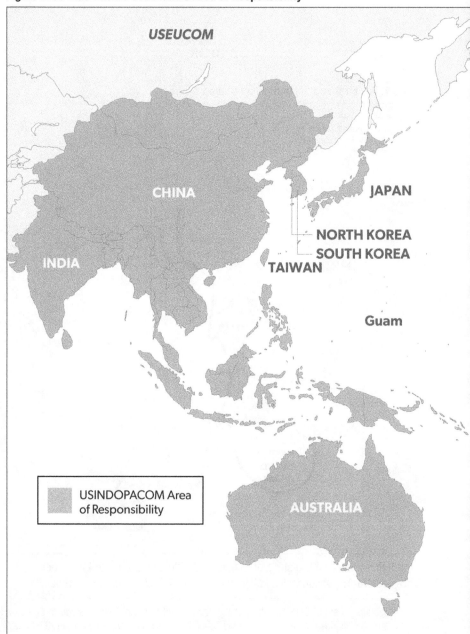

Note: This map shows all or part of the territory of US Indo-Pacific Command (USINDOPACOM), US European Command (USEUCOM), and US Northern Command (USNORTHCOM).

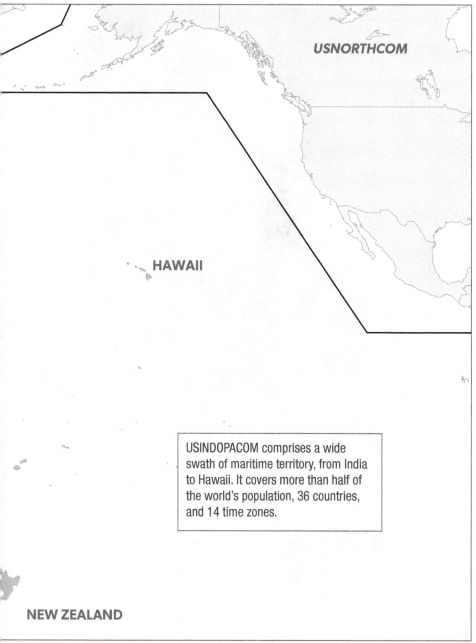

USNORTHCOM

HAWAII

USINDOPACOM comprises a wide swath of maritime territory, from India to Hawaii. It covers more than half of the world's population, 36 countries, and 14 time zones.

NEW ZEALAND

Source: US Indo-Pacific Command, "USINDOPACOM," https://www.pacom.mil/Portals/55/Images/USINDOPACOM-MAP-H1_Oct-2018.jpg.

Figure 3. The Chinese Missile Threat

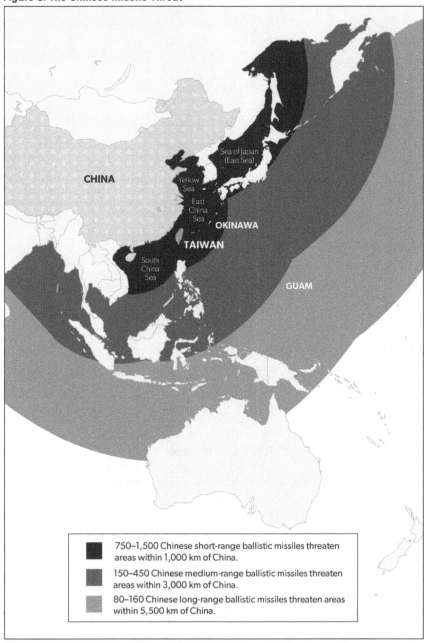

750–1,500 Chinese short-range ballistic missiles threaten areas within 1,000 km of China.

150–450 Chinese medium-range ballistic missiles threaten areas within 3,000 km of China.

80–160 Chinese long-range ballistic missiles threaten areas within 5,500 km of China.

Source: Center for Strategic and International Studies, Missile Defense Project, "China's Ballistic & Cruise Missiles," April 19, 2017, https://missilethreat.csis.org/missile-maps-infographics/#jp-carousel-6273.

Figure 4. Most At-Risk Taiwanese Islands

CHINA

Taiwan Strait

Taipei

Quemoy

Pescadores
Islands

TAIWAN

Pratas Islands

There are various islands governed by Taiwan that would be at immediate risk in the event of a Chinese invasion. These island groups include Quemoy, the Pescadores Islands, and the Pratas Islands.

Source: American Enterprise Institute.

Figure 5. Disputed Islands in the South China Sea

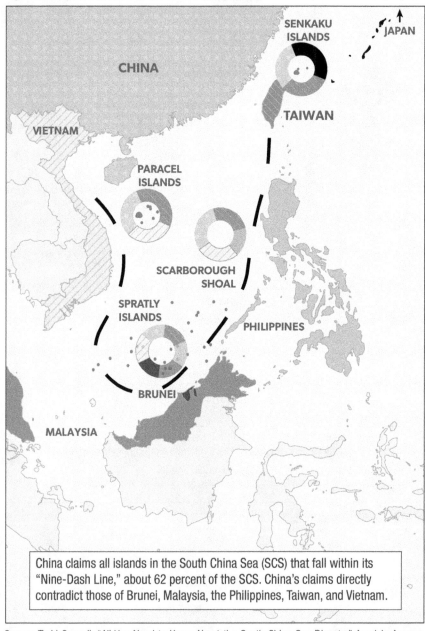

China claims all islands in the South China Sea (SCS) that fall within its "Nine-Dash Line," about 62 percent of the SCS. China's claims directly contradict those of Brunei, Malaysia, the Philippines, Taiwan, and Vietnam.

Source: Todd Crowell, "All You Need to Know About the South China Sea Dispute," Anadolu Agency, April 8, 2015, https://www.aa.com.tr/en/politics/all-you-need-to-know-about-the-south-china-sea-dispute/19877.

Is Taiwan Part of China?

MICHAEL RUBIN

That Taiwan is an inalienable part of China remains a sine qua non of Beijing's diplomacy. Since Mao Zedong proclaimed the People's Republic of China (PRC) on October 1, 1949, no Communist Chinese leader has brokered any compromise on the issue.

Speaking to the Supreme State Council in 1958, Mao declared, "Taiwan is ours, and we will never compromise on this issue, which is an issue of internal affairs."[1] He warned the United States that the only way to avoid a catastrophic defeat was to withdraw from the island. Just a year later, when he met Soviet Premier Nikita Khrushchev, Mao reiterated, "Taiwan is an internal PRC issue."[2]

Across the decades, Chinese Communist policy has been diplomatically, economically, and culturally fluid. The experience of the mainland Chinese under Mao's rule and during the Cultural Revolution differed wildly from their aspirations under Deng Xiaoping, and Xi Jinping, the current leader, abrogates the social compacts and diplomatic agreements signed by his predecessors. But through it all, the PRC's position has remained consistent on Taiwan: As the Chinese Foreign Ministry website still declares, "Taiwan is a sacred and inseparable part of China's territory."[3]

Chinese leaders might hope that repetition will breed acceptance, but the historical reality is that the "One China" concept is a lie. While American policymakers in pursuit of compromise and détente with the PRC have wavered over the decades in their commitment to Taiwan, the reality is that mainland China's historical and legal claims to Taiwan do not stand up to scrutiny.

What's in a Name?

Taiwan lies approximately 100 miles off the coast of mainland China, but for much of Chinese history, it might as well have been 1,000 miles away. Before the early 17th century, there was no appreciable Chinese control of—let alone interest in—Taiwan. Theories regarding the island's very name reflect this.

There is no consensus about the roots of the name "Taiwan." In 1937, the Japanese scholar Akiyoshi Abe, of the Aboriginal Languages Research Institute of Taihoku, speculated the word to be a bastardization of the Taiwanese aboriginal words *taian* and *tayoan*, which meant "foreigners" or "aliens" and likely referred to Chinese settlers.[4] The Dutch may have been pragmatic and simply adopted the name after Tayouan island, where the Dutch built Fort Zeelandia in what is now the Anping District of Tainan.[5]

Another theory is that the name derives from the Chinese for a "bent dais rising from the river," but this ignores that the resulting Chinese word would then be *wan-tai* rather than *tai-wan*. Likewise, the notion that "Taiwan" comes from the Chinese for "terraced bay" falls flat, as there is no obvious candidate for such a feature on the island.[6]

Others speculate that the word is a bastardization of the Chinese *tung hwan*, or "eastern barbarians." Indeed, from the perspective of mainland Chinese, Taiwan was always the "other." A Chinese chronicle from the third century BC refers to Taiwan as "I Chou," "a barbarous region to the East."[7] Until the seventh century AD, many Chinese cartographers confused the island with Okinawa (which is part of present-day Japan), hardly a sign of its historical centrality.[8]

Historically, other names stuck. The name "Formosa" was an invention of 16th-century Portuguese traders who, struck by the island's beauty, christened it "Ilha Formosa"—"beautiful island."[9] Spaniards who briefly colonized the northern coast simply used the Spanish equivalent, "Isla Hermosa." Aborigines in the south of the island, meanwhile, often called their home "Pekan," a word that means a "haven gained after long wandering." This, in turn, highlights the divergent origins of those who call Taiwan home and came to the island far earlier and from greater distances than did Han settlers coming from across the Taiwan Strait.[10]

Are Taiwanese Chinese?

In 1978, a debate about what constituted native literature transcended Taiwanese academe and sparked a broader debate in Taiwan about whether Taiwanese and Chinese identities were mutually exclusive.[11] The issue remains a cultural and political fault line in Taiwan today, surfacing in nearly every presidential election.

The preponderance of evidence suggests Taiwan is not Chinese. Many in Taiwan traditionally differentiated between *waishengren*, who migrated to Taiwan from China between the end of the Japanese occupation and the 1949 Communist victory on the mainland, and *benshengren*, or "people of this province." These could be both Han Chinese whose settlement predated World War II and those from the Minnan or Hakka ethnic groups.[12] There is a separate debate about how distinct the Minnan and Hakka are from each other, but there is no argument over whether they are distinct from the Han.[13]

If the Taiwanese do not share a common origin with the Han Chinese in the premodern period, then where did they come from? Two main theories exist about the population of both Taiwan and the islands of Southeast Asia.

From the 1970s until the 1990s, linguists proposed the "Out of Taiwan" theory, which posited two waves of migration. The first occurred during the Ice Age, around 50,000 years ago, when lower sea levels meant not only that Taiwan was connected to mainland China but also that much of Indonesia was joined by land to the Southeast Asian mainland. The sea level rise that accompanied the end of the Ice Age ultimately cut off these populations. Then, in the late Holocene, between 5,500 and 4,000 years ago, another population wave allegedly left Taiwan for what is now Indonesia, Malaysia, and the Philippines, as the population sought new land for rice cultivation, bringing the prototypical forms of the languages now spoken in these locations.

Beginning in 1998, however, multiple genetic studies returned to the question about the origins of Taiwan's peoples. Their findings question the notion that Taiwan served as a base for the dispersal of people across the region and instead suggest that climate change and the closing of land bridges led to differences in the evolution of various peoples and cultures.[14]

However, when researchers overlay genetic studies with linguistic and cultural traits, a different picture emerges in which there was a common ancestry among Taiwanese aborigines and the peoples of the islands of Southeast Asia, with only minor migrations in the late Holocene from both Southeast Asia and southern China to and through Taiwan.[15] These findings undermine the claims of some Chinese nationalists that Taiwan was always just an extension of China.

While scientists, linguists, and anthropologists may debate the timing and direction of migrations, what is beyond dispute is the great interplay over the centuries between Taiwan and the other islands of Southeast Asia and that Taiwan's native population has significant genetic and linguistic ties to peoples now living in Indonesia, Malaysia, and the Philippines.

In their pursuit of the "One China" policy and *Anschluss* with Taiwan, Chinese authorities have imposed an ideological and political prism through which Chinese researchers operate. Chinese academics date the colonization of Taiwan to an agricultural revolution among the Han: Over the centuries, a Han lust for new farmland led to a concerted effort to subjugate or force the migration of the Guizhou "barbarians" along their borders. The Guizhou fled south and west to what are now the Chinese provinces of Sichuan and Yunnan and northern Burma, Cambodia, Laos, and Vietnam. There is broad consensus that this migration marks the origin of the Yue people, who, over subsequent centuries, excelled at navigation and trade.

Chinese Communists are not the only ones to emphasize the connection between the Guizhou and some Taiwanese aborigines. In the 1950s, for example, historian Chang Chi-yun, who between 1954 and 1958 served as the Republic of China's education minister, cited common customs among the Guizhou and northern Taiwan's Atayal people to suggest that the Guizhou had not stopped on China's southern coast but instead continued their migration to Taiwan between the eighth and fifth centuries BC.[16]

Even if this is true, it does not create a basis for contemporary Chinese claims over the island; otherwise, Malaysia could make a similar claim. As India grew militarily and culturally stronger in the first four centuries AD, its commanders and princes traveled across Southeast Asia, the Philippines, and the Indonesian archipelago, often establishing petty kingdoms. This created a ripple effect of migration, as Malays chose to migrate rather than assimilate into the Indian interpolators' culture as the Indians increasingly demanded land. Ultimately, this led to an ethnic Malay colonization of southern Taiwan.[17]

Did China Govern Taiwan?

In his 1990 history *The Search for Modern China*, Jonathan Spence, long a doyen of Chinese studies, suggested that China's interest in Taiwan was a relatively recent phenomenon. "The integration of Taiwan into China's history dates from the early seventeenth century," he observed.[18] Most Chinese at the time still avoided the island, writing it off as an inhospitable place blighted by malaria and battered by storms and rough seas. Those who did make it to Taiwan faced aborigines hostile to exploration, let alone settlement and cultivation by mainlanders.

That said, there was some interplay. Some late Ming dynasty traders established small trading posts in the southwest, seeking to profit off deer hides and the powdered deer horns that were the Viagra of the day. Some Chinese and Japanese pirates would also seek shelter among the marshes and inlets of the southwestern Taiwanese coast.

Ming rulers were never able to defeat the pirates, but in the early 17th century, they decided to make common cause with them against their enemy, the Dutch settlers in southern Taiwan. The Ming court approached Cheng Chihlung, whom it appointed first commodore of the imperial fleet and then admiral, with responsibility to stamp out (others') piracy.[19] His son, Koxinga, became increasingly important to the Ming as the Manchus captured first Beijing, then Nanjing, and, in 1646, Fuzhou. Both the remaining Ming and Qing courted Koxinga, who maintained his fleet and ruled over an exclave along the southern Chinese coast.

While Koxinga repulsed numerous land attacks and even pressed several successful ones of his own, he understood time was against him and, by 1659, was looking to stage a retreat from his mainland base near Xiamen to Taiwan. Two years later, he launched his invasion, laying siege to Fort Zeelandia, the Dutch trading center on the southwestern coast. Finally, on February 1, 1662, the Dutch surrendered, retreating to Batavia (present-day Jakarta, Indonesia) and ceding Taiwan to Koxinga. To suggest that Koxinga's victory was Chinese, however, ignores that his mother was Japanese, something many Taiwanese readily point out.

It also ignores what followed: The Kangxi emperor—the Qing dynasty's third—assumed the throne in 1661, at age 6. He and the regents operating in his name sought to uproot the coastal population of mainland China, but it was not until 1683 that they forced Taiwan into submission. There followed a debate in the Qing court about what to do next. Admiral Shi wanted to fortify Taiwan to prevent a Dutch return. Other courtiers counseled abandoning the island altogether. "Taiwan is nothing but an isolated island on the sea far away from China, it has long since been a hideout of pirates, escaped convicts, deserters and ruffians, therefore, there is nothing to gain from retaining it," one report read.[20] The Qing deployed many of Koxinga's troops instead to northern China to counter Russian encroachment.

Even after Kangxi incorporated Taiwan as a prefecture of the Fujian province, with an 8,000-man garrison of Qing soldiers, he ordered that Chinese emigration to the island be limited.[21] In effect, the Qing quarantined Taiwan.[22] Certainly, the debate about Taiwan's status and Kangxi's ultimate ambivalence showed the general Chinese ambivalence toward, if not the othering of, Taiwan.

In 1721, Chu Yi-kuei, a native of the Zhangzhou prefecture in Fujian who had settled in Taiwan eight years earlier and until then led a fairly placid life raising ducks, headed a revolt against Qing rule after Wang Chen, the local magistrate, imposed a particularly harsh tax regime. The revolt quickly escalated. Chu and his rebel allies briefly took control of the island, although internal rivalries and a Qing counterattack from the mainland ultimately doomed his two-month rule.[23]

It was not the last rebellion against the Qing. In December 1731, Taiwan's aborigines revolted, joined quickly by Han immigrants on the island. This time, it took the Qing eight months to reassert control. The resistance to Chinese rule was so great that, by 1738, the governor restricted farming or settlement of aborigine lands and, the following year, restricted Han immigration to Taiwan.[24]

Over the next several decades, Han immigration nevertheless increased—much of it illegal. Still, this did not mean Chinese domination, especially as many Chinese continued to pay rent to aborigine landowners.

Nor did it end strife on the island. Communal violence erupted in 1782, and four years later, locals again rebelled against the Qing.

For Chinese officials today to look at Qing-era rule in Taiwan as proof that Taiwan is Chinese territory is hypocritical on another front: The Qing dynasty that established itself after Manchurian forces defeated the Ming was only the second major Chinese dynasty that the Han did not rule. While the Qing sought to prove themselves as more Chinese than the Ming were in terms of customs and practices during their reign, after Qing rule fractured, the Han Chinese argued that the Qing were really foreign interlopers. Chinese officials' efforts now to suggest that intermittent mainland rule in the 17th and 18th centuries proves China's right to incorporate Taiwan fall apart when Han leaders question the legitimacy of the Qing's pedigree.

Were the Chinese Alone in Influencing Taiwan?

While Beijing may amplify fleeting and incomplete Chinese rule of Taiwan during the Qing dynasty to justify current claims that Taiwan is part of "One China," such logic also falls flat given the longer duration of foreign rule in Taiwan than the duration of Chinese rule there. Long before Chinese authorities showed any interest in Taiwan, Portuguese sailors did. Their attention, however, was short-lived. Portugal's motivation was, like that of many other European powers, less conquest for its own sake but rather enrichment. Here, the prize was trade with mainland China. As the Portuguese consolidated control over and ultimately settled in Macao, they lost interest in investment in the more distant Taiwan.

What Portugal ignored, Spain did not. By the mid-16th century, the Spanish had already conquered most of the Philippines. Between 1626 and 1642, Spaniards established a small colony in the northern tip of Taiwan.

For the Dutch, this was unacceptable. The Dutch chartered the Dutch East India Company in 1602 and nine years later established a trading post in Batavia from which the company would ultimately coordinate its operations, which quickly expanded throughout the region. In 1622, after failing to oust the Portuguese from Macao, the Dutch seized the Pescadores Islands, just over 100 miles off the southeast coast of China. Skirmishing ensued between the Dutch, who erected a fort in the Pescadores, and Chinese forces from the mainland coastal province of Fujian.

Finally, in 1624, the Dutch East India Company came to an agreement with Fujian's governor, Shang Zhouzuo, for the Dutch to leave the Pescadores Islands, with the Ming in exchange recognizing Dutch ownership of Taiwan. The logic of the bargain was telling. Foreign presence in the Pescadores threatened the Ming. Taiwan, however, was too distant and barbarous to be their concern.[25] For the next 38 years, the Dutch governed much of southern Taiwan from Fort Zeelandia, expelled other foreigners who sought safe haven on the island, and, even after the 1662 fall of Fort Zeelandia, managed to maintain a presence in the northern town of Keelung until 1668.

So while the Spanish presence in Taiwan was never on the scale of the Dutch settlement there, given the Dutch history on Taiwan, the presence of any other foreign power was unacceptable to the Dutch East India Company, and fighting erupted. Dutch troops failed in their first attempts to oust the Spanish from Fort San Domingo, in what is today Taipei, but in 1642, they succeeded. In the 18th and early 19th centuries, other Europeans also ended up on the island, more by accident than design. Often, such encounters did not end well, with aborigines chaining and ultimately executing British sailors or other prisoners who sought refuge after mishaps at sea.

While neither the British nor French sought to colonize Taiwan, they were not indifferent to the island. After Qing officials illegally searched a British-flagged Chinese junk in Guangzhou on October 8, 1856, a diplomatic spat ensued, which escalated quickly. The British first seized Guangzhou and, as the Chinese continued to refuse British terms, eventually marched on Beijing itself before the Qing court accepted the Treaty of Tientsin, under which the Qing agreed to open four Taiwanese ports to foreign traders and allow Christian missionaries to proselytize. This led to the opening of a British consulate in Fort San Domingo.

Taiwan was of interest to not only European powers but Japan as well. Japanese seamen faced the same perils in Taiwan that their European counterparts did: When shipwrecked or forced to flee into a Taiwanese harbor, they often suffered gruesome attacks by aboriginal tribes. After Taiwan's Botan tribe massacred Japanese shipwreck survivors in December 1871 (ironically, believing the crew of the ill-fated *Miyako* were Chinese), the Chinese officials disavowed responsibility, stating that Chinese sovereignty on Taiwan itself only extended to the western flatlands and not the rugged and untamed central and eastern portion of the island.[26] That sovereignty was tenuous, as the French invasion of Taiwan against the backdrop of the 1884–85 Sino-French War demonstrated.

The French ultimately withdrew, but Japanese interest grew. In 1894, Chinese and Japanese troops faced off in Korea; Japanese forces prevailed. In the resulting Treaty of Shimonoseki, China ceded claims to both Taiwan and the Pescadores Islands "in perpetuity."[27] That Japanese control would continue through World War II, and it continues to imprint itself deeply on Taiwanese culture and society.

Put another way, Taiwan's separation from China occurred a half century before the dissolution of most of the British and French Empires. From a Taiwanese standpoint, the notion of returning to Beijing's control would be akin to Australia, which gained its independence in 1901, returning to the direct control of the United Kingdom or Algeria, which gained its independence from France in 1962, again becoming a French department. Every nation that colonized Taiwan left an imprint that, over the years, amplified Taiwan's differences with mainland Chinese culture, especially as Western powers and Japan sought to modernize the country in ways different from the mainland's development.

Is China's Legal Case Valid?

Chiang Kai-shek led the Republic of China from 1928 until his death in 1975. He may have been an American ally, but American officials questioned his competence and trustworthiness. This was a main reason Franklin D. Roosevelt's administration denied Chiang a seat at Yalta or Potsdam, as Allied leaders sought to chart Asia's future,[28] though at the 1943 Cairo Conference, Chiang got what he wanted. The joint declaration concluding that conference declared, "All the territories Japan has stolen from the Chinese, such as Manchuria, Formosa, and the Pescadores, shall be returned to the Republic of China."[29]

Nor can the PRC claim that the UN accepts Beijing's "One China" interpretation. While Secretary-General Kofi Annan created a UN "One China" policy out of whole cloth, the UN Charter does not give the secretary-general or the broader UN that power. This instead is the realm of international treaties, the last of which was the 1951 Treaty of San Francisco. To finalize peace with Japan, it declared, "Japan renounces all right, title and claim to Formosa and the Pescadores." The treaty did not transfer sovereignty to another state, however.[30]

Today, Chinese authorities argue that the Cairo Declaration awards them control over Taiwan.[31] In effect, however, this is just a legal syllogism based on their insistence that they are the sole representatives of China. While Roosevelt, British Prime Minister Winston Churchill, and Soviet Premier Joseph Stalin sought to revert Taiwan to China, at the time, they did not envision more than one China. After the victory of Chinese Communists on the mainland and the 1949 declaration of the PRC, the seat of the Republic of China mentioned in both the Cairo Declaration and the Supreme Commander for the Allied Powers' General Order No. 1 was the Republic of China, which had relocated its government to Taiwan.[32]

Beijing may dispute Taiwan's sovereignty and the legitimacy of its government, but two facts remain: First, periods in which governance in Taiwan is distinct from the mainland are greater than the time the two have had united authority. And second, the People's Republic has never had sovereignty in Taiwan. Ironically, on this, the Taiwanese can use Mao's words against Beijing. In a 1936 interview with journalist and author Edgar Snow, Mao treated Taiwan as distinct from China. "It is the immediate task of China to regain all our lost territories, not merely to defend our sovereignty below the Great Wall," he said.

> We do not, however, include Korea, formerly a Chinese colony, but when we have re-established the independence of the lost territories of China, and if the Koreans wish to break away from the chains of Japanese imperialism, we will extend them our enthusiastic help in their struggle for independence. The same thing applies to Formosa.[33]

Precedent undermines the "One China" concept for other reasons. Ethnic arguments do not support China's claims. The Arab League has 22 members; both the international community and most Arab leaders rejected former Egyptian President Gamal Abdel Nasser's concept of Arab nationalism. Both Albania and Kosovo have ethnic Albanian populations, while Romania and Moldova remain separate countries despite their common ethnicity. Few countries recognize Russia's annexation of Crimea, notwithstanding Russian President Vladimir Putin's argument that its population is Russian. Conversely, for Beijing to use ethnicity as the basis for its claim to legitimacy over Taiwan would undermine the logic of its claims to Inner Mongolia, Tibet, and Xinjiang.

During his first meeting with Premier Zhou Enlai, in 1971, Secretary of State Henry Kissinger remarked, "There's no question that if the Korean war hadn't occurred . . . Taiwan would probably be today a part of the PRC."[34] That may be true, but it is immaterial to the present day. The histories of Taiwan and mainland China diverged, frankly, centuries before Kissinger's pursuit of his China diplomacy. Taiwan has an identity, culture, and political history as different from China as most of China's other neighbors have. The biggest mistake any American leader could make is to buy into what essentially has become Beijing's big lie: that Taiwan is a part of China.

Notes

1. Mao Zedong, "Speech, Mao Zedong at the Fifteenth Meeting of the Supreme State Council (Excerpt)," Wilson Center, Digital Archive, https://digitalarchive.wilsoncenter.org/document/117015.

2. Nikita Sergeevich Khrushchev et al., "Discussion Between N.S. Khrushchev and Mao Zedong," Wilson Center, Digital Archive, http://digitalarchive.wilsoncenter.org/document/112088.

3. Chinese Ministry of Foreign Affairs, "A Policy of 'One Country, Two Systems' on Taiwan," https://web.archive.org/web/20140828134501/https://www.fmprc.gov.cn/mfa_eng/ziliao_665539/3602_665543/3604_665547/t18027.shtml.

4. Akiyoshi Abe, *Taiwan chimei kenkyū* [*The Study of the Place Names in Taiwan*] (Taihoku-shi, Taiwan: Bango Kenkyūkai: Hatsubaijo Sugita Shoten, 1938).

5. Shih-Shan Henry Tsai, *Maritime Taiwan: Historical Encounters with the East and the West* (New York: Routledge, 2009), 105.

6. *Taiwan Review*, "What's New in a Name," March 1, 1971, https://taiwantoday.tw/news.php?unit=20,29,35,45&post=25821.

7. Jonathan Manthorpe, *Forbidden Nation: A History of Taiwan* (New York: Palgrave MacMillan, 2005), 21–22.

8. Manthorpe, *Forbidden Nation*, 22.

9. Manthorpe, *Forbidden Nation*, 22–23.

10. Manthorpe, *Forbidden Nation*, 23.

11. Feng-yi Chu, "Chinese and Taiwanese Identities in Taiwan as Epistemic Challengers," *International Journal of Taiwan Studies* 4, no. 2 (July 2021): 267–68, https://brill.com/view/journals/ijts/4/2/article-p265_265.xml.

12. Chu, "Chinese and Taiwanese Identities in Taiwan as Epistemic Challengers," 267.

13. Lin-yao Chi, "Minnan and Hakka Are the Same," *Taipei Times*, May 11, 2001, http://www.taipeitimes.com/News/editorials/archives/2001/05/11/0000085315.

14. Pedro Soares et al., "Climate Change and Postglacial Human Dispersals in Southeast Asia," *Molecular Biology and Evolution* 25, no. 6 (June 2008): 1209–18, https://academic.oup.com/mbe/article/25/6/1209/1134230.

15. Pedro A. Soares et al., "Resolving the Ancestry of Austronesian-Speaking Populations," *Human Genetics* 135 (2016): 309–26, https://doi.org/10.1007/s00439-015-1620-z.

16. Manthorpe, *Forbidden Nation*, 31–32.

17. Manthorpe, *Forbidden Nation*, 32–33.

18. Jonathan Spence, *The Search for Modern China* (New York: W. W. Norton, 1990), 53.

19. Manthorpe, *Forbidden Nation*, 54.

20. Manthorpe, *Forbidden Nation*, 111.

21. Spence, *The Search for Modern China*, 56–57.

22. John R. Shephard, "The Island Frontier of the Ch'ing, 1684–1780," in *Taiwan: A New History*, ed. Murray A. Rubinstein (Armonk, NY: M. E. Sharpe, 1999), 112–13.

23. Shephard, "The Island Frontier of the Ch'ing, 1684–1780," 114–15.

24. Shephard, "The Island Frontier of the Ch'ing, 1684–1780," 117–19.

25. Manthorpe, *Forbidden Nation*, 50.

26. Manthorpe, *Forbidden Nation*, 134–36.

27. Spence, *The Search for Modern China*, 223.

28. John Pomfret, *The Beautiful Country and the Middle Kingdom: America and China, 1776 to the Present* (New York: Henry Holt, 2016), 303.

29. J. P. Jain, "The Legal Status of Formosa: A Study of British, Chinese and Indian Views," *American Journal of International Law* 57, no. 1 (January 1963): 25, https://www.cambridge.org/core/journals/american-journal-of-international-law/article/abs/legal-status-of-formosa-a-study-of-british-chinese-and-indian-views/137D56F749DFE-E606446CDD7D37AC513.

30. Michael Mazza and Gary J. Schmitt, "Righting a Wrong: Taiwan, the United Nations, and United States Policy," Project 2049 Institute, October 25, 2021, https://project2049.net/2021/10/25/righting-a-wrong-taiwan-the-united-nations-and-united-states-policy.

31. Xinhua News Agency, "Cairo Declaration Sets Legal Basis for Taiwan as Part of China: Expert," November 28, 2003, http://www.china.org.cn/english/taiwan/81136.htm.

32. Jain, "The Legal Status of Formosa," 25–26.

33. Mao Zedong, *China: The March Toward Unity* (New York: Workers Library Publishers, 1937), 40.

34. National Security Archive, "Memcon, Kissinger and Zhou, 9 July 1971, 4:35–11:20 PM, Top Secret/Sensitive/Exclusively Eyes Only, with Cover Memo by Lord," July 29, 1971, https://nsarchive2.gwu.edu/NSAEBB/NSAEBB66/ch-34.pdf.

The Rise of the "China Threat"

GISELLE DONNELLY

Mirror, mirror on the wall, what's the biggest threat of all?

In March 2021, the Pew Research Center found that nine in 10 Americans had come to see the People's Republic of China as either an outright "enemy" or a strategic "competitor." Half consider that "limiting China's power and influence" should be the principal purpose of US foreign policy.[1] That is a remarkable turnaround since 83 members of the US Senate voted to grant China permanent most-favored trading status in 2000.

But even at the time of the Senate vote, which would open the way for Beijing to enter the World Trade Organization, skeptical members of Congress insisted on what might be called "trust but verify" caveats to welcoming China into the post–Cold War liberal international order. Two provisions of the 2000 National Defense Authorization Act accompanied the Clinton administration's push on opening Chinese trade: One chartered the US-China Economic and Security Review Commission to "review the national security implications" of the deal,[2] and the second directed the Department of Defense to issue an annual report on the state of the Chinese military. Over the intervening two decades, the commission and the report have mirrored the increasingly fretful and ambiguous American understanding of the People's Republic of China, and the Pentagon report, in particular, both charts and has shaped the scope and nature of the emerging China threat.

The New Consensus

The latest Pentagon report shows just how far the pendulum has swung. It concludes that Beijing views the United States as not just a "rival" great power but a "clash of opposing systems" of political beliefs.[3] Such strong language also marks a swing from President Joe Biden. As recently as the 2019 primaries, candidate Biden held the benign view that had been reflected in his Senate vote in favor of the 2000 trade pact, stating that Beijing was "not competition" for America. "China is going to eat our lunch? Come on, man," he declared on the campaign trail in Iowa. "I mean, you know, they're not bad folks."[4]

The 2021 China military power study, however, is a portrait of pretty bad folks with a voracious geopolitical appetite. It describes China as an ideologically revisionist power bent on creating an "international order . . . more advantageous to Beijing's authoritarian system,"[5] a conclusion that echoes Cold War rhetoric about the Soviet Union. And for several years, the report has concentrated on the "Chinese dream" of General Secretary Xi Jinping, the "great rejuvenation of the Chinese nation" to, in the report's summation, "surpass U.S. global influence and power, [and] displace U.S. alliances . . . in the Indo-Pacific region."[6]

The new report also reverses past assessments of China's nuclear forces, doctrine, and strategic purpose. Whereas the 2020 edition put the estimate of Beijing's nuclear arsenal at just 200 warheads—a minimally deterrent, second-strike force—the 2021 report indicates an accelerating pace of nuclear modernization that would make 1,000 warheads within the decade and "three solid-fueled ICBM [intercontinental ballistic missile] silo fields, which will cumulatively contain hundreds of new ICBM silos."[7] This would put China "on the cusp of a large silo-based ICBM force . . . comparable to . . . other major powers"—that is, Russia and the United States, the two nuclear superpowers.[8] The reemerging balance of nuclear terror is reinforced by the fact that the Chinese People's Liberation Army (PLA) is adopting "a launch-on-warning posture, called 'early warning counterstrike.'"[9] This is, essentially, Dr. Strangelove with Chinese characteristics.[10]

Two other elements of the 2021 report stand out. While previous reports have long contained detailed reporting of Chinese missile-building programs, in this version the estimates of the number of short-range (less than 1,000 kilometers) and medium-range (1,000–3,000 kilometers) missiles have risen substantially, by several hundred missiles in each case. These are systems ideal for blanketing Taiwan, American and Japanese military bases, and the waters of the Philippine Sea that would be crucial in any US naval response to a Taiwan crisis.

Further, after several years of heavy hints about the Chinese military's growing footprint and expanding operations, the Pentagon has started naming names, sketching out the network of potential Chinese bases and supply depots that would support global power projection, particularly naval power projection. The report observes that, at 355 ships, the PLA Navy's battle force is the "largest navy in the world" and on course to reach 420 ships by 2025 and 460 by 2030.[11] Moreover, the quality of Chinese ships is advancing rapidly, with Beijing's first large-deck aircraft carrier, the Type 003, which is capable of catapult launches—essential for adding larger and more capable naval aircraft to the fleet—to enter service by 2024.

Yet the annual Pentagon report has been something of a trailing-edge indicator, reflecting the hopes that, by bringing Beijing into the post–Cold War economic order and opening trade, geopolitical stability—if not necessarily domestic democratic political reform in China—would continue; it would be in China's national interest to join the world America had made. These hopes persisted through the Clinton, Bush, and Obama administrations and remained strong among Donald Trump's economic advisers. Each administration tended to arrive in office with a set and nearly unchangeable view of China policy. Thus, each set of military power reports contained almost identical rhetoric. And despite the 2021 report's stark assessment, the Biden administration clearly is likewise of two minds, balancing the realities of rising strategic and military competition and Beijing's aggressive "wolf warrior" diplomacy, manipulation of the COVID-19 pandemic, theft of technology and intellectual property, and ideological assertiveness with the desire for cooperation on climate change and other supposedly "win-win" opportunities.

Pleading Ignorance

The Pentagon was also clearly unprepared to respond to Congress's concerns about China's military modernization, which had begun in the mid-1990s; the Chinese were as shocked and awed as anyone to see the ease with which the US military defeated the Iraqi army in Operation Desert Storm. The first Chinese military power report's first section was subtitled "Gaps and Uncertainties," remarking on "how little is known about the most significant aspects of Chinese military power. Chinese secrecy is extensive." The report was even in the dark about the Chinese defense budget, estimating that it might be as much as four times the official amount of $20 billion. "Since the 1980s," the Pentagon admitted, "U.S. military exchange delegations to China have been shown only 'showcase' units, never any advanced units or any operational training or realistic exercises."[12]

The Pentagon sorted its ignorance into three categories. It confessed it could not calculate how the Chinese military stacked up against Taiwan—a principal interest for Congress. It lacked understanding of almost every aspect of a net assessment:

> There is much more the United States can learn about both sides' ideas of statecraft, their approaches to the use of force, their perceived vulnerabilities, and their preferred operational methods, as well as about the political and military organizations that produce military assessments and plans.[13]

Nor did it grasp the levels of PLA training, logistics, doctrine, command and control, special operations, and mine warfare. Lastly, while it thought it had identified worrisome "emerging methods of warfare that appear likely to be increasingly important in the future—particularly missiles and information warfare," it didn't know what to make of these developments.[14] Indeed, these two measures have turned out to be a constant and growing problem for the US military. The report did estimate that the PLA had about 350 short-range ballistic missiles in its arsenal and was building about 50 per year while "developing variants . . . that enable attacks against [US bases on] Okinawa."[15]

The report assumed greater confidence in understanding the ends and means of Beijing's strategy. This, the Pentagon concluded, was essentially conservative, content to modernize and increase its "comprehensive national power" within the "*shi*," translated as the existing "strategic configuration of power"[16]—that is, the American-led international order. This was based on the "24-character strategy" of Deng Xiaoping, China's leader during the reforms of the 1980s and whose followers still held the highest posts in government and the Chinese Communist Party (CCP). The Deng strategy was translated as "keep cool-headed to observe, be composed to make reactions, stand firmly, *hide our capabilities and bide our time*, never try to take the lead, and be able to accomplish something."[17] (The Defense Department added its own italics for emphasis.)

While acknowledging that Beijing "believes that the United States poses a significant long-term challenge,"[18] the existing balance of military power heavily favored the United States, especially in the wake of the Gulf War, the 1990s intervention in the Balkans, and the 1995 and 1996 Taiwan Strait crises. "Chinese analyses," the Pentagon was convinced, "indicate a concern that Beijing would have difficulty in managing potential U.S. military intervention" in the western Pacific or South China Sea.[19]

The "Responsible Stakeholder" Years

The George W. Bush administration put a consistent stamp on the reports from 2004 to 2009. These were the high point of the strategy of encouraging Beijing to become a "responsible stakeholder"—a phrase coined by Deputy Secretary of State Robert Zoellick[20]—playing a constructive role in the liberal international order under Hu Jintao's leadership of China. Hu was the first general secretary and president from the generation that came after the Maoist revolution, and he promoted Beijing's "peaceful rise" as a great power.[21] Thus, the Bush administration adopted a variant of Ronald Reagan's trust-but-verify approach to Beijing, acknowledging the dichotomy between China's increasing ambitions and capabilities and its continuing desire for the US-guaranteed security that had framed its economic growth and integration into the international trade regime.

These years were also a high-water mark of Bush military self-confidence—of "Mission Accomplished" after the successful invasions to topple the Taliban from power in Afghanistan and then Saddam Hussein in Iraq. Indeed, first among the "key developments between the 2003 and 2004 reports to Congress" was an appraisal of China's "'lessons learned' from Operation Iraqi Freedom."[22] In this assessment, the PLA was "rethinking" its conclusion in the wake of the Balkan wars of the 1990s that "airpower alone is sufficient to prevail in a conflict" and, in particular, reevaluating "their assumptions about the value of long-range precision strikes, independent of ground forces, in any Taiwan conflict scenario." Whether this assessment reflected the administration's pride in "the success of Coalition joint operations" and "allied weapon system integration/interoperability" or improved intelligence is unclear.[23] The report also admitted that the Pentagon had "much to learn about the motivations and decisionmaking behind China's military modernization"[24]— but the conclusion was that the Chinese had begun an "ambitious, long-term . . . effort to develop capabilities to fight and win short-duration, high-intensity conflicts along its periphery."[25]

The PLA was likewise said to believe that American intervention "in conflict scenarios involving China, such as Taiwan and the South China Sea, is increasingly likely."[26] Thus, the framework of China's pursuit of a crafty "assassin's mace"[27] to raise the cost of US power projection formally entered the department's lexicon, as did a focus on PLA anti-access and area-denial (A2AD) systems. Discussing "PLA counters to foreign intervention," the report speculated that "China could consider a sea-denial strategy to hold at risk US naval forces approaching the Taiwan Strait. Deep-water naval mines, submarines, cruise missiles, and even special forces could be employed to threaten a US aircraft carrier."[28]

Despite its claims of uncertainty in its assessments, the Bush administration continued to revise and raise its estimates of Chinse defense spending (thought to be as high as $80 billion per year at the time, climbing to almost $300 billion in the 2020s) and missile inventories (about 500 short-range ballistic missiles and development of medium- and solid-fueled intercontinental-range systems). These forces were "likely to increase substantially over the next few years," as were their "accuracy and lethality."[29] The report also added several sections on "information operations," which might be seen as a precursor to the broader current concern with gray-zone warfare.

With the 2008 report, however, the hopes that China would act as a responsible pillar of the international order had faded. The Pentagon report had taken on an almost plaintive quality: "No country has done more to assist, facilitate, and encourage China's national development and its integration in the international system." Yet Beijing's "expanding and improving military capabilities [were] changing East Asian military balances" that had "implications beyond the Asia-Pacific region." The administration was clearly worried: "The lack of transparency in China's military and security affairs poses risks to stability"—that is, America's status as a global superpower. This, in turn, presaged a darker future: "This situation will naturally and understandably lead to hedging" behavior by the United States and its allies.[30]

The Barack Obama "Pivot"

Barack Obama entered the White House in 2009 promising a "Pacific pivot." While this was in good measure a move away from Europe, where the administration embarked on a slow but steady reduction of US forces, and the Middle East, especially from the "surge" of troops in support of a counterinsurgency campaign late in the Bush administration, it also reflected a fundamental reassessment of America's strategic interests. Speaking in Japan in November 2009, Obama recalled his Hawaiian birth and childhood in Indonesia and declared himself to be the "first Pacific president," stating that "the Pacific rim has helped shape my view of the world." But his view was of a modulated form of American attention, with an emphasis on achieving a consensually derived order, implemented through multilateral organizations that would "advance the security and prosperity of this region." And in this, he imagined a constructive role for China: "The rise of a strong, prosperous China can be a source of strength for the community of nations." He added, "In Beijing and beyond, we will work to deepen our Strategic and Economic Dialogue, and improve communication between our militaries."[31]

The administration's 2010 China military power report dutifully followed suit, further quoting the November speech: The relationship with Beijing "has not been without disagreement and difficulty. But the notion that we must be adversaries is not pre-destined." The report even found a silver lining in China's increasing power-projection capabilities. "China began a new phase of military development by articulating roles and missions for the People's Liberation Army . . . that go beyond China's immediate territorial interests," it observed, noting Beijing's contributions to international peacekeeping missions, humanitarian and disaster relief, and counter-piracy operations in the Arabian Sea. "The United States recognizes and welcomes these contributions." In sum, the Pentagon was encouraged—spouting a line common to its theater commanders—that military-to-military ties could help with "reducing mistrust, enhancing mutual understanding and broadening cooperation."[32] What the initial military power reports had regarded as Potemkin village shows by the PLA were now taken as tokens of transparency.

Obama's hopeful attitude continued through the term of Hu's leadership, yet the military facts of PLA modernization began to stack up against the administration's narrative. The 2012 report included a full-blown exposition of A2AD framework that increasingly was entrenched in the Defense Department through the advocacy of Navy Under Secretary Robert Work, who would become deputy secretary of defense in 2014. That year's review also cataloged

> the inaugural flight testing of the J-20 stealth fighter; limited power projection, with the launch of China's first aircraft carrier for sea trials; integrated air defenses; undersea warfare; nuclear deterrence and strategic strike; improved command and control; and more sophisticated training and exercises across China's air, naval, and land forces.[33]

Sotto voce, the Pentagon admitted that the Chinese military was on a path to becoming a global rival, a great power in capability and capacity.

Xi's general secretaryship almost immediately made for a hardening line in the White House and the Defense Department. The new Chinese leader had, in his June 2013 "Sunnylands summit" with Obama, framed a "new pattern of major power relations,"[34] though what that meant was anyone's guess. Initial reviews were positive, even among sober-minded China analysts.[35] Yet by the time the subsequent annual reports to Congress were written, Xi had also announced his "Chinese dream" of national rejuvenation and consolidated CCP domestic control and ambition to be a rule-maker and simply a "stakeholder" in international affairs.

The 2015 report, in particular, marked a watershed. "China's military modernization has the potential to reduce core U.S. military . . . advantages," it warned, noting that the PLA budget had increased at an annual rate approaching 10 percent and predicting similar increases "for the foreseeable future." Beijing was "investing in capabilities designed to defeat adversary power projection and counter third-party—including U.S.—intervention during a crisis or conflict."[36] Two other factors gained increased emphasis. "China is also focusing on counter-space, offensive cyber operations, and electronic warfare capabilities meant to deny . . . the advantages of modern, informationized warfare" that characterized US military operations. Second, "China also started reclaiming land and building infrastructure at its outposts in the Spratly Islands" in the South China Sea, enabling the PLA "to use them as persistent . . . military bases of operation" in waters claimed by several nations, including the US treaty ally in the Philippines.[37]

Yet, even in 2016, the Obama administration could not get itself to a point of openly acknowledging strategic competition with China. Yes, "China [had] demonstrated a willingness to tolerate higher levels of tension in the pursuit of its interests," but it "still seeks to avoid direct and explicit conflict with the United States." Xi, like his more moderate predecessors, remained an essentially rational actor.

> China's leaders understand that instability or conflict would jeopardize the peaceful external environment that has enabled China's economic development, which is central to the perpetuation of the CCP's domestic legitimacy. In the near-term, China is using coercive tactics short of armed conflict, such as the use of law enforcement vessels to enforce maritime claims, to advance their interests in ways that are calculated to fall below the threshold of provoking conflict.[38]

The Era of "Great-Power Competition"

Trump has left his mark on American politics in numerous ways. Many have been enraging, but some remain enlightening—none more so than the introduction of the idea that the current geopolitical moment should be defined by the return of great-power competition as post–Cold War Pax Americana ebbs. Debating whether the president ever read his 2017

National Security Strategy has long been a Washington parlor game, but the document, produced during Lt. Gen. H. R. McMaster's brief and stormy tenure as national security adviser, has reframed America's understanding of China's rise; even the Biden administration cannot escape its shadow, much as it loathes all things Trump.[39]

The great-power framework provided the context for Trump-era Pentagon reports, which became more direct in tone and included "special topic" supplements that were deeper dives into subjects that reflected the US military's emerging concerns. The reports typically began with a straightforward assessment of Chinese security strategy; the pretense that China's motives and means were ambiguous was a thing of the past. "China's leaders are leveraging China's growing economic, diplomatic, and military clout to establish regional preeminence and expand the country's international influence," declared the 2019 edition. Among that year's "special topics" was a dissection of Beijing's "influence operations." These included the PLA's traditional "Three Warfares" doctrines—psychological, public opinion, and legal—but involved the whole of the Chinese government and people. These operations were directed against "cultural institutions, media organizations, and the business, academic, and policy communities of the United States, other countries, and international institutions" and included appeals to "overseas Chinese citizens or ethnic Chinese citizens of other countries . . . through soft power or, sometimes, coercion and blackmail." The goal was to establish networks of overseas "power brokers" to "facilitate China's rise."[40]

Trump-era reports also concluded that the goals of Chinese military modernization were no longer simply local. Although the Taiwan scenario remained the PLA's main "strategic direction,"[41] it was not just a direct cross-Strait bean count but a larger, multi-theater view that included the China-India border and the East China Sea and South China Sea—in all, encompassing five separate commands.

Taken as a whole, the annual Chinese military power reports have tracked a sea change in what can be said in polite company in Washington about China; the shift from potential "stakeholder" to geopolitical "great-power competitor" is neither complete nor irreversible. The business community, for example, still covets the prospect of profits from Beijing. But attitudes among national security elites have hardened, and the report release is a reliable headline-making event. In this respect, the design of the original legislation has been fulfilled. However, the larger intent—to frame America's defense investments—has not been realized.

The Trump administration boasted that it would "adapt its forces, posture, investments, and operational concepts to ensure it retains the ability to . . . deter aggression, protect our allies and partners, and preserve regional peace, prosperity, and freedom."[42] This it did not do, nor did its predecessors or successors. Since the end of the Cold War, US defense budgets have been cut roughly in half, from the Reagan-era peak of more than 6 percent of gross domestic product to a projected 2.7 percent; the increases of the second Bush administration were devoted to waging the post-9/11 wars in the Middle East, not responding to the China challenge.[43]

Neither has any administration followed the model of the Reagan-era *Soviet Military Power* report that inspired the China reports' authors. The Russia report was, as even its critics lamented, a "call to action" that buttressed the Reagan administration's buildup.[44] The China report has produced a conventional-wisdom consensus about the dark side of China's rise, but that has yet to translate into appreciable action.

Notes

1. Laura Silver, Kat Devlin, and Christine Huang, *Most Americans Support Tough Stance Toward China on Human Rights, Economic Issues*, Pew Research Center, March 4, 2021, https://www.pewresearch.org/global/2021/03/04/most-americans-support-tough-stance-toward-china-on-human-rights-economic-issues.

2. National Defense Authorization, Fiscal Year 2001, Pub. L. No. 106-398, § 1238, https://www.govinfo.gov/content/pkg/PLAW-106publ398/pdf/PLAW-106publ398.pdf.

3. US Department of Defense, Office of the Secretary of Defense, *Military and Security Developments Involving the People's Republic of China*, November 2021, i, https://media.defense.gov/2021/Nov/03/2002885874/-1/-1/0/2021-CMPR-FINAL.PDF.

4. Adam Edelman, "Biden's Comments Downplaying China Threat to U.S. Fire Up Pols on Both Sides," NBC News, May 2, 2019, https://www.nbcnews.com/politics/2020-election/biden-s-comments-downplaying-china-threat-u-s-fires-pols-n1001236.

5. US Department of Defense, Office of the Secretary of Defense, *Military and Security Developments Involving the People's Republic of China*, November 2021, iii.

6. US Department of Defense, Office of the Secretary of Defense, *Military and Security Developments Involving the People's Republic of China*, November 2021, iii.

7. US Department of Defense, Office of the Secretary of Defense, *Military and Security Developments Involving the People's Republic of China*, November 2021, vii.

8. US Department of Defense, Office of the Secretary of Defense, *Military and Security Developments Involving the People's Republic of China*, November 2021, 94.

9. US Department of Defense, Office of the Secretary of Defense, *Military and Security Developments Involving the People's Republic of China*, November 2021, 93.

10. For a fuller explication of this and other salient aspects of the 2021 report, see Zack Cooper and Emily Young Carr, "5 Key Updates in the Pentagon's 2021 China Military Power Report," AEIdeas, November 8, 2021, https://www.aei.org/foreign-and-defense-policy/5-key-updates-in-the-pentagons-2021-china-military-power-report.

11. US Department of Defense, Office of the Secretary of Defense, *Military and Security Developments Involving the People's Republic of China*, November 2021, 49.

12. See US Department of Defense, *Annual Report on the Military Power of the People's Republic of China*, GlobalSecurity.org, July 2002, 1, https://www.globalsecurity.org/military/library/report/2002/d20020712china.pdf.

13. US Department of Defense, *Annual Report on the Military Power of the People's Republic of China*, July 2002, 2.

14. US Department of Defense, *Annual Report on the Military Power of the People's Republic of China*, July 2002.

15. US Department of Defense, *Annual Report on the Military Power of the People's Republic of China*, July 2002.

16. US Department of Defense, *Annual Report on the Military Power of the People's Republic of China*, July 2002, 5–6.

17. US Department of Defense, *Annual Report on the Military Power of the People's Republic of China*, July 2002, 7.

18. US Department of Defense, *Annual Report on the Military Power of the People's Republic of China*, July 2002, 8.

19. US Department of Defense, *Annual Report on the Military Power of the People's Republic of China*, July 2002, 9.

20. See Robert B. Zoellick, "Whither China? From Membership to Responsibility" (keynote address, National Committee on US-China Relations, New York, September 21, 2005), https://www.ncuscr.org/sites/default/files/migration/Zoellick_remarks_notes06_winter_spring.pdf.

21. See Zheng Bijian, "China's 'Peaceful Rise' to Great-Power Status," *Foreign Affairs* (September/October 2005), https://www.foreignaffairs.com/articles/asia/2005-09-01/chinas-peaceful-rise-great-power-status.

22. US Department of Defense, *Annual Report on the Military Power of the People's Republic of China*, GlobalSecurity.org, May 2004, 4, https://www.globalsecurity.org/military/library/report/2004/d20040528prc.pdf.

23. US Department of Defense, *Annual Report on the Military Power of the People's Republic of China*, May 2004.

24. US Department of Defense, *Annual Report on the Military Power of the People's Republic of China*, May 2004, 7.

25. US Department of Defense, *Annual Report on the Military Power of the People's Republic of China*, May 2004.

26. US Department of Defense, *Annual Report on the Military Power of the People's Republic of China*, May 2004, 13.

27. US Department of Defense, *Annual Report on the Military Power of the People's Republic of China*, May 2004, 14.

28. US Department of Defense, *Annual Report on the Military Power of the People's Republic of China*, May 2004, 51.

29. US Department of Defense, *Annual Report on the Military Power of the People's Republic of China*, May 2004, 37.

30. US Department of Defense, Office of the Secretary of Defense, *Military Power of the People's Republic of China*, 2008, 1, https://nuke.fas.org/guide/china/dod-2008.pdf.

31. Mike Allen, "'America's First Pacific President,'" *Politico*, November 13, 2009, https://www.politico.com/story/2009/11/americas-first-pacific-president-029511.

32. US Department of Defense, Office of the Secretary of Defense, *Military and Security Developments Involving the People's Republic of China*, 2010, GlobalSecurity.org, 2010, i, https://www.globalsecurity.org/military/library/report/2010/2010-prc-military-power.pdf.

33. US Department of Defense, Office of the Secretary of Defense, *Military and Security Developments Involving the People's Republic of China 2012*, May 2012, iv, https://dod.defense.gov/Portals/1/Documents/pubs/2012_CMPR_Final.pdf.

34. Richard C. Bush, "Obama and Xi at Sunnylands: A New Pattern of Relations?," Brookings Institution, June 4, 2013, https://www.brookings.edu/blog/up-front/2013/06/04/obama-and-xi-at-sunnylands-a-new-pattern-of-relations.

35. See Elizabeth Economy, "The Xi-Obama Summit: As Good as Expected—and Maybe Even Better," *Atlantic*, June 11, 2013, https://www.theatlantic.com/china/archive/2013/06/the-xi-obama-summit-as-good-as-expected-and-maybe-even-better/276733.

36. US Department of Defense, Office of the Secretary of Defense, *Military and Security Developments Involving the People's Republic of China 2015*, April 7, 2015, i, https://dod.defense.gov/Portals/1/Documents/pubs/2015_China_Military_Power_Report.pdf.

37. US Department of Defense, Office of the Secretary of Defense, *Military and Security Developments Involving the People's Republic of China 2015*, i–ii.

38. US Department of Defense, Office of the Secretary of Defense, *Military and Security Developments Involving the People's Republic of China 2016*, April 26, 2016, i, https://dod.defense.gov/Portals/1/Documents/pubs/2016%20China%20Military%20Power%20Report.pdf.

39. White House, *National Security Strategy of the United States of America*, December 2017, https://trumpwhitehouse.archives.gov/wp-content/uploads/2017/12/NSS-Final-12-18-2017-0905.pdf.

40. US Department of Defense, Office of the Secretary of Defense, *Military and Security Developments Involving the People's Republic of China 2019*, May 2, 2019, i, iv–v, https://media.defense.gov/2019/May/02/2002127082/-1/-1/1/2019_CHINA_MILITARY_POWER_REPORT.pdf.

41. US Department of Defense, Office of the Secretary of Defense, *Military and Security Developments Involving the People's Republic of China 2019*, 14.

42. US Department of Defense, Office of the Secretary of Defense, *Military and Security Developments Involving the People's Republic of China 2019*, iv.

43. See US Department of Defense, "Defense Spending as a % of Gross Domestic Product (GDP)," https://www.defense.gov/Multimedia/Photos/igphoto/2002099941.

44. Kyle Mizokami, "How the Pentagon Exaggerated Russia's Cold War Super Weapons," *National Interest*, June 5, 2016, https://nationalinterest.org/blog/the-buzz/how-the-pentagon-exaggerated-russias-cold-war-super-weapons-16468.

China's Three Roads to Controlling Taiwan

DAN BLUMENTHAL AND FREDERICK W. KAGAN

China has been moving along three roads to fully integrating Taiwan into the People's Republic of China (PRC) and extinguishing Taiwan's autonomy: persuasion, coercion, and compellence.[1] American policy has focused increasingly on preventing China from seizing Taiwan by force—blocking the compellence road. But China can still secure its goals through persuasion and coercion.

General Secretary of the Chinese Communist Party (CCP) Xi Jinping likely prefers those roads to the much riskier path of overt military attack on the island. Blocking the Chinese roads through persuasion and coercion is not a marginal task, nor is it inherent in the effort to deter or defeat a Chinese invasion of Taiwan. The current US approach to blocking the compellence road may in fact increase the likelihood that Xi will reach his objectives by these other two paths. The US must urgently rethink its approach to the problem of defending Taiwan's autonomy so that it blocks all three roads to PRC victory rather than focusing on only one—at the expense or to the detriment of defending Taiwan against ongoing persuasion and coercion campaigns.

Persuasion

One can easily overstate the Chinese preference for "winning without fighting" or ascribe to Chinese military thought an intellectual patent on an idea that other societies and cultures value and share. Frequent and facile references to Sun Tzu's aphorism that "those who render others' armies helpless without fighting are the best of all"[2] contribute to this danger.

The fact that repetition of this aphorism has made it seem trite, however, does not strip it of its force in Chinese thought. The concept of *buzhan ersheng* (不战而胜)—to "subdue the enemy without fighting"—has been a cornerstone of Chinese strategic thinking for centuries.[3] The People's Liberation Army (PLA) has pursued a massive military reform and modernization program since 1993[4] in preparation for modern, great-power warfare, even as Beijing has intensified a coercion campaign that uses real and threatened power to achieve its aims. But China has not abandoned the psychological strategies that helped the CCP successfully topple the Republic of China (ROC) during the Chinese civil war and take over mainland China.[5]

The aim of so shaping an adversary's understanding of the world that it voluntarily chooses one's own preferred course of action is a highly evolved part of Chinese strategic thought and practice. The idea of causing the enemy to perceive its own benefit in choosing the path most favorable to oneself is heavily discussed in Sun Tzu, encapsulated in the observation that "what causes opponents to come of their own accord is the prospect of gain."[6] Mao Zedong translated that aphorism into an accessible analogy, describing

> three ways to make a cat eat a hot pepper: stuff it down the cat's throat, disguise the pepper by wrapping it in cheese, or grind the pepper up and spread it on the cat's back. In the latter case, the cat will lick itself, thinking it is doing something for itself when it is actually doing what you want. This is the essence of strategy.[7]

Soviet theorists expanded on this idea in considerable and meticulous detail under the rubric of "reflexive control." Soviet writer Vladimir Lefebvre described reflexive control in the following manner:

> In making his decision the adversary uses information about the area of conflict, about his own troops and ours, about their ability to fight, etc. We can influence his channels of information and send messages, which shift the flow of information in a way favorable for us. The adversary uses the most contemporary method of optimization and finds the optimal decision. However, it will not be a true optimum, but a decision predetermined by us.[8]

Reflexive control is at the heart of Russian information operations and hybrid war theories. The CCP has long studied and learned from Russian thought and experiences.

Mao's theory of how to prevail in war was based on what he called the "three magic weapons." The CCP, or politics, is in the lead. It wields armed force together with "the united front" to "storm and shatter the enemy's positions."[9] Armed force is calibrated to support the ongoing work of political struggle to defeat an enemy.

The PLA has always had robust political warfare units alongside its conventional units. Its General Political Department (GPD) was devoted to undermining enemy morale and building international support. The GPD helped build the United Front with the Kuomintang (KMT) against the Japanese while subverting the KMT military to further its aims in the Chinese civil war. The GPD was reorganized in 2015 into the Central Military Commission's Political Work Department. Its responsibilities are to conduct the "three warfares": public opinion warfare, legal warfare, and psychological warfare.[10] This department, along with the new Strategic Support Force, where the PLA's cyber, space, electronic warfare, and information warfare units reside, is responsible for conducting political warfare in peace and war, including the ongoing coercive campaign against Taiwan.[11]

Beijing's theory of victory rests on the destruction of Taiwan's morale: If Taiwan believes that the US will not or cannot help undermine China's escalating threats, it will have to accede to Beijing's demands. Taiwan is a small, isolated island with little acceptance as an independent state. It is sui generis in international relations. Absent US support, it is not difficult to imagine morale on the island collapsing.

China's persuasion campaign is thus aimed at not only Taiwan but also the US and its key allies and partners. Beijing continues to use all the tools at its disposal to drive general acceptance of the reality it desires to instantiate—that Taiwan is part of China, not an independent country, and that all other states agree with that premise. Its goal in doing so is to achieve preemptive recognition of its objectives and thereby collapse Taipei's will to resist by demonstrating that Taiwan is fully isolated and alone.

This objective is the primary motivation behind the CCP's constant efforts to rewrite history and current events in what often appears to be a

ham-fisted way. The CCP has thus continually portrayed itself as the victim and the US and Taiwan as the aggressors in the cross-Strait dispute,
despite enormous concessions and diplomatic generosity by Washington
and Taipei. This argument resonates in parts of the nonaligned world and
among potential US partners who would rather stay neutral in a conflict
over Taiwan and more broadly in the US-China global competition.

Even as the CCP engages in highly destabilizing shows of force, it
accuses the US and Taiwan of violating an "agreement" that was never
made, in which the US supposedly recognized Beijing's right to control
Taiwan's affairs. A brief excursion into the actual history of PRC-ROC
relations—and America's relations with both—is necessary to understand
the scope and scale of Beijing's revisionism as part of its persuasion campaign to isolate Taiwan.

The ROC, not the PRC, was China's sovereign government after the
fall of the Qing dynasty. Though the ROC never controlled all the lands it
claimed, it had all the trappings and juridical elements of a state for most
of the period in which it ruled mainland China.[12] The ROC conducted all
official diplomatic business for China before the CCP's victory in 1949. The
ROC was part of the grand alliance in World War II and a charter member
of the United Nations Security Council. Consistent with the prominent role
it was to have after the war, the ROC, not the CCP, accepted the surrender
of the Japanese on Taiwan. The CCP came to power only after its violent
rebellion against the duly constituted ROC government run by the KMT.

The CCP prevailed on the mainland, but the ROC survived and retreated
to Taiwan. The CCP governed, had sovereignty, and was the legitimate
ruler over only the mainland of China, while the KMT had sovereignty and
legitimate rule over the island of Taiwan and the offshore Matsu, Pescadores, and Quemoy islands.[13]

The CCP consistently denies and attempts to persuade others to deny
the historical and geopolitical reality that there have been two Chinas since
1949: an ROC on Taiwan and a PRC on the mainland. The US recognized
the ROC (including its claims to rule all of China) from 1949 to 1979 and
the PRC (which also claims to rule all of China) from 1979 onward.[14]

The shift in US recognition did not change the reality of the two Chinas. The US made a policy choice to accommodate the PRC, a decision
that had no bearing on the continued reality that the ROC legitimately

governed Taiwan.[15] Though the US made an enormous concession to its erstwhile enemy by switching its official recognition from the ROC to the PRC and abrogating its treaty with the island, the ROC still ruled Taiwan and had sovereignty over its people. The shift in US recognition was not accompanied by a formal agreement that the CCP was the legitimate ruler of Taiwan and that the ROC was therefore illegitimate. Beijing demanded such an agreement, but it received only an "acknowledgment" from Washington of the CCP's position that Taiwan was a sovereign part of China.[16]

Even when the US broke formal ties with Taipei—but still refused to recognize the CCP's formal claims—the US Congress protested and enacted with bipartisan support the Taiwan Relations Act (TRA), which provides the legal basis for strong if unofficial relations with Taiwan today. The US thus never officially recognized China's claim of sovereignty over Taiwan.[17] Washington's robust political, commercial, cultural, and educational ties with Taiwan are required by law. The PRC knows this yet insists that the US can somehow stop supporting Taiwan. Further, the US has a legal requirement to help Taiwan resist coercion. The TRA was passed in 1979, yet China continued with the process of diplomatic normalization. It thus implicitly acknowledged that US unofficial relations with Taiwan are part of what Washington calls "our one China policy."[18]

The CCP not only denies this reality but also portrays itself as an aggrieved party, despite the concessions the US has made to its demands. The US shifted its recognition from the ROC to the PRC at a time when China was especially weak: ravaged by Mao's Cultural Revolution, threatened by the Soviets with nuclear war, and readying for war with a Vietnam that was becoming hegemonic and hostile. It has still not acknowledged this tremendous US concession, but rather continues trying to force more change.

To understand Beijing's persuasion campaign, it is useful to understand what the US did *not* agree to in its "One China" policy and what Congress insisted on through the TRA and associated actions. First, the US does not take a position on Taiwan's sovereignty. It insists that the dispute over sovereignty between Taipei and Beijing is to be worked out peacefully, without preconditions. That is why the TRA's language requiring the US to resist Chinese coercion of Taiwan is so crucial: Washington has always maintained that Taiwan should not have to negotiate with a gun pointed at its head. That the US does not take a position on sovereignty does not negate

Taiwan's sovereignty; under international law, Taiwan is a sovereign entity. The US is making a reversible policy concession to the PRC in not officially recognizing the ROC, and it certainly never agreed to the "One China" *principle* (as opposed to America's "One China" *policy*), which Beijing tries to persuade countries to accept. The supposed "principle" is that Taiwan has always been part of the PRC. The principle is a lie—Taiwan has *never* been part of the People's Republic of China. It has been part of past Chinese empires (as well as Dutch, Portuguese, and Japanese empires), but it has never been part of the political entity that is the PRC.

Second, the US never agreed to cut off unofficial ties with Taiwan or limit the seniority of officials who conduct the operations of this unofficial relationship. Indeed, the presidents of Taiwan and the US can meet if they so choose. Such meetings cannot have the trappings of official state meetings because treating the Taiwanese leader as the president of Taiwan would violate America's definition of its "One China" policy—not because it would violate international law or any promise to Beijing.[19] Yet the PRC protests meetings between lower levels of the US government and Taiwanese officials, increasingly through demonstrations of force.

Third, while the US stated in a 1982 diplomatic communiqué that it would cap arms sales to Taiwan, it made abundantly clear that this cap was contingent on China's commitment to peace as manifested in China's military posture. But China's military posture has grown more menacing. Given Washington's historic position that it will calibrate its Taiwan policy based on the threat China poses to Taiwan, the US has no formal obligation to limit its military relationship with Taiwan. It has limited this relationship as a concession to China. But it can exercise with and train the ROC armed forces, and it can sell any military equipment it deems necessary to keep the peace across the strait.

Fourth, the US never agreed to limit Taiwan's international political and economic identity. Washington can push for Taiwan's participation in any international organization for which statehood is not a requirement. China has in the past acquiesced to Taiwan's participation as a separate legal entity in the World Trade Organization.[20] China, not the US, has changed policy. Beijing is trying to persuade the US and its allies that the "One China" principle governs cross-Strait relations, that Taiwan is part of the PRC, and that the US is abrogating promises to China to this effect.

The US must undermine this persuasion campaign and provide its allies with the political cover to develop the kind of relations with Taiwan that they want, free from Chinese intimidation. There is simply nothing provocative about this policy. The US promised not to unilaterally confer diplomatic recognition on the ROC, and it is abiding by that promise. On the other hand, the PRC is not abiding by its promise of peacefully resolving its differences with Taiwan.

Coercion

The CCP has not been content to rely on persuasion to secure final control of Taiwan, of course. It has long accompanied its persuasion campaign with an expanding coercion effort. This effort fits with Thomas Schelling's definition of coercion as a kind of "violent communications about intentions and commitment."[21] Schelling's insight was that the power to hurt gives states tremendous bargaining power. Expounding on his work, scholar Tami Davis Biddle evokes one of the most memorable scenes in modern cinematic history to explain how coercion works: In *The Godfather*, Don Corleone tells his consigliere that he will make a noncompliant movie producer an "offer he cannot refuse"[22] to get him to do something he otherwise would not do. Following a famous scene involving a decapitated horse's head, the producer subsequently hires the don's friend for an important role in an upcoming movie.

The movie producer felt[23] he had to comply or face more harm. This cinematic example helps illustrate the PRC's coercion tactics toward the US and Taiwan. No serious analyst doubts that Beijing is willing and able to inflict harm against Taiwan and the US if they do not comply with its demands. The act of being coerced is thus a psychological process. The coercer must manipulate the mind of the coerced.[24] As Schelling says, the power to hurt is a bargaining power. The willingness to use it is diplomacy—"vicious diplomacy, but diplomacy."[25] This strategy is an exploitation of fear. Arguably, a state's leverage over another is at its greatest when its adversary believes it has not yet used all its power, that any display of force is a *restrained* one.

The PLA's Theory of Coercion. The PLA has been interested in US theories of coercion since the first Gulf War. Coercive strategies fit well with a CCP strategic culture that emphasizes the ability to manipulate an adversary's psyche through stratagems. According to Mark Stokes, in the late 1990s the PLA began to theorize that US aerospace coercion was related to China's own concepts of stratagem, which it calls *mouliie* (谋略). Military force could be used to attack "an opponent's cognitive processes."[26] Military strategies of this kind require specific calculations of where pressure or manipulation can be applied to achieve political objectives. The PLA theorizing about coercive tactics closely resembled Mao's writing about the so-called magic weapons of warfare. Force and political manipulation were tightly sewn into strategies that manipulate the enemy and make them concede before all-out warfare is needed.

PLA theorists wrote about the coercion of Taiwan in the context of achieving limited political objectives, short of what could be achieved through an invasion and occupation of the island. Force would be modulated based on the objective and level of resistance to it. Deterring de jure independence requires a certain level of force; forcing agreement with different forms of unification requires more force.

These PLA writings coincided with the onset of the PLA modernization program in 1993. By the beginning of the 21st century, the PLA was deploying a lethal, precision-guided missile force positioned across the Taiwan Strait, enabled by a modernizing comprehensive command, control, communications, and computers and intelligence, surveillance, and reconnaissance (known as C4ISR) program. Indeed, the PLA aerospace force was the leading edge of the modernization program. At the same time, the PLA was developing anti-access and area-denial (A2AD) capabilities that raised the costs of US intervention on Taiwan's behalf. The political message to Taiwan was clear: The PLA could inflict great harm on the island, and the US would not want to risk making a costly defense of it.

As the PLA acquired new capabilities, it developed new options to deter Taipei's moves to formalize its de facto independent status, co-opt Washington to contain such perceived moves by Taiwan, and set conditions for intensification of the use of force across the strait. PLA authors stressed that the threat or actual application of force is necessary to ensure its goals regarding Taiwan, and Washington understood the consequences of crossing Beijing's ever-changing political thresholds.

The PLA continues to debate the efficacy of demonstrations of power to affect political dynamics. The 2020 version of the *Science of Military Strategy* describes *weishe* (威慑), often translated as "deterrence," as

> a method of military conflict to achieve a political goal based on military strength . . . and determination to use strength [that] makes the other side face unworthy or even unbearable consequences.[27]

The intended political outcome of this method of military conflict is to make the adversary "give in, compromise, or surrender," ideally without having to engage in large-scale fighting.[28]

The PLA may use military conflict at a low level to achieve a political goal. The *Science of Military Strategy* identifies "warning military strikes" as part of strategies to both forestall adversary actions and coerce compliance. Indeed, limited uses of military strikes against precise and specific targets can showcase the ability and determination to achieve military and political objectives and may obviate the need for larger military campaigns and operations. The PLA does not see itself as moving through distinct phases of war, from "shaping" and "influence" operations to "kinetic" use of force operations.[29] Rather, it intertwines shaping and influence operations with kinetic operations.

All militaries are instruments of politics, but in the PRC the relationship has historically been more direct. The PLA is the party's armed wing, not China's professional military. The PLA's foundational purpose is to help the party win political struggles and develop new political realities. In turn, the CCP's main purpose is to expand its power over territory and peoples. The party's history as an insurgency engaged in "people's war" informs its current conduct as it expands its writ over Hong Kong, Tibet, and Xinjiang.

In Taiwan's case, the CCP seeks to expand its political power over new territory and 24 million additional people that it has never ruled. This is difficult to do and would require much more force than any of the other populations and territories it now controls. The PLA is thus a crucial tool, and intensifying applications of actual—rather than "only" demonstrations of—force may be necessary.

The coercive campaign offers the PRC distinct advantages over a campaign to invade and occupy Taiwan. It also provides Beijing flexibility to continually redefine what it considers the bounds of acceptable political behavior by Taipei and Washington. First, unlike a campaign of brute force annihilation, Beijing can redefine success if it needs to. Second, Beijing's negotiating leverage keeps increasing as the PLA grows stronger.

The CCP's coercion campaign has expanded even as Taipei has made concessions. The ROC abandoned its claim to be the sole legitimate ruler of all of China in 1991. In effect, Taiwan declared peace, abandoning its stated policy of unification through force, and aligned its polity with geopolitical realities. The overwhelming majority of Taiwanese residents did not come to Taiwan during the KMT retreat, and they had no say and little interest in perpetuating the Chinese civil war. They disagree with Washington's "One China" policy and never had a say in its foundational 1972 statement that "all Chinese on either side of the Taiwan Strait maintain there is but One China."[30] Yet they have accepted it.

A substantial group of voters now supports Taiwan's newer Democratic Progressive Party (DPP), an erstwhile opposition party that rose to power as part of the independence movement in Taiwan. But the once-oppressed DPP voters made an enormous concession by accepting that they were citizens of the ROC, not of a new state called Taiwan. The ROC is a preexisting political entity whose existence the CCP recognizes in practice even while denying its right to rule over anything. Any declaration of the existence of a new Republic of Taiwan would seem to Beijing a declaration of independence and therefore an escalation rather than a concession.[31] But the US does not support such a political escalation and thus this option is all but impossible. Rather, the US supports the political status quo, which means that the ROC rules Taiwan and the PRC rules mainland China.

Taipei also suspended martial law in 1987, which had been put in place to fight Communist subversion and infiltration. It made political changes to better reflect the reality that its government only has sovereignty over the people and territory of Taiwan, though it did not formally amend its constitution to relinquish its claims to mainland China, which ironically would have angered the PRC. The ROC thus set the conditions for a diplomatic breakthrough across the strait. Officials from each side of the strait met to work out practical matters of cooperation, from the governance of postal services to consular services. The two sides implicitly agreed to compromise on a political formulation, now referred to as the 1992 Consensus. They agreed to disagree on the meaning of "One China."[32]

The ROC's unilateral abandonment of the threat of force and the forfeiture of claims of jurisdiction over the mainland should have been the basis for a lasting peace. But Beijing's response to Taipei's cessation of a state of hostilities was an escalation of its coercion campaign. Before Taiwan's first democratic election in June 1995, Taiwan's president, Lee Teng-hui, made a high-profile visit to his alma mater, Cornell University. The PRC then conducted a series of missile tests in the waters surrounding Taiwan and other military maneuvers in response to what CCP leaders called Lee's attempts to "split the motherland."[33] The US and Taiwan had never formally agreed to limit the visits of Taiwan presidents, and the US does not agree that there is a "motherland" that Taiwan is trying to "split." There has never been a single political CCP-run entity that included Taiwan. This was a provocative escalation by Beijing.

The PRC initiated another set of missile tests in the run-up to Taiwan's first presidential election in 1996 in an attempt to frighten Taiwan's electorate into voting against Lee and compel the US to rein in what China called Taiwan's pro-independence forces.[34] In 1999, Lee suggested the two sides negotiate on a "special state-to-state basis"[35] in an effort to break Taipei and Beijing out of a diplomatic stalemate, just seven years after its partial breakthrough. The response from Beijing was a stepped-up rhetorical assault with escalating military maneuvers. Beijing focused on Lee's use of the term "state-to-state," despite Lee's use of the modifier "special" to connote something less than official country-to-country relations. His creative formulation was meant to co-opt independence-minded Taiwanese while providing Beijing with a face-saving way to conduct relations with Taiwan.

Taiwan's efforts to normalize relations based on a reasonable diplomatic formula that recognized CCP rule over the mainland while avoiding declaring Taiwanese independence were seen in Beijing as dangerous "splittism" (the term the CCP uses for political separatism). Beijing pocketed Taiwanese concessions as it had previous American concessions, but it failed to make any concessions of its own. Moreover, the PRC treated these concessions as provocations justifying further demands and coercion.

This response was delivered by the Chinese General Secretary Jiang Zemin at the height of the US effort to integrate China into the global economy and establish warm commercial relations with Beijing. It occurred as the US dramatically downsized its military following the end of the Cold War. There was certainly cause for Beijing to worry about the military balance with the US after America's thumping of Saddam Hussein's military in 1991—and the prodemocratic rhetoric of both the George H. W. Bush and Clinton administrations. But US actions indicated that the threat to the PRC was receding rather than growing. The Chinese coercion campaign thus began during a time of peace and prosperity for Beijing, when it enjoyed friendly relations with the West.

Countries and companies had rushed into China to explore commercial opportunities while the PRC embraced foreign expertise and know-how. The Soviet Union had collapsed, removing a long-standing threat to Beijing's north. Beijing's ideological problem remained, however: Democracy in Taiwan undermines the CCP's core tenet that democracy is unsuitable for the Chinese cultural context. The existence of a legitimate constitutional government actually ruling Taiwan, moreover, discredited the CCP's claim to speak for all Chinese people.

Having received US and Taiwanese concessions as if they were acts of escalation, the CCP learned during this period of peace and Western outreach and engagement that threats of force could push the US to pressure Taipei. The US sent ships to the Taiwan Strait in response to Chinese missile tests in 1995 and 1996, to be sure. But the PRC convinced then-President Clinton to publicly affirm China's position on Taiwan, rather than Taipei's or Washington's, while speaking on Chinese soil in Shanghai.[36] Beijing demanded that President Clinton repeat the so-called three nos: that the US would not support (1) Taiwan independence, (2) "Two Chinas" or "One China One Taiwan," or (3) Taiwan's efforts to participate in international organizations in which statehood is a requirement.[37]

The events of 1995–97 also exposed the PRC's relative military impotence at that time, as the PLA had no military answer to the arrival of US warships in the strait. But Beijing accomplished the political outcome it sought, despite its military weakness, through an apparent escalation that was not backed by actual capability. It made a political demand of Washington based on a military bluff, and Washington complied.

A DPP government under Chen Shui-bian was elected in 2000, partially in reaction to China's military intimidation. As the CCP's pressure grew on the Chen government, Taipei pushed for greater recognition of Taiwan's independence. Yet Beijing convinced President George W. Bush to publicly rebuke Taiwan's president in the company of PRC Premier Wen Jiabao, humiliating Chen in the process.[38]

When Xi became general secretary of the CCP in 2012, his initial approach to Taiwan was relatively moderate. Taiwan was governed by a KMT leader, Ma Ying-jeou, who sought more conciliation with Beijing. Xi and Ma met in Singapore in 2015, the first meeting between the leaders of Taiwan and China and a notable Chinese diplomatic olive branch to Taiwan. Moreover, Xi did not protest when Ma took the public position that the two sides had "agreed to disagree" about the meaning of "One China," another apparent PRC concession.[39] The formula of "One China, different interpretations" was apparently back on the table. This formulation was in essence the same as Lee's "special state-to-state relations" comment in 1999, as the leaders of the government of Taiwan and China met as coequals.

This history is not merely of academic interest. To counter CCP revisionism, US policymakers need to understand it. And, as a matter of policy, the US should insist that Beijing does not get to choose which elected leaders of the ROC it deals with. To date, the US has not called on the PRC to return to the negotiating table with the current Taiwanese President Tsai Ing-wen based on this precedent.

Xi's relatively conciliatory approach to Taiwan did not survive Ma's presidency, however. When Tsai succeeded Ma in 2016, Xi reverted to the previous CCP posture of threats and demands. During his meeting with Ma, Xi said that "as long as the 1992 Consensus and its core values are acknowledged, we stand ready to have contact."[40] Tsai did not explicitly accept the language of the 1992 Consensus, charting a different course from an agreement made by her political opponent's party. This is, of course, the prerogative of any new government. China's Taiwan Affairs Office criticized her and demanded that she recognize the PRC's "One China" principle.[41] Tsai nevertheless went as far toward conciliation as Taiwan's new politics would allow. By 2016, the electorate in Taiwan had little connection to mainland China. The grandchildren of the old KMT were voters who had grown up in a democratic Taiwan. Ties with China were akin to those of Canadians with the US: a shared culture, history, and language but little else, despite the CCP's insistence otherwise.

While Beijing was warning Washington about Tsai's "separatist" and independence proclivities, Tsai conceded in her May 2016 inauguration speech that "the new government will conduct cross-Strait affairs in accordance with the Republic of China Constitution, the Act Governing Relations between the People of Taiwan Area and the Mainland Area, and other relevant legislation."[42]

This statement was another major concession by a Taiwanese leader. That Tsai represented the native Taiwanese DPP yet accepted that the ROC and Taiwan were the same entity was a difficult internal political maneuver. Crucially, she embraced the reality that the PRC governs the mainland and the ROC on Taiwan does not; she thereby opened the door to diplomatic solutions similar to those of her predecessors. But for Tsai, the meaning of "One China" was to be negotiated, not simply conceded to the PRC. Washington encouraged Tsai's concession, but it never insisted that the CCP make any similar compromise or live up to Xi's implicit acceptance of the "different interpretations."[43]

Xi has years of experience dealing with Taiwan as a former party secretary of Fujian province, directly across the strait from Taiwan. He is versed in Taiwanese politics and knows that Tsai went as far as she could go on the issue of "One China." Yet he chose to escalate the coercion campaign, blaming Tsai for recalcitrance. The US and its allies should have made a more concerted effort, beginning then to call on Xi to return to the negotiating table and not escalate his disagreements with Taiwan's new government through force and diplomatic pressure.

Soon after Tsai was elected, Beijing pressured Panama and São Tomé and Príncipe to shift diplomatic relations from the ROC to the PRC.[44] Beijing shut Taiwan out of international organizations, such as the International Civil Aviation Organization[45] and the International Criminal Police Organization,[46] among others. During Tsai's presidency, the CCP has pressured companies ranging from United Airlines to Snickers to call Taiwan a province of China or face economic penalty.[47]

Beijing also accelerated its campaign of military coercion following Tsai's accession. The PLA increased the frequency of bomber circum-navigations of Taiwan in late 2016 and made such circumnavigations an enduring reality for the Tsai administration.[48] By late 2017, PLA bombers and support aircraft circumnavigated the island.[49] Beijing modified a civil aviation route near the centerline of the Taiwan Strait in January 2018 to allow commercial airlines to fly over open ocean in the strait, severely tax-ing Taiwan's air defense system and air traffic controls.[50] Since February 2018, the People's Liberation Army Air Force (PLAAF) intensified a pat-tern of flights through the Miyako Strait, off the east coast of Taiwan in the Philippine Sea, and the Bashi Channel. These flights demonstrate the PLAAF's ability to "break" the first island chain and establish air domi-nance over key lifelines for Taiwan and its geographical connection to the outside world.[51]

In March 2019, two PLAAF fighters crossed into Taiwan's side of the median line—an unofficial boundary between Taiwan and the PRC not challenged by the Chinese military since 1999.[52] The military maneuvers were accompanied by statements from China's Taiwan Affairs Office and the PLA's Eastern Theater Command about their necessity to guard against "separatists," as if the PLA were conducting legitimate counterterror operations.[53] In September 2020, a Chinese Foreign Ministry spokesman stated, "There is no so-called median line in the Strait."[54]

This line had been another means of keeping peace and stability across the Taiwan Strait. The CCP's violation and rejection of it was an incremen-tal move to claim the waters and air around Taiwan as its own. The PRC continued this coercive campaign by increasing air incursions into the Taiwanese Air Defense Identification Zone (ADIZ). Taiwan recorded 969 incursions by Chinese warplanes into its ADIZ in 2021—more than double the roughly 380 carried out in 2020.[55] In 2022, total Chinese air incursions into the ADIZ were 1,115.[56] The PLA continually issues threatening mes-sages in native Taiwanese dialects and allows military commentators to describe the ability of their jets to decapitate the Taiwanese leadership.[57]

These PLA operations are part of Chinese cognitive warfare, what Tai-wan calls "cognitive domain warfare" or *renzhi yu zuozhan* (认知域作战). A Taiwan defense analyst has captured the purpose of this aerospace cam-paign: "PLA exercises first create an environment of fear, and then the responsibility of causing tension is blamed on 'Taiwan's ambitious politicians.'"[58] The CCP aims to influence Taiwanese and American politics through the tension it creates. In manipulating the information space through demonstrations of force, its goal is to get important audiences in Taipei, Washington, and allied capitals to believe more pliant Taiwanese leaders could make this threat go away.[59]

The CCP has thus put the Taiwanese under the constant threat of ever-escalating violence and political pressure. One purpose of these shows of force across the strait is to coerce the US to change its policy, curtail its relations with Taiwan, come closer to the CCP's definition of what "One China" means, and force Taipei to come with it on that journey of concessions. The second purpose is to wear down Taiwan's resistance, undermine DPP rule, and persuade the Taiwanese of their own accord to elect and follow leaders who will concede to China's demands.

The PRC can fully secure its objectives vis-à-vis Taiwan if it achieves either aim. Taiwan cannot continue to resist growing PRC pressure without the active support of Washington and its allies in and beyond the region. If Beijing can reduce or *break* that support, Taiwan will have no option but to give the PRC what it desires. The CCP can succeed even more fully if it can actually break the will of Taiwanese supporters of policies of autonomy and resistance and elevate compliant Taiwanese politicians to power.

US policy risks making a grave error by seeing China's expanding military operations around Taiwan only through the prism of preparations for an invasion. Those operations may be part of such preparations and may help with them in various ways, but they are also strategic undertakings in their own right and are directly aimed at accomplishing Beijing's goals. Developing strategies to deter or defeat a Chinese invasion of Taiwan may be ineffective or even counterproductive in preventing the PRC from subjugating Taiwan through a combination of these coercion efforts and the continuing persuasion efforts that accompany them, as we consider below.

A strategy to protect Taiwan's autonomy and freedom from Chinese control requires blocking the persuasion and coercion roads to PRC domination of the island and deterring or defeating the compellence road. A US counter-persuasion and -coercion strategy should be focused, tightly sequenced and phased, and deliberate. Chinese political and economic moves to undermine Taiwan's isolation should be coordinated with demonstrations of US and allied force that can ensure open strategic lines of communication and resupply around Taiwan. The increasingly myopic focus on the supposedly imminent Chinese invasion threat can seriously hinder or prevent entirely the development and implementation of such a strategy. This outcome may be in part what China seeks.

Compellence

The PRC has unquestionably been developing the capability to compel Taiwanese capitulation by force if coercion and persuasion fail, but Xi's determination to move to compellence and the imminence of a Chinese invasion of Taiwan both require more rigorous interrogation than either is currently receiving. It would be more strategically apposite for the US to approach concerns about an impending Chinese invasion in the context of ongoing Chinese persuasion and coercion approaches. An invasion or other compellent strategies are possible, but such scenarios would be escalations of current campaigns carrying significant risks and downsides for Beijing.

The narrow focus on the threat of Chinese invasion, moreover, marginalizes an alternative compellence strategy that would flow far more naturally from China's persuasion and coercion efforts—a strategy of isolation. The US would do well, therefore, to take a step back from the increasingly frantic discussion of ways and means to deter or stop a cross-Strait invasion and instead reconsider the PRC strategic context from which any such decision and operation would emerge.

China did not begin its military modernization with the express purpose of invading Taiwan. As we have stated, the PLA modernization campaign started in the early 1990s, when the PRC observed America's military modernization demonstrated in the deserts of Iraq and Kuwait.[60] The Gulf War shocked the world's major militaries by demonstrating that a highly trained, professional, all-volunteer force equipped with precision strike and stealth capabilities could humiliate the world's fourth largest army rapidly and with extremely low casualties.

Russian military theorists were seized by this phenomenon and pushed for the modernization and professionalization of the Russian military in the following decades. Many other countries began abandoning long-held conscription practices and turning to professional volunteer militaries equipped with more advanced technology. The Chinese did the same and for the same reasons.

Defense analysts have grown increasingly concerned that the PLA has a set goal of 2027 to invade Taiwan, based on comments by outgoing commander of US Indo-Pacific Command Adm. Phil Davidson (ret.).[61] But the primary importance of 2027 is that it is the 100-year anniversary of the PLA's founding and is thus likely a deadline for it to reach new modernization milestones. The PLA can likely already conduct an invasion if ordered, albeit with high risk; as the modernization process continues, and in every year that passes, the PLA will have more capability to do so.[62]

The PLA's modernization effort is general-purpose, rather than narrowly optimized for a cross-Strait invasion. It began at a time when the PRC was pocketing US and Taiwanese concessions and increasing its demands; it continued through periods of apparent Taiwanese and American conciliation of Beijing and through periods of easing of tensions between Beijing and Taipei. Xi may have accelerated the expected date of completion of this decades-long general military buildup, shifting it into a specific preparation for a particular invasion scenario, but there is no direct and publicly available evidence of this assessment.[63] US policymakers would do well to question the notion that this program's date of completion represents some kind of specified invasion date.

The modernization program naturally enhances the PRC's military abilities to invade Taiwan even against US resistance, but it also enhances the PLA's abilities to pursue another form of compellence—isolation.

Isolation. A strategy of isolating Taiwan by air and sea flows naturally from China's ongoing persuasion and coercion efforts. Those efforts explicitly aim to get the last few states that diplomatically recognize Taiwan to shift their recognition to Beijing. They aim to cajole states and businesses to accept and promulgate the Chinese version of the Beijing-Taipei relationship, rather than Taiwan's—a form of informational isolation. That aim includes efforts to prevent other heads and senior leaders of foreign states from visiting Taipei or receiving Taiwanese officials in their capitals.

It is thus in part also a strategy of diplomatic isolation. And Beijing constantly presses other countries to refrain from providing Taiwan with military equipment—a form of military-cooperation isolation. One set of aims of the current coercion and persuasion efforts is thus to use means short of the actual use of force to cut Taipei's connections to the outside world, other than those that might run through Beijing.

The natural next escalation in these efforts is not invasion, but rather adding the overt use of force to complete the isolation. Beijing could declare a quarantine or blockade of Taiwan on some pretext and deploy its maritime power and airpower to enforce such a policy. The blockade need not be total from the start. The PRC could begin by deploying ships covered by aircraft around the island to inspect all vessels entering and leaving Taiwan's ports for some claimed contraband—advanced weapons systems, perhaps. Beijing could similarly insist on inspecting aircraft, although attempting to enforce such a demand without actually shooting down civilian aircraft would be challenging. How many civilian aircraft, on the other hand, would continue operating through skies full of PLAAF aircraft threatening to down them?

If such initial efforts failed to bring Taipei to a position satisfactory to Beijing, the PRC could escalate further to an actual blockade. Taiwan is unalterably dependent on external resources to survive, so it is almost impossible to imagine that a protracted blockade could fail to secure Taipei's surrender on almost any terms Beijing might dictate. Moreover, given its unique lack of official status in international affairs, it may be especially vulnerable to demonstrations that it can be isolated. It would be difficult to muster the kind of defiance that Britain did under attack from Nazi Germany: Taiwan lacks Britain's long history and strategic traditions, general cohesion, and unbreakable morale.

This form of compellence not only is the most natural and obvious progression from the current PRC campaigns but also seems to present a far more attractive balance of risk and reward to Beijing. It does not in principle require the PLA to engage in combat. If Taiwan's supporters make clear they will not challenge such a blockade, then Taiwan might surrender without fighting. If either Taiwan or its supporters decide to challenge it, moreover, they run the risk of appearing to have fired the first shot, provided the PRC has arranged matters such that running the blockade requires shooting at ships or aircraft blocking routes to ports or airfields.[64]

If the PRC has not managed such an arrangement, then the PLA might need to shoot first, but it might begin by hitting a civilian plane or ship. Such an action would obviously incur outrage and opprobrium, on the one hand, but it would also place Taiwan and its partners in the position of having to decide how to respond. That position would likely be uncomfortable, as competing pressures to respond to the Chinese action and support Taiwan would be offset by fears that the pro-Taiwan coalition would be initiating a war. To see this dynamic at work, we have only to look at the extensive Western discourse about the fears of prompting Russian escalation by providing defensive systems to Ukraine following Moscow's unprovoked and illegal invasion. The West's early wavering about supporting Ukraine against a blatantly illegal and unjust invasion requires considerably more attention than it has received, since it offers Beijing encouragement as it considers escalation toward Taiwan.

This isolation strategy has some downsides for Beijing, to be sure. It would be an obvious escalation to the use of force and could trigger the US and regional states to mobilize for war, thereby depriving the PRC of the element of surprise it might otherwise hope to achieve at some level in a no-notice invasion scenario. If the US and its partners responded to the isolation rapidly and in force, Beijing could find it has made the prospects of a successful invasion much worse by bringing its adversaries' advanced military capabilities into the vicinity of Taiwan without interdicting them.

The PRC would thus need to be prepared to choose either of the two most plausible actions in response to the deployment of considerable US and allied firepower toward Taiwan: de-escalate and await another moment or escalate to regional war. If the strength and determination of the US and partner response seemed to Beijing too high to challenge, then the PRC could back away, accept a temporary defeat, and develop alternative approaches for another try later on. Beijing could prepare in advance to mitigate the unpleasantness of having to climb down by defining a lesser political objective that it could be reasonably sure to accomplish—or plausibly claim to have accomplished—before it had to back away.

The PRC could alternatively ensure that its initial preparations for the isolation campaign include preparations to escalate to major conflict if a

US-led coalition challenged it seriously. This approach might not be easily distinguishable from preparations for a full-scale invasion in that it would likely include putting in place all the capabilities needed to exclude US-led forces from the vicinity of Taiwan and drive off or destroy any already near the island. It might include the preparation of an invasion force, depending on whether Beijing believed it could achieve its aims by the escalatory application of the isolation approach. The PLA would face a potentially much worse military position at the start of such an escalation than it could hope to face in a surprise invasion scenario, but Beijing might also calculate that the threat of invasion could reduce the willingness of the US-led coalition to push matters to full-scale war.

Time-space relationships could also be central to any PRC isolation approach. The PRC appears to believe it is developing a strong network of collaborators and fellow travelers in Taiwan and that its own political warfare elements on the island may be able to paralyze initial Taiwanese responses and quickly sap the island's will to resist. An isolation strategy would almost certainly begin with the successful isolation of the island by air and sea; any response to break blockades or quarantines would likely take days or weeks to negotiate and then bring into effect.

The initial shock of isolation could engender strong psychological effects, especially if China manages to cut Taiwan's internet connectivity and other means of communicating with the outside world. Beijing might calculate that its efforts and agents could bring Taiwan to surrender before the US is able to break through Taiwan's isolation. The PRC leadership is moderately likely to be wrong in such a calculation; overestimating one's ability to break the will of an adversary is one of the most common mistakes in coercion and compellence strategies. But miscalculation would change the outcome, not the decision to make the attempt.

If Beijing pursued an isolation strategy, it would undermine the prospects of an immediate escalation to full-scale attack. But this approach is still attractive as it offers the possibility of achieving Beijing's aims without having to engage in a complicated amphibious invasion. An isolation strategy poses a potentially higher risk that the PRC might have to back down in an embarrassing fashion, but it offsets that risk by offering a climbdown before major hostilities break out and therefore before China suffers significant combat losses. It also flows most naturally from the long-standing persuasion and coercion campaigns China has been pursuing.

Invasion. Xi might nevertheless decide not to bother with isolation efforts, instead driving straight toward his final objective via invasion. The Chinese idealized version of this strategy would of course be attractive to Beijing: A brief period of increased tension covers the execution of well-planned and rehearsed PLA mobilization for an invasion. A short air-missile campaign shatters Taiwan's defense and government structures while Chinese political warfare agents on the island become active, wrecking any hope of coherent Taiwanese preparations for defense. The massive Chinese fleet sweeps quickly across the strait and begins disembarking troops and vehicles onto Taiwanese beaches almost before Taipei knows what's happening, and Chinese troops raise the PRC flag over government buildings in Taipei while policymakers in Washington and Tokyo debate what to do. Xi makes a speech from the Presidential Office in Taipei, and "splittism" is forever defeated.

It is unlikely that even Xi seriously entertains this fantasy. The statements and actions of American and Japanese leaders and officials offer no reason for Xi to be confident that the US and Japan (or Australia) would stand idly by and watch this spectacle. On the contrary, from the PRC's perspective, President Joe Biden has been setting informational and military conditions to prepare to defend Taiwan against an invasion.

Xi has clearly also been observing the disastrous Russian invasion of Ukraine that highlighted additional factors of concern. The Russians thought they had thoroughly penetrated Ukrainian society and government with their own agents and fellow travelers and built a campaign on the assumption that Ukrainians would not fight. They were wrong on all counts. The Russians also wildly overestimated their own military capabilities and competence and underestimated the inevitable effects of battlefield friction. The PLA is almost certainly more competent and able to handle friction than the Potemkin army with which Russia invaded, but friction is real in any war and the more so in complex large-scale amphibious invasions.

Chinese military leaders and Xi himself must therefore take seriously the possibilities that Taiwan will fight and that the political warfare efforts on the island will be only partially successful, that the US and its allies will respond with force rapidly and determinedly, that the PLA will not perform optimally, and, even if nothing else does, that the friction inherent in war will lead to setbacks and losses. None of these observations are groundbreaking. They serve only to say that Xi must recognize the high risks associated with invading Taiwan—unless he is a thoroughgoing fool, which he does not in any way appear to be.

It is clear enough that an island of 24 million people cannot hope to defeat the massed forces of a country of 1.4 billion. The best that Taiwan on its own could hope would be to inflict painful losses on an invading Chinese force. Properly equipped and determined to fight, Taiwan might be able to do so. We shall set aside further consideration of this aspect of the scenario, however, to focus on those that are more dangerous to Beijing.

Debate roils the US national security establishment about America's capacity to stop a Chinese invasion of Taiwan. Some argue that the PLA's ballistic, cruise, and now hypersonic missiles render America's aircraft carriers hopelessly vulnerable and that China's air and missile arsenal and A2AD systems force the US to rely on bases far from Taiwan and on long-range standoff missiles alone, ultimately dooming any chance the US might have to stop the attack.[65]

Much hinges in these scenarios on when and whether Beijing would attack US bases at Guam and Okinawa, at least, and on assumptions about America's ability to use bases in South Korea and the Japanese home islands. If the US retains the ability to use Guam and Okinawa, so the reasoning often goes, then it might be able to challenge the PLA's ability to cross the strait or at least to impose losses that Beijing would find unbearable.[66]

These discussions are important for considerations of invasion scenarios. One struggles to recall a successful amphibious invasion in the era of combat aircraft conducted without at least localized air supremacy. Amphibious ships are large, vulnerable targets whose sinking entails the deaths of hundreds or thousands of soldiers and the loss of large amounts of vehicles and supplies. Few if any militaries have been willing to risk sailing them to shore in the face of enemy aircraft or an enemy's ability to concentrate volumes of high-payload munitions on them.

China cannot deprive the US of all ability to strike a PLA landing force. Long-range stealth bombers can refuel out of the A2AD bubble and fire missiles, some of which will almost surely hit and destroy their targets. US attack submarines and other platforms can fire volleys of cruise missiles that PLA air defenses will not completely shoot down. If China invades and the US is determined to defend Taiwan, the PLA will take losses.

The scale and consequences of those losses depend heavily, however, on whether the US can use its carriers and regional bases. The more of those assets the American military can use, the more severe the damage it can impose on the invasion force, possibly up to and including its destruction. That is one of the reasons many discussions of a Chinese invasion scenario assume that the PLA would attack US bases on Guam and Okinawa, at least, and possibly on the Japanese home islands.[67] They often assume that South Korea would not allow the US to use its bases on the Korean Peninsula in a war that, in principle, interests Seoul very little.[68]

Chinese military technocrats would likely prefer to begin the attack in this fashion and deprive the US of as much regional capacity as possible. The geostrategic advisability of doing so, however, rests on political rather than military considerations. Would the US absorb an attack on Guam and not thereafter regard itself as at war with China? Would Tokyo regard attacks on US bases on Japanese territory as bilateral US-China affairs that do not constitute acts of war against Japan? Would the US, having lost immediate use of its other regional bases, not activate the US–Republic of Korea mutual defense treaty (which, unlike the US treaty with Japan, actually is mutual and obliges Seoul to come to the aid of the US if the US is attacked in the region)?[69] Would Seoul refuse that activation, thereby risking the loss of its most important ally?

As both Russia and the allies have learned, no prewar assumption holds after a war begins. Ukraine's fighting will is beyond what analysts imagined before the conflict, the US and NATO are equipping Ukraine far beyond what was thought possible, Washington has reinforced NATO forces on the eastern flank, and there are now two new NATO members under consideration. Turning back to Asia, it is hard to imagine South Korea wanting to remain neutral once Australia, Japan, and the US (and possibly some other NATO countries) are in the fight; in a scenario in which US ships, territory, and allies are struck, the US will likely pay whatever price its allies Thailand and the Philippines demand for the use of their airspace and bases in their territory. The issue of South Korean sympathy for Taiwan (or lack thereof) is a red herring. Seoul will have to make decisions in the context of the viability of its long-term reliance on the US and America's allies—and the possible impact of refusing US requests for help on that reliance.

Surely Xi and his lieutenants have considered the geopolitical consequences of trying to succeed operationally. If not, the China problem may be bigger than most analysts realize. In that case, either Xi is as isolated and delusional as Putin was before invading Ukraine, and therefore is undeterrable, or his grand strategic objectives have changed. From building up comprehensive national power and making incremental gains to undermine US alliances and reshape the world order, Xi would have transformed his grand strategy into one of forcefully obtaining hegemony in Asia. If Xi's objectives have changed in such a fashion, then the US should not be preparing to counter only an invasion of Taiwan but rather a series of Chinese campaigns for hegemony. The assumption of this report is that China's strategy toward Taiwan is part of a unification campaign, a close cousin of the successful Hong Kong, Tibet, and Xinjiang campaigns, and that any other gains Xi thinks he can secure from successful unification are secondary and opportunistic.

One might restate these considerations more straightforwardly. A PRC invasion plan that relies on attacking Guam and US positions in Japan early in the conflict would immediately bring China into open war with the US, Japan, and possibly South Korea. US policy analysts might broodingly fear that the US and its regional allies would allow even such attacks to glance off them from a geopolitical standpoint and work to treat the war as a "Taiwan crisis" with no larger ramifications. We needn't get into that argument ourselves to observe that Xi would, again, be a complete fool to be confident of such a response.

Serious political and military leaders in Beijing must thus consider that a decision to invade Taiwan immediately confronts them with a second extremely thorny decision: Either Xi accepts the much greater risks to the success of the military operation if China does not attack US bases at once, or he must accept the real possibility that the limited invasion of Taiwan could rapidly become a full-scale regional or even global war with the US and its allies.

We do not by any means intend to suggest that Xi might not decide that either risk is acceptable; he might. We certainly do not mean to say that strong and prompt US responses or US and American-allied escalations are certain or would be successful. Those arguing that, as things stand today, China could invade Taiwan and the US couldn't stop the invasion might be right. Calls for increasing America's military capabilities to defeat such a Chinese attack at acceptable costs to the US and its allies are surely cogent and should be heeded.

But even this cursory examination of some of the invasion-scenario implications suggests that it would be an extraordinarily risky undertaking to any Chinese leader not besotted with his own power and deluded by stupid or dishonest generals and political advisers. Most leaders would prefer less risky approaches that offer the promise of securing the same outcome at lower cost.

US policy therefore cannot accept as a given that Xi is simply preparing to invade and that, when the PLA is ready, he will. We must instead reopen the aperture to see other plausible roads Xi could take to seizing Taiwan and develop strategies to block all of them rather than focusing on only one.

Implications

This discussion would be of merely academic interest if preparations to defeat the cross-Strait invasion also included blocking the persuasion, coercion, and isolation-compellence roads. Unfortunately, though, the approaches generally advocated to stop the invasion actively undermine efforts to block Xi's other roads.

If the invasion scenario is the only one the US and its allies plan to block, the temptation will grow to pull back from the Chinese A2AD bubble, abandon reliance on Guam and Okinawa, and focus on increasing America's long-range strike capabilities.[70] Maximizing perceived operational effectiveness would override geopolitical necessity. Such a move would potentiate the PRC's persuasion, coercion, and isolation efforts. It could be the case that these efforts actually enhance America's ability to defend Taiwan and therefore increase the likelihood the US would come to Taiwan's defense, although we question both assumptions. But would it seem that way to the Taiwanese?

The actual optics of that strategy involve withdrawing visible US presence from the near vicinity of Taiwan, after all. The more imminent war becomes, under this approach, the faster US carrier battle groups steam away from the island, the more US strike aircraft fly north and west from Okinawa and Guam, and the more American military bases throughout the region move into defensive rather than offensive postures. The Taiwanese would be remarkable people indeed to observe those phenomena, see the growing concentration of Chinese military assets around their island, and conclude that they should be ready to fight to the death, confident that America will be with them.

Openly accepting the premise that US carriers cannot survive Chinese attacks also means openly stating that moving carriers toward Taiwan, Japan, or through the strait is always an American bluff and should not be seen as a serious demonstration of Washington's willingness or ability to fight.[71] The utility of such freedom of navigation operations could be questioned in any event, but accepting the widely held premises about the poor US prospects for defeating a cross-Strait invasion today makes them worse than meaningless.[72]

These discussions all tend to undermine the likely effectiveness of any strategies the US and its partners might develop to try to block the persuasion and coercion roads to the conquest of Taiwan, but they don't preclude the construction and implementation of such strategies. Even advocates of the standoff approach to defending Taiwan against invasion, after all, generally agree that the US should develop such counterstrategies even if they also generally dismiss the significance of Chinese persuasion and coercion campaigns through their confidence that invasion is inevitable and even imminent.[73]

The most serious problem with focusing narrowly on preventing the cross-Strait invasion from standoff ranges is that it almost invites Xi to try the isolation strategy. Breaking blockades requires presence. The US certainly could use long-range precision weapons to sink Chinese ships blocking or interfering with merchant vessels trying to move into and out of Taiwan's ports—until those Chinese ships move too close to those merchant vessels to permit their safe destruction. And driving PLAAF aircraft out of Taiwan's skies is not likely a task that can be undertaken from far-over-the-horizon bases except by destroying all the PLAAF bases on the mainland from which such operations are conducted.

Even assuming that that is a feasible military undertaking, it nevertheless would move the US rapidly toward the tremendously escalatory step of conducting a large-scale air attack on the Chinese homeland. Any approach to breaking the blockade with standoff munitions, finally, requires the US to use an immediate lethal approach to respond to a Chinese effort conducted, possibly, with less-than-lethal force. It could put the responsibility for escalating to a shooting war on the US, even though China created the crisis.

The main problem with approaches seeking to break a blockade from standoff distances is not that doing so is impossible but rather that promising to do so is insufficiently credible. It is almost impossible to imagine a scenario in which the Chinese begin to interfere with Taiwan's communications and trade with the rest of the world, whereafter the US instantly responds by sinking Chinese ships. Beijing's isolation strategy would almost inevitably have some time to work before a serious US response along these lines even started—let alone before it succeeded, if it could. Xi might miscalculate the odds of securing Taiwan's concession in that interval, as we have observed above, but the relatively low risks he would run compared with those entailed in a full-scale invasion make it more plausible that he would accept the risk of miscalculation here.

There is a solution to the conundrum these challenges pose to the US: Design a counterinvasion strategy that includes a counter-isolation strategy. The far-over-the-horizon counterinvasion strategy is a problem only if it precludes or excludes counter-isolation efforts. The US should and, indeed, must have far-over-the-horizon capabilities in any scenario. But it must also develop ways to operate within China's A2AD zone, including within the range of China's hypersonic missiles. It must be able to meet a Chinese blockade effort centered on nonlethal force with a nonlethal counter-isolation effort of its own. It must avoid the optics of withdrawing its military power from the theater as the threat of Chinese attack grows and instead, ideally, create the object of credible military power flowing toward Taiwan.

We recognize that these demands are easy to make and hard to meet. We have no specific suggestions about how to do so technically or tactically.

Our purpose in this report, rather, is to say that actually keeping Taiwan free is even harder than it seems to many. We cannot reduce the problem to one specific scenario, and we actually must focus on solving extraordinarily hard military problems to enable strategies that can defeat not only the most dangerous courses of action Beijing might pursue but also the most likely.

Notes

1. By "persuasion," we mean attempts through information operations and diplomacy, backed by the threat of force, to convince all relevant players to accept China's definition of "One China," which is that Taiwan is and has always been a part of China. China is trying to persuade key international stakeholders that the costs of not accepting its preferred reality are high. By "coercion," we mean more intense military intimidation and threats short of invasion to force Taiwan to accede to China's demands. In a successful coercion campaign, Taiwan would still have a military that could resist, but one or both of its political leadership and military would have lost the willpower to do so. By "compellence," we mean the use of force to degrade or destroy Taiwan's means and will to resist. For example, this could be an invasion and occupation or a blockade accompanied by strikes. The key is that China is forcefully making Taiwan do something it would otherwise not do. Note that this chapter was originally published as a research report for the Coalition Defense of Taiwan, a project of the American Enterprise Institute and the Institute for the Study of War. See American Enterprise Institute, "Coalition Defense of Taiwan," https://www.aei.org/coalition-defense-of-taiwan.

2. Sun Tzu, *The Art of War*, https://web.mit.edu/~dcltdw/AOW/3.html.

3. Mark A. Stokes, "The Chinese Joint Aerospace Campaign: Strategy, Doctrine, and Force Modernization," in *China's Revolution in Doctrinal Affairs: Emerging Trends in the Operational Art of the Chinese People's Liberation Army*, ed. James Mulvenon and David M. Finkelstein (Arlington, VA: CNA Corporation, 2005), 222.

4. Dean Cheng, "Chinese Lessons from the Gulf Wars," in *Chinese Lessons from Other People's Wars*, ed. Andrew Scobell, David Lai, and Roy Kamphausen (Carlisle, PA: US Army War College Strategic Studies Institute, 2011), 153–99, https://apps.dtic.mil/sti/pdfs/ADA553490.pdf.

5. For an excellent analysis of the People's Liberation Army's (PLA) changes in strategy and doctrine, see Joel Wuthnow and M. Taylor Fravel, "China's Military Strategy for a 'New Era': Some Change, More Continuity, and Tantalizing Hints," *Journal of Strategic Studies* (March 2022), https://www.tandfonline.com/doi/full/10.1080/014023 90.2022.2043850. The PLA is modernizing to fight "joint integrated operations" under conditions of "informatization." It has been doing so since 1993, driven by a theory that it may have to fight the US. Taiwan is the main theater the PLA is preparing for, but the possible "big war" can start over other issues as well. This general-purpose

modernization program is often confused with the Chinese Communist Party's ongoing, and more comprehensive, Taiwan strategy.

6. Sun Tzu, *The Art of War*.

7. This is Timothy Thomas's paraphrase of Li Bingyan. See Timothy L. Thomas, "China's Concept of Military Strategy," ETH Zürich, Center for Security Studies, https://css.ethz.ch/en/services/digital-library/articles/article.html/190449; and Li Bingyan, "Applying Military Strategy in the Age of the New Revolution in Military Affairs," in *The Chinese Revolution in Military Affairs*, ed. Shen Weiguang (Beijing, China: New China Press, 2004), 2–31.

8. Vladimir A. Lefebvre, *Reflexive Control: The Soviet Concept of Influencing an Adversary's Decision Making Process* (Moscow, Soviet Union: Science Applications, 1984); and Maria Snegovaya, *Putin's Information Warfare in Ukraine: Soviet Origins of Russia's Hybrid Warfare*, Institute for the Study of War, September 2015, https://www.understandingwar.org/report/putins-information-warfare-ukraine-soviet-origins-russias-hybrid-warfare.

9. Mao Zedong, "Introducing the Communist," in *Selected Works of Mao Tse-Tung* (Beijing, China: Foreign Languages Press, 1960), https://www.marxists.org/reference/archive/mao/selected-works/volume-2/mswv2_20.htm.

10. Dean Cheng, "PLA Perspectives on Network Warfare in 'Informationized Local Wars,'" testimony before the US-China Economic and Security Review Commission, February 17, 2022, https://www.uscc.gov/sites/default/files/2022-02/Dean_Cheng_Testimony.pdf.

11. Cheng, "PLA Perspectives on Network Warfare in 'Informationized Local Wars'"; and John Costello and Joe McReynolds, *China's Strategic Support Force: A Force for a New Era* (Washington, DC: National Defense University Press, 2018), 17, https://ndupress.ndu.edu/Portals/68/Documents/stratperspective/china/china-perspectives_13.pdf.

12. The Republic of China was the successor state to the Qing dynasty. Its stability was challenged during its tumultuous early years by warlords, attempts to reinstate the Qing dynasty, and, finally, the Communist insurgency.

13. By "legitimate" we do not mean "just" or "decent"; we only mean that under international custom and law, both would be seen as sovereign states.

14. Consistent with its anti-Communist Cold War policy, the US was part of this distortion of reality, and it further acquiesced in it by recognizing the People's Republic of China (PRC). It brought itself to the brink of recognizing the reality of two Chinas and then decided that such a move would undermine its recognition of the PRC. See John W. Garver, *The Sino-American Alliance: Nationalist China and American Cold War Strategy in Asia* (New York: Routledge, 2015), 218–19, 221–24, 230–31, 249, 256–61, 271, 295.

15. The point is worth restating by the United States government as clearly as possible. The removal of US recognition of the Republic of China (ROC) has no bearing on the ROC's international legal status as a nation-state. It is, by all indices of international law, a country.

16. Michael J. Green and Bonnie S. Glaser, "What Is the U.S. 'One China' Policy, and Why Does It Matter?," Center for Strategic and International Studies, January 13, 2017, https://www.csis.org/analysis/what-us-one-china-policy-and-why-does-it-matter.

17. Russell Hsiao and David An, "What Is the U.S. 'One China' Policy?," *National Interest*, December 28, 2016, https://nationalinterest.org/blog/the-buzz/what-the-us-%E2%80%9Cone-china%E2%80%9D-policy-18882.

18. James A. Kelly, "Overview of U.S. Policy Toward Taiwan," testimony before the House International Relations Committee, April 21, 2004, https://2001-2009.state. gov/p/eap/rls/rm/2004/31649.htm. The whole point of the diplomatic formulation that Beijing and Washington agreed to during the long normalization negotiations was that each side would have its own definition of "One China." For an excellent recent history of Washington's interpretation of the "One China" policy, see William Inboden, *The Peacemaker: Ronald Reagan, the Cold War, and the World on the Brink* (New York: Dutton 2022), 27, 76–77, 95–97, 125–26, 170–71, 400.

19. For example, a US president can meet with Taiwan's president in her capacity as head of government rather than head of state.

20. Elizabeth Olson, "Taiwan is Cleared for Membership in W.T.O.," *New York Times*, September 19, 2001, https://www.nytimes.com/2001/09/19/business/taiwan-is-cleared-for-membership-in-wto.html.

21. Tami Davis Biddle, "Coercion Theory: A Basic Introduction for Practitioners," *Texas National Security Review* 3, no. 2 (2020): 95, https://doi.org/http://dx.doi. org/10.26153/tsw/8864. Tami Davis Biddle notes the discomfort military officers have with the idea of killing and dying as a form of "communications."

22. *The Godfather* (Los Angeles: Paramount Pictures, 1972).

23. The key here is his feeling—his perception that he did not have other choices.

24. It is no accident that Taiwan President Tsai Ing-wen recently stated that Taiwan is under a Chinese cognitive attack, one that is trying to "create disturbance in minds of people." Huizhong Wu, "Taiwan Leader Cites Threat of Chinese 'Cognitive Warfare,'" September 6, 2022, Associated Press, https://apnews.com/article/taiwan-technology-china-misinformation-f9b030d8c11f2250a2a516d73059b257.

25. Thomas C. Schelling, *Arms and Influence* (New Haven, CT: Yale University Press, 2008); and Biddle, "Coercion Theory," 98.

26. See the quote from Wang Qiming and Chen Feng, "*Daying gaojishu jubu zhanzheng*," in Mark Stokes, "The Evolution of China's Military Strategy," in *China's Revolution in Doctrinal Affairs: Emerging Trends in the Operational Art of the Chinese People's Liberation Army*, ed. James Mulvenon and David M. Finkelstein (Arlington, VA: CNA Corporation, 2005), 226.

27. The translation of *weishe* is akin to both "compellence" and "deterrence" in English. It is used as "deterrence," as in forestalling an unwanted action; it is also used as "compellence," as in forcing an action that is unwanted by an adversary. Xiao Tianlang et al., *In Their Own Words: Science of Military Strategy 2020* (Washington, DC: National Defense University Press, 2020), 126, https://www.airuniversity.af.edu/Portals/10/CASI/ documents/Translations/2022-01-26%202020%20Science%20of%20Military%20 Strategy.pdf.

28. Here the PLA moves beyond threats of force in a coercive campaign to "methods of military conflict" to create, according to the PLA's 2019 defense white paper, the means to "use fear to stop." Xiao, *In Their Own Words*.

29. Xiao, *In Their Own Words*, 138.

30. Wilson Center Digital Archive, "Joint Communique Between the United States and China," February 27, 1972, https://digitalarchive.wilsoncenter.org/document/joint-communique-between-united-states-and-china.

31. Ironically, given Beijing's intransigence toward Tsai, the PRC's new grievance is that a Democratic Progressive Party successor will not accept her careful formulations and instead push for formal independence as a new nation-state. The US should consider telling Beijing that should it continue to unilaterally attempt to change the status quo, threaten Taiwan, or attack Taiwan, the US will no longer feel obligated to keep its promises on nonrecognition of Taiwan.

32. Yu-Jie Chen and Jerome A. Cohen, "China-Taiwan Relations Re-Examined: The '1992 Consensus' and Cross-Strait Agreements," *Asian Law Review* 14 (2019): 10, https://scholarship.law.upenn.edu/cgi/viewcontent.cgi?article=1039&context=alr.

33. Rone Tempest, "Taiwan Crisis Tied to China Power Struggle," *Los Angeles Times*, March 9, 1996, https://www.latimes.com/archives/la-xpm-1996-03-09-mn-44883-story.html.

34. CNN, "Nations Condemn Chinese Missile Tests," March 8, 1996, http://edition.cnn.com/WORLD/9603/china_taiwan/08.

35. Chen and Cohen, "China-Taiwan Relations Re-Examined," 15.

36. Barton Gellman, "Reappraisal Led to New China Policy," *Washington Post*, June 22, 1998, https://www.washingtonpost.com/wp-srv/inatl/longterm/china/stories/china062298.htm.

37. Jonathan Peterson and Tyler Marshall, "Clinton Backs China on Issue of Free Taiwan," *Los Angeles Times*, June 30, 1998, https://www.latimes.com/archives/la-xpm-1998-jun-30-mn-65011-story.html.

38. White House, "President Bush and Premier Wen Jiabao Remarks to the Press: Remarks by President Bush and Premier Wen Jiabao in Photo Opportunity," press release, December 9, 2003, https://georgewbush-whitehouse.archives.gov/news/releases/2003/12/20031209-2.html; and Michael D. Swaine, "Trouble in Taiwan," Carnegie Endowment for International Peace, February 23, 2004, https://carnegieendowment.org/2004/02/23/trouble-in-taiwan-pub-1460.

39. Ma Ying Jeou, "When I Said 'Mr. Xi': Ma Ying Jeou," *USA Today*, November 22, 2015, https://www.usatoday.com/story/opinion/2015/11/22/taiwan-china-xi-jinping-ma-ying-jeou-1992-consensus-column/76215872.

40. Shannon Tiezzi, "Did China Just Kill Cross-Strait Relations?," *Diplomat*, June 26, 2016, https://thediplomat.com/2016/06/did-china-just-kill-cross-strait-relations.

41. Reuters, "'One China' Principle Must Be Basis for Relations with Taiwan: Xinhua," May 21, 2016, https://www.reuters.com/article/us-china-politics-taiwan/one-china-principle-must-be-basis-for-relations-with-taiwan-xinhua-idUSKCN0YC05X.

42. Tsai Ing-wen, "Inaugural Address of ROC 14th-Term President Tsai Ing-wen" (speech, Presidential Office Building, Taipei, Taiwan, May 5, 2020), https://english.president.gov.tw/News/4893.

43. Stacy Hsu, "MAC Releases Ma-Xi Meeting Transcript," *Taipei Times*, November 10, 2015, https://www.taipeitimes.com/News/front/archives/2015/11/10/2003632096.

44. BBC, "Panama Cuts Ties with Taiwan in Favour of China," June 13, 2017, https://www.bbc.com/news/world-latin-america-40256499.

45. Allison Lampert and J. R. Wu, "U.N. Agency Snubs Taiwan, Recognizing Beijing's 'One China,'" Reuters, September 22, 2016, https://www.reuters.com/article/us-taiwan-china/u-n-agency-snubs-taiwan-recognizing-beijings-one-china-idUSKCN11T08P.

46. *Taipei Times*, "Foreign Ministry Slams Interpol Snub," October 19, 2022, https://www.taipeitimes.com/News/taiwan/archives/2022/10/19/2003787329.

47. Tara Francis Chan, "US Airlines Just Gave Into China's 'Orwellian' Demands over Taiwan—Here's Every Company That's Done the Same," Insider, July 25, 2018, https://www.businessinsider.com/which-companies-have-changed-taiwan-description-china-2018-7.

48. Derek Grossman et al., "China's Long-Range Bomber Flights: Drivers and Implications," RAND Corporation, 2018, 22, https://www.rand.org/content/dam/rand/pubs/research_reports/RR2500/RR2567/RAND_RR2567.pdf.

49. Grossman et al., "China's Long-Range Bomber Flights."

50. Colby Ferland, "Under the Radar: China's Coercive Air Power in the Taiwan Strait," Project 2049 Institute, March 9, 2018, https://project2049.net/2018/03/09/under-the-radar-chinas-coercive-air-power-in-the-taiwan-strait.

51. Ferland, "Under the Radar."

52. *Taipei Times*, "Fighter Incursion a Display of China's Displeasure at Taiwan-US Ties: Expert," April 3, 2019, https://www.taipeitimes.com/News/taiwan/archives/2019/04/03/2003712719.

53. Mathieu Duchâtel, "Anticipating China's Military Coercion of Taiwan," Institut Montaigne, September 15, 2020, https://www.institutmontaigne.org/en/blog/anticipating-chinas-military-coercion-taiwan.

54. Joel Wuthnow et al., eds., *Crossing the Strait: China's Military Prepares for War with Taiwan* (Washington, DC: National Defense University Press, 2022), 95, https://ndupress.ndu.edu/Portals/68/Documents/Books/crossing-the-strait/crossing-the-strait.pdf.

55. CBS News, "China Flies 39 Warplanes into Taiwan's Air Defense Zone in a Day," January 24, 2022, https://www.cbsnews.com/news/china-taiwan-warplanes-fly-incursions-air-defense-zone. The PLA had been setting conditions for the kind of reaction it had to the visit of Speaker Nancy Pelosi to Taiwan in August 2022. It had already begun wiping away the median line in the strait and increasing its incursions into Taiwan's Air Defense Identification Zone. It was thus ready to portray its provocative activity in the strait as "merely" a reaction to a US provocation. This psychological warfare strategy succeeds as it counts on lack of regular attention to its incremental provocations.

56. According to Missile Defense Advocacy Alliance, Taiwan Incursion Updates, https://missiledefenseadvocacy.org/missile-threat-and-proliferation/todays-missile-threat/taiwan-missile-updates. The Chinese used Speaker Pelosi's visit to Taiwan to escalate this activity. Beijing would sooner or later have found another excuse to operate in this fashion.

57. Grossman et al., "China's Long-Range Bomber Flights," 24.

58. Kuan-Chen Lee, "*zhonggong dui tai junshi donghe yu huyu kezhi de liangshou celue*" [The CCP's Dual Strategies of Military Intimidation Against Taiwan and Calling for Restraint], *National Defense Security Biweekly* 11 (2020): 19–25; and Wuthnow et al., eds., *Crossing the Strait*.

59. Wuthnow et al., eds., *Crossing the Strait*, 99–100. The PLA tends to exaggerate the aerospace campaign's geographic scope.

60. Cheng, "Chinese Lessons from the Gulf Wars."

61. Philip S. Davidson, testimony before the Senate Armed Services Committee, March 9, 2021, https://www.armed-services.senate.gov/imo/media/doc/Davidson_03-09-21.pdf.

62. See Lonnie Henley, "PLA Operational Concepts and Centers of Gravity in a Taiwan Conflict," testimony before the US-China Economic and Security Review Commission, February 18, 2021 https://www.uscc.gov/sites/default/files/2021-02/Lonnie_Henley_Testimony.pdf. In 2004, the PLA may have been ordered to be ready for an invasion by 2020. There are other years identified as milestones for the PLA, including 2035. It is highly unlikely that Xi Jinping would have locked himself in to a set deadline for an invasion; instead, he would seek maximum flexibility and condition his decision for war on the trend of Taiwan's politics; an assessment of US, Japanese, and other coalition responses; and his assessment of PLA readiness.

63. Thomas Shugart has made a compelling case that the combination of capabilities the PLA will have in the next five years and the degradation of relevant US capabilities heightens the danger that Beijing will start a major war over Taiwan. But this scenario implies Xi's willingness to start World War III over Taiwan by attacking US allies throughout the region. See Thomas H. Shugart III, "Trends, Timelines, and Uncertainty: An Assessment of the Military Balance in the Indo-Pacific," testimony before the Senate Foreign Relations Committee, March 17, 2021, https://www.cnas.org/publications/congressional-testimony/trends-timelines-and-uncertainty-an-assessment-of-the-military-balance-in-the-indo-pacific. There is no evidence that this is Beijing's strategic intent.

64. Beijing will make the case that the Taiwan issue is a "domestic" one and therefore blockading it is not an act of war.

65. For a review of why some believe this, see Michael Kofman, "Getting the Fait Accompli Problem Right in U.S. Strategy," War on the Rocks, November 3, 2020, https://warontherocks.com/2020/11/getting-the-fait-accompli-problem-right-in-u-s-strategy.

66. Oriana Skylar Mastro, "Defense, Deterrence, and the Role of Guam," in *Defending Guam*, ed. Rebeccah Heinrichs (Washington, DC: Hudson Institute, 2022), 44–48, https://fsi.stanford.edu/publication/defending-guam.

67. Elbridge Colby, "How to Win America's Next War," *Foreign Policy*, May 5, 2019, https://foreignpolicy.com/2019/05/05/how-to-win-americas-next-war-china-russia-military-infrastructure.

68. Zack Cooper and Sheena Chestnut Greitens, "Asian Allies and Partners in a Taiwan Contingency: What Should the United States Expect?," American Enterprise Institute, 2022, https://www.defendingtaiwan.com/asian-allies-and-partners-in-a-taiwan-contingency-what-should-the-united-states-expect.

69. "Mutual Defense Treaty Between the United States and the Republic of Korea; October 1, 1953," in *American Foreign Policy 1950–1955: Basic Documents Volumes I and II* (Washington, DC: US Government Printing Office, 1953), https://www.usfk.mil/Portals/105/Documents/SOFA/H_Mutual%20Defense%20Treaty_1953.pdf.

70. A limited number of experts have experimented with arguments along these lines. We have no indications that US policy or strategy has embraced this approach, however, and merely wish to warn against the dangers of doing so.

71. Some experts have made such claims, often referring to hypersonic systems the Chinese may bring online. We have no concrete indications that the US military accepts such claims, but the presentation of such claims without loud and clear contestation by the US military unintentionally strengthens Chinese coercion and persuasion campaigns. For a summary of both sides of the carrier survivability debate, see Jon Harper, "Incoming: Can Aircraft Carriers Survive Hypersonic Weapons?," *National Defense*, March 22, 2019, https://www.nationaldefensemagazine.org/articles/2019/3/22/incoming-can-aircraft-carriers-survive-hypersonic-weapons.

72. "While Chinese strategists acknowledge US military superiority generally, the conventional wisdom is that China's proximity to Taiwan, corresponding access to operational resources and resolute stance makes the local balance of power favorable to Beijing." See Oriana Skylar Mastro, "The Precarious State of Cross-Strait Deterrence," testimony before the US-China Economic and Security Review Commission, February 18, 2021, https://www.uscc.gov/sites/default/files/2021-02/Oriana_Skylar_Mastro_Testimony.pdf.

73. Elbridge Colby, "America Can Defend Taiwan," *Wall Street Journal*, January 26, 2021, https://www.wsj.com/articles/america-can-defend-taiwan-11611684038.

Gray-Zone Subjugation of Taiwan:
A More Acute Risk Than Invasion?

ELISABETH BRAW

Taiwan is no stranger to gray-zone aggression. Indeed, it could be said that ever since the island established itself as a self-ruling nation, it has had to defend against Chinese attempts to harm it below the threshold of armed conflict. Today, though, China's increasing harassment of Taiwan, using tools in the gray zone between war and peace on one hand and Taiwan's openness and significant dependence on the Chinese market on the other, make it more likely a concerted Chinese gray-zone campaign against the island will happen.

In late February 2021, Beijing announced it was banning imports of pineapples from Taiwan, claiming to have found "harmful creatures" in the tropical fruit.[1] Even though Chinese authorities never proved the presence of such creatures, on March 1 the ban came into force. Given that 90 percent of Taiwan's exports go to mainland China, this was a devastating turn of events for Taiwan's pineapple growers.[2] It was also a move that Taipei could do little to counter. To be sure, the Taiwanese government repeatedly argued that the ban violated World Trade Organization (WTO) rules, but even when appeals to the WTO are successful, as several complaints against China have been, the organization has little enforcement power.

Indeed, this is not the first time Beijing has suspended imports of agricultural products to punish a country for a perceived offense. As Ivar Kolstad notes, after the Norwegian Nobel Committee awarded the Nobel Peace Prize to Chinese dissident Liu Xiaobo in late 2010,

> Overt Chinese sanctions against Norwegian exports to China would have been in conflict with WTO rules. There can

nevertheless be little doubt that non-tariff barriers to Norwegian exports were introduced following the Nobel peace
prize. . . . Norwegian exports of salmon were subjected to more
stringent and time-consuming sanitation and veterinary controls at the border, and importers were unable to get licences
for larger quantities of Norwegian salmon.[3]

Between 2011 and 2013 alone, this resulted in losses of up to $176 million
for Norway's fishermen.[4] In November 2020, Beijing imposed tariffs of up
to 200 percent on Australian wine, an apparent retaliation after Australia's government called for an independent investigation into the origin
of COVID-19. This, too, was a devastating turn of events for the farmers
affected, as China is Australian vintners' main export market.[5] And following its ban of Taiwanese pineapples, in September 2021, Beijing banned
imports of Taiwanese wax apples and sugar apples. This time, the move
appeared to be retaliation against Taiwanese efforts to change the name
of its representative office in Washington, DC, to one including the word
"Taiwan," rather than the customary "Taipei."[6]

China has also punished companies in other sectors after their home
governments offended Beijing. In the spring and summer of 2021, the
Swedish telecommunications equipment giant Ericsson saw its sales
drop in China even though they rose in the rest of the world as Chinese
companies—no doubt acting on Beijing's instructions—withheld business in retaliation against Sweden's decision not to include Huawei in its
5G network.[7] And at the end of 2021, following Lithuania's decision to
allow Taiwan to open a representative office bearing the name of Taiwan,
China retaliated by blocking all imports containing Lithuanian components. While Lithuania's exports to China are negligible, countless companies across the world—especially those from other EU member states—use
Lithuanian components in their products. To these companies' shock,
they discovered that their products were being blocked at Chinese ports.
"Imports from Lithuania are no longer being processed by the Chinese
customs authority. . . . Apparently the Chinese customs authority doesn't
process goods from other EU member states if they contain parts made in
Lithuania," the EU's trade commissioner, Valdis Dombrovskis, explained
in a media interview just before Christmas 2021.[8]

In all cases, the punished countries and industries acutely felt the pain, but there was little they could do to change China's behavior or even call it out. They could not prove that Chinese authorities had found no harmful creatures, and Chinese officials flatly denied blocking any cargo containing Lithuanian components. These examples are so instructive because they illustrate the nature and potential of gray-zone aggression. It exploits modern societies' extreme interconnectedness and liberal democracies' openness and adherence to international agreements and the rule of law.

To be sure, there are many examples of liberal democracies using subversive means to harm another country—US attempts to remove democratically elected foreign leaders such as Patrice Lumumba and Mohammad Mosaddegh come to mind—but they do not use gray-zone aggression as extensively as do authoritarian states such as China and Russia. Perhaps even more importantly, gray-zone aggression is attractive to China and Russia as they seek to weaken the West because it is both inexpensive and hard to detect. Indeed, gray-zone aggression is the geopolitical version of gaslighting: The aggression's ambiguous nature leaves the targeted country unsure of whether it is experiencing gray-zone aggression or merely the hustle and bustle of the globalized economy.

This reality faces every liberal democracy. Taiwan, though, occupies a particularly precarious position. China is Taiwan's largest trading partner; in 2020, it accounted for 26.3 percent of total trade and 22.2 percent of Taiwan's imports. That makes China far more important to Taiwan, in trading terms, than Japan (10.9 percent) and the European Union (8.2 percent) are, especially when one considers that the Hong Kong special administrative region accounts for another 7.9 percent of Taiwan's trade.[9] What is more, China is by far the most important export market for Taiwanese companies. Taiwan, though, is not one of China's five biggest markets, neither for imports nor for exports.[10] This means that China can afford to suspend imports of a range of Taiwanese goods and suspend its own exports to Taiwan without feeling much pain. (A few crucial goods are exceptions: Like all other countries, China depends on computer chips made by Taiwan Semiconductor Manufacturing Company.)[11]

Taiwan's precarious situation extends beyond the economy. Like all other liberal democracies, it is vulnerable precisely because it is a democracy. Indeed, China has for decades exploited this openness through disinformation directed against the island nation. Jude Blanchette et al. note,

> The United Front Work Department (UFWD), which reports directly to the CCP Central Committee and acts as a traffic cop for the various domestic and global united front exertions, has long been active in, and focused on, Taiwan and its political dynamics. Traditional channels of influence, including domestic political parties, overseas Taiwanese businesspeople and their extended families, and proliferating ownership of domestic media outlets have allowed the CCP to slowly and methodically build up its influence network in Taiwan since the early-1980s.[12]

But especially since Taiwan's 2016 election of the outspokenly pro-independence Tsai Ing-wen as president, these influence efforts have grown and morphed. Blanchette et al. go on to observe that

> the UFWD and the larger ecosystem of United Front actors have become an important conduit and messaging channel for Beijing's preferred narratives and for active efforts to *disinform* Taiwan citizens, especially as public discourse has shifted onto digital and social media platforms and become increasingly commercialized.[13] (Emphasis in the original.)

Disinforming a country's citizens is, of course, a relatively easy task when the country is open and democratic, with vibrant and often animated debate among citizens on any matter under the sun.

Taiwan is an extremely open and democratic country. In its 2022 "Freedom in the World" report, Freedom House gives Taiwan a 94 of 100 rating, which means the country counts as fully free. At the time of writing, the full 2022 report had not yet been published, but in its 2021 report, Freedom House notes that "Taiwan's vibrant and competitive democratic system has allowed three peaceful transfers of power between rival parties since 2000, and protections for civil liberties are generally robust."[14] It adds, though, that ongoing concerns include foreign migrant workers' vulnerability to exploitation and the Chinese government's efforts to influence policymaking, the media, and democratic infrastructure in Taiwan.

. . . In January, incumbent president Tsai Ing-wen and her Democratic Progressive Party (DPP) were returned to power in general elections that drew the highest voter turnout since 2008, despite online disinformation and influence operations targeting the vote that were attributed to the Chinese government.[15]

A 2019 report by Varieties of Democracy, an international group of academics, concluded that Taiwan was, along with the United States and Latvia, the country most targeted by disinformation. "By circulating misleading information on social media and investing in Taiwanese media outlets, China seeks to interfere in Taiwan's domestic politics and to engineer a complete unification," the researchers noted.[16] The report also highlighted how China funds Taiwanese media that adopt pro-Beijing messaging, concluding that "Chinese disinformation strategy and resulting online information fractionalization is likely to have a detrimental impact on Taiwan's democracy."[17] Recent disinformation campaigns have seen hackers and bots spread disinformation on Facebook, Weibo, and similar platforms, and in 2018, Chinese media outlets shared a damning but false story about a Taiwanese diplomat in Japan. The news coverage contributed to the diplomat's subsequent suicide.[18]

It is against this background that those interested in the safety of Taiwan should view the current situation. This situation also includes regular incursions by Chinese military aircraft—often several at a time—into Taiwan's air defense identification zone (ADIZ). While an ADIZ is not identical with national airspace, Taiwan's proximity to mainland China means it patrols its ADIZ more conscientiously than many countries with more geographically distant adversaries patrol the space immediately adjacent to their national airspace. China regularly sends aircraft into Taiwan's ADIZ in an apparent effort to wear Taiwanese aircraft and crews out. In a mere four days in October 2021, Chinese military aircraft conducted no fewer than 149 sorties into Taiwan's ADIZ.[19] Similarly, Chinese sand-dredging vessels have been extracting sand off the Matsu archipelago, which belongs to Taiwan. Like most countries, China uses sand for construction, but the vessels' main purpose appears to be to wear Taiwan down by forcing its coast guard to respond to their intrusions.[20]

A Hypothetical Scenario

If China wanted to act on its long-standing goal of forcing Taiwan into submission and turning it into a real province of China, not just a theoretical one, it could build on these already existing forms of gray-zone aggression. Consider, for example, the following hypothetical scenario.

China continues its disinformation campaign against Tsai and her government. But instead of focusing primarily on the president, the Chinese hackers, bots, and news outlets single out diplomats, civil servants, and junior political officials unaccustomed to the spotlight. As with the Tokyo-based diplomat, they invent malefactions allegedly committed by specific officials and bureaucrats, who are individually hounded in media and on social media. Some see no choice but to resign, which removes crucial expertise from the ranks of the government.

The atmosphere of constant fear, in which any official or civil servant can become the next target of disinformation campaigns, creates nervousness and unhappiness in the civil service and among political officials. They begin suggesting to their superiors that Tsai's government should make clear and unequivocal statements that it won't move toward an official declaration of independence. Tsai and her ministers refuse.

Meanwhile, though, a small but increasingly vocal share of the Taiwanese population, including foreign migrant workers, has been infected by Chinese disinformation and begins to stage demonstrations. While the demonstrators lack a coherent message, they are noisy and voice sundry grievances, including ones invented by the Chinese disinformation campaigns.

At the same time, China again punishes Tsai's government for an allegedly offensive decision by suspending imports of more Taiwanese products. However, this time Beijing does not announce the punishment: Taiwanese exporters simply discover that Chinese customers no longer buy their products. Beijing's new, surreptitious approach means the ban lacks a poignancy the world can unite behind. The world has moved on and has no appetite for absorbing the Taiwanese goods now no longer reaching the Chinese market, especially because the goods in question—perhaps plastics—do not easily lend themselves to the type of solidarity campaigns the "freedom pineapples" (or "freedom wine," in support of Australian vintners) did. "Freedom plastic" would not be a winning campaign.

Although Taiwanese business leaders initially do not criticize Tsai's policies, after several rounds of suspended exports, they grow exasperated and plead with her government to change course. Tsai's government, refusing to be blackmailed by China, stands by its position. Unhappiness with the Tsai government grows in the Taiwanese business community, and some executives start talking about relocating their companies' headquarters to China or another country. Chinese news outlets and social media accounts begin reporting a corporate exodus from Taiwan, inflating Taiwanese business leaders' concerns.

The Taiwanese public, aware of China's tactics, knows not to trust Chinese media, but in the muddled media landscape, they struggle to discern which news outlets have Chinese connections and which social media accounts operate on China's behalf. Knowing of Taiwanese business leaders' concerns, many Taiwanese citizens conclude that their country's economy risks ruin because of Tsai's policies. Some begin protesting in front of government buildings, where migrant foreign workers and others are already airing their grievances. While the protesters do not have any complaints or solutions in common, their protests project to the rest of the country an overpowering fear that Taiwan is facing doom.

The fear is compounded by increasing Chinese sorties into Taiwan's ADIZ, which puts the Taiwanese air force—air crews, ground crews, and aircraft—under extreme strain. Meanwhile, Chinese diggers increase their sand dredging in the Matsu archipelago, causing Taiwan Coast Guard Administration vessels to spend even more resources patrolling the area. The coast guard vessels, though, cannot force the sand dredgers to leave, as doing so would provoke an incident that could escalate to an armed conflict. The Taiwanese public is thus forced to watch Chinese sand dredgers systematically dig up Taiwanese sand under the eyes of

Taiwanese authorities. With slogans like "stop the sand steal," concerned citizens begin protesting, not just in Taipei but across the country.

Within weeks, the country is engulfed in citizen protests and private-sector lament, and the coast guard and air force are exhausted, the latter even running short of aircraft because of wear and tear caused by constant scrambles. Even with the public deserting her, Tsai does not budge. The Kuomintang opposition party, meanwhile, struggles to identify how the country should respond to the Chinese provocations. Taiwan's decision-making is paralyzed, even as the protests escalate and the air force and coast guard exhaustion increase.

Out of the ranks of private-sector leaders, though, a voice emerges that seems to have a solution. The CEO of a hitherto unknown company in the high-tech sector presents a package of evidently sensible ideas that will help Taiwan emerge from its precarious situation. Indeed, he forms a new party based on these ideas. Even as it emerges that he has links to the Chinese government, large parts of the Taiwanese public decide that he and his suddenly assembled party are the island's best chance for the people of Taiwan to be able to live in continued prosperity and relative freedom. Yes, they realize that with a political novice in charge of Taiwan, Beijing could exert considerable influence, but worn down as they are from China's campaign to weaken their country, they decide that supporting him is the lesser evil.

Tsai, faced with a rebelling country and massive support going to the new political strongman, steps down, leaving a weakened government in charge. In the subsequent general elections, the new party wins an outright majority, and their leader wins the presidency. He immediately declares that Taiwan will join China as a Hong Kong–style autonomous region. Many Taiwanese citizens protest against the move—indeed, their demonstrations dwarf those that protested against Tsai's government—but the new government pays them no mind.

Conclusion

This hypothetical chain of events is clearly not inevitable or even likely. It is, however, no less likely to occur than a Chinese military invasion of

Taiwan. Indeed, aggression in the gray zone would be far more attractive to China than a military assault, primarily because China would incur minimal loss of blood or treasure. It would also be attractive because the Taiwanese government and public would struggle to determine whether a concerted gray-zone campaign against their country was taking place.

Taiwan is highly accustomed to Chinese harassment in the gray zone between war and peace, but even moderate gray-zone harassment is hard to counter, precisely because responding with force would escalate the situation. While it is clearly desirable to forcefully respond to a gray-zone campaign aimed at a country's subjugation, it is virtually impossible to distinguish such an assault from the regular drumbeat of gray-zone harassment. For the same reason, it would also be difficult for Taiwan's friends and allies to respond to a campaign of this kind.

This is also the reason that an often-proposed "economic Article 5,"[21] akin to NATO's military Article 5 that asserts an attack on one member is an attack on all members, is unrealistic. An attack on another country's economy does not present itself as starkly as a military attack does. Indeed, like almost all gray-zone aggression, it arrives gradually, with the targeted country unable to discern whether what is taking place is simply another imperfection of the globalized economy or, on the contrary, gray-zone aggression. Because China has denied punishing the economies of Australia, Lithuania, Norway, and Taiwan, the targeted countries and their allies have struggled to respond.

The challenge liberal democracies face is that they can never fully prevent gray-zone aggression. Indeed, their openness and adherence to rule of law and international diplomatic standards mean that in the gray zone, they are always at a disadvantage vis-à-vis authoritarian countries wishing to harm them. This clearly does not mean that liberal democracy is doomed or that liberal democracies should retreat from the globalized economy. In the case of Taiwan, however, it does mean that it should increase its already impressive efforts to involve all parts of society in keeping the country safe. Especially in light of Beijing's gradual but ironfisted reversal of democratic liberties in Hong Kong, most citizens of Taiwan are bound to appreciate the benefits of their free and open country and see the need for everyone to do their part to help it continue to prosper.

Notes

1. Yimou Lee, "Forbidden Fruit: Taiwan Urges People to Eat More Pineapples After China Ban," Reuters, February 26, 2021, https://www.reuters.com/world/china/forbidden-fruit-taiwan-urges-people-eat-more-pineapples-after-china-ban-2021-02-26.

2. Lee, "Forbidden Fruit."

3. Ivar Kolstad, "Too Big to Fault? Effects of the 2010 Nobel Peace Prize on Norwegian Exports to China and Foreign Policy" (working paper, Chr. Michelsen Institute, Bergen, Norway, 2016), https://www.cmi.no/publications/5805-too-big-to-fault.

4. Kolstad, "Too Big to Fault?"

5. BBC, "Australia Takes Wine Dispute with China to WTO," June 19, 2021, https://www.bbc.com/news/world-australia-57536422.

6. Dong Xing, "First Pineapples, Now Sugar Apples. Taiwan Threatens to Take China to WTO over New Fruit Import Ban," Australian Broadcasting Corporation, September 21, 2021, https://www.abc.net.au/news/2021-09-21/china-taiwan-fruit-ban-may-jeopardise-application/100479612.

7. Elisabeth Braw, "How Do You Stop Beijing from Bullying? Take Away Its Prada Bags," *Wall Street Journal*, August 10, 2021, https://www.wsj.com/articles/ericcson-beijing-australia-sweden-denmark-5g-national-security-trade-luxury-goods-zte-huawei-11628631680.

8. Tobias Kaiser, "Autozulieferer zwischen den Fronten—Litauens Streit mit China trifft deutsche Firmen" [Automotive Suppliers Between the Fronts—Lithuania's Dispute with China Hits German Firms], *Die Welt*, December 23, 2021, https://www.welt.de/wirtschaft/article235849914/China-Warum-deutsche-Firmen-unter-der-Blockade-gegen-Litauen-leiden.html.

9. US Department of Commerce, International Trade Administration, "Taiwan—Country Commercial Guide," September 13, 2021, https://www.trade.gov/country-commercial-guides/taiwan-market-overview.

10. World Bank, World Integrated Trade Solution, "Trade Summary for China 2019," 2019, https://wits.worldbank.org/CountrySnapshot/en/CHN.

11. Yimou Lee, Norihiko Shirouzu, and David Lague, *Silicon Fortress: T-Day, the Battle for Taiwan*, Reuters, December 27, 2021, https://www.reuters.com/investigates/special-report/taiwan-china-chips/.

12. Jude Blanchette et al., *Protecting Democracy in an Age of Disinformation: Lessons from Taiwan*, Center for Strategic and International Studies, January 2021, 6, https://csis-website-prod.s3.amazonaws.com/s3fs-public/publication/210127_Blanchette_Age_Disinformation.pdf.

13. Blanchette et al., *Protecting Democracy in an Age of Disinformation*.

14. Freedom House, "Freedom in the World 2021: Taiwan," https://freedomhouse.org/country/taiwan/freedom-world/2021.

15. Freedom House, "Freedom in the World 2021."

16. University of Gothenburg, Varieties of Democracy, *Democracy Facing Global Challenges: V-Dem Annual Democracy Report 2019*, 35, https://www.v-dem.net/static/website/files/dr/dr_2019.pdf.

17. University of Gothenburg, Varieties of Democracy, *Democracy Facing Global Challenges*.

18. Joshua Kurlantzick, "How China Is Interfering in Taiwan's Election," Council on Foreign Relations, November 7, 2019, https://www.cfr.org/in-brief/how-china-interfering-taiwans-election.

19. Adrian Ang U-Jin and Olli Pekka Suorsa, "Explaining the PLA's Record-Setting Air Incursions into Taiwan's ADIZ," *Diplomat*, October 14, 2021, https://thediplomat.com/2021/10/explaining-the-plas-record-setting-air-incursions-into-taiwans-adiz.

20. Elisabeth Braw, *The Defender's Dilemma: Identifying and Deterring Gray-Zone Aggression* (Washington, DC: AEI Press, 2022), 139.

21. Jonas Parello-Plesner, "An 'Economic Article 5' to Counter China," *Wall Street Journal*, February 11, 2021, https://www.wsj.com/articles/an-economic-article-5-to-counter-china-11613084046.

Deterring Coercion and Conflict
Across the Taiwan Strait

MICHAEL BECKLEY, ZACK COOPER, AND ALLISON SCHWARTZ

How can the United States continue to deter coercion and conflict across the Taiwan Strait? This is perhaps the most important and difficult question that the American defense community faces today. The Biden administration has called China "the pacing challenge" for the US military, and US officials have labeled an invasion of Taiwan "the pacing scenario."

Nonetheless, many are concerned that the current approach to cross-Strait deterrence may not be sustainable, because the military balance is rapidly shifting in China's favor.[1] Many now argue that the United States is losing—or has already lost—military primacy in East Asia. In this chapter, we assert that the United States does not need to have primacy throughout maritime Asia, with full air and sea control, to attain its military objectives in the Taiwan Strait. This chapter explains why and how this is the case by examining four key trends, four Chinese military options, and four potential US responses.

Four Cross-Strait Trends

Four fundamental trends are underway across the Taiwan Strait, each of which has substantial implications for cross-Strait stability. The first two—political dynamics and military imbalances—make conflict more likely. The second two—geographic features and technological innovations—make conflict less likely. Understanding the interactions among these four factors is crucial to managing cross-Strait risks.

First, political dynamics across the Taiwan Strait are becoming more difficult to manage because Beijing's actions have all but eliminated mainland China's hopes for peaceful unification. The Communist Party's repressive actions in Hong Kong have undercut its insistence that the "one country, two systems" model should appeal to those living in Taiwan. As this political solution becomes less realistic, leaders in China are considering alternatives that might force unification. Beijing's recent political warfare, diplomatic and economic pressure, air sorties around Taiwan, landing drills opposite Taiwan, and naval exercises in the East China Sea all serve as reminders of Beijing's coercive options against Taiwan. In short, China's prospects for a peaceful political solution to the Taiwan situation are receding and triggering a renewed debate in China about whether Beijing should use military tools to forcibly unify Taiwan with the mainland.

Second, there is a growing military imbalance between China and Taiwan. The gap in defense spending is widening: China now spends 13 times as much on its military as Taiwan spends on its own, to say nothing of the Communist Party's internal security forces, which could also be used in a conflict. Taiwan's standing military consists of 190,000 troops, less than a tenth of China's two million active military personnel. The Pentagon's most recent Chinese military power report assesses that China has 416,000 ground-force personnel near the Taiwan Strait, while Taiwan has only 88,000.[2] In wartime, Taiwan could hope to mobilize its two million reservists, but only 300,000 of Taiwan's reservists are required to participate in yearly refresher training.[3] It is unclear whether Taiwan's entire force would be prepared and capable of fighting under high-intensity combat conditions. There are real questions, therefore, about whether Taiwan will be capable of deterring China on its own. Thus, the prospect of US military involvement is increasingly important for cross-Strait deterrence.

These political and military factors imply that conflict between China and Taiwan is all but inevitable, yet two key trends are pushing in the other direction. One is Taiwan's geography, which would challenge an invading force. The main island of Taiwan is 245 miles long and 90 miles across at its widest point—roughly the same size as the Taiwan Strait that Chinese forces would have to cross.[4] The terrain is highly mountainous, including 258 mountain peaks taller than 9,800 feet. And there are only a handful of deep-water ports, most of which are at the island's north and south ends. Taiwan is also urbanized, with a population of 23.6 million in under 36,000 square kilometers—roughly the same population as Australia but in 0.5 percent of its territory.[5]

Therefore, China would have to cross a large body of water to launch an invasion against a densely populated island spread across mountainous territory. Amphibious invasions are notoriously difficult, so observers should not expect that China could carry out such an operation without substantial operational risk.

In addition, attempting an invasion of Taiwan would put China on the costlier side of the power-projection curve; Beijing would have to project power against an entrenched adversary that is trying to deny it. Power projection is fundamentally platform-centric, and therefore expensive, whereas anti-access and area denial are more munitions-centric and thus comparatively cheap. Precision-guided munitions enable even relatively weak forces to sink surface ships, hit fixed bases, and shoot down aircraft.

To invade Taiwan successfully, China would need to maintain forces in contested areas for extended periods, a mission that would require a panoply of pricey platforms (and skilled operators)—potentially including amphibious ships, aircraft carriers, submarines, anti-submarine warfare forces, surveillance aircraft, refueling tankers, and replenishment vessels. Taiwan or the United States could threaten these platforms by using cheaper denial systems, such as advanced missiles that, according to a recent RAND Corporation study, cost on average 1/50th the amount of the power-projection systems they could neutralize in war.[6]

These four trends focus on one central question: Can the United States use geographic and technological asymmetries to offset the Taiwan Strait's worsening political and military situations? We now turn to this question, focusing in more detail on China's four military options and how smart choices from US leaders could deter each.

Four Chinese Military Options

The most high-intensity scenario involving Taiwan would be an outright invasion of its main island. Conquering Taiwan is the People's Liberation Army's (PLA) top warfighting mission, but the China military power report asserts that the PLA is not currently capable of mounting a successful invasion of Taiwan.[7] The report does, however, assess that China "has a range of options for military campaigns against Taiwan, from an air and maritime blockade to a full-scale amphibious invasion to seize and occupy some or all of Taiwan or its offshore islands."[8] This section looks at four options China has for doing this: barraging Taiwan with missile strikes, blockading it, seizing its outlying islands, and launching an amphibious invasion of its main island.

Air and Missile Strikes. According to some PLA strategy documents, China would begin a war with Taiwan by bombing its air and naval bases, missile batteries, and command centers with ground- and air-launched missiles. The purpose would be to destroy most of Taiwan's air defenses and offensive forces before they could fight back.

In 2000, the PLA had only a few hundred inaccurate missiles and a few dozen advanced aircraft. Today, however, China has 1,500 accurate missiles aimed at Taiwan and more than 1,000 advanced fighter aircraft.[9] This raises the risk that China could annihilate Taiwan's air defenses, ground its air force, and sink most of its warships.

The success of a Chinese air-and-missile bombardment would depend on several factors, the first of which is how much notice Taiwan would have ahead of the attack. Taiwan has two dozen fixed early warning radars, 10 ground-mobile radars, six E-2 Hawkeye aircraft, thousands of spies on the Chinese mainland, and satellite intelligence provided by the United States.

Taiwanese intelligence has often detected PLA actions in advance. In 2013, for example, the Taiwanese government had early warning about China's pending announcement of an air defense identification zone in the East China Sea. If China planned an all-out assault on Taiwan, it would require an operation involving hundreds of thousands of personnel, and Taiwan's military would probably discover it days, if not weeks, in advance. Conversely, for a smaller Chinese attack, such as an assault on offshore islands, Taiwan might have little, if any, warning.

Second, the success of a Chinese attack would depend on how quickly Taiwan could deploy its navy and disperse its combat aircraft among the dozens of airfields scattered around the island. Some of these locations have aircraft facilities built inside mountains. Others have hardened aircraft shelters with thick concrete walls. If PLA missiles disabled Taiwan's air bases early in a conflict, Taiwanese aircraft could still operate from a dozen civilian airstrips and numerous highways, where Taiwanese forces have already deployed fuel and supplies.

Taiwan also could shoot down some Chinese missiles and aircraft and strike Chinese bases and missile batteries. Taiwan has dozens of surface-to-air missile batteries, nearly all of which are road mobile, and at least 400 road-mobile antiaircraft guns.[10] In addition, Taiwan has at least 12 road-mobile cruise-missile launchers; 50 short-range ballistic-missile launchers; several hundred howitzers located on Quemoy, an offshore island a few miles from China; and several hundred fighter aircraft and dozens of ships that can fire long-range cruise missiles.[11]

Some of Taiwan's major weapons systems would likely survive a Chinese missile bombardment. In the Gulf War and the war in Kosovo, the United States and its allies pummeled Iraq and Serbia for weeks, yet some of each adversary's road-mobile missile launchers survived. The same has been true in Russia's war against Ukraine. But if China has greater success and destroys most of Taiwan's air and naval forces in a surprise attack, it would quickly establish air and sea dominance and could then move on to an invasion or coercive campaign.

An alternative coercive tactic would be a strategic bombing campaign, in which the PLA tries to prevent Taiwan from declaring independence by leveling some of its cities and infrastructure. Opinion polls show that most Taiwanese are willing to risk conflict with China to maintain Taiwan's de facto independence but not to achieve de jure independence.[12] Thus, China could seek to deter Taiwan from officially declaring independence (or compel it to reverse any move toward formal independence) by carrying out a bombing campaign.

But it would be difficult for China to compel Taiwan to give up its de facto sovereignty by bombing its cities. Strategic bombing alone has never forced an opponent to surrender its sovereignty. Modern states adapt to the loss of critical infrastructure, and civilian populations react by digging in and rallying around their home government. Strategic bombing not only is historically ineffective, as seen by history's 14 unsuccessful strategic bombing campaigns, but also does not neatly serve China's ultimate political objectives.[13] In past bombing campaigns, the attacker simply wanted the defender to halt some action, a goal that theoretically could be achieved by bombing the defender into ruin. China, by contrast, wants to absorb Taiwan as a prosperous Chinese province and turn Taiwan's people into loyal Chinese citizens. Leveling Taipei and killing thousands of Taiwanese civilians would not achieve that end.

Maritime Blockade. An alternative option would be for China to coerce Taiwan into submission through a blockade in which the PLA tries to strangle Taiwan's economy by preventing commercial ships from reaching its ports. Taiwan imports most of its food and 98 percent of its energy resources and has only a four-month emergency supply of food and a three-month supply of oil.[14] Its small coastline requires large container ships to take predictable paths to seven major ports, four of which are located on Taiwan's west coast—facing China.

China's most aggressive option would be to destroy Taiwan's offensive forces, ports, and offshore oil terminals in a surprise missile attack and then have PLA submarines and combat aircraft sink cargo ships and scatter mines near Taiwan's ports. If China's surprise attack destroyed all of Taiwan's offensive forces and port infrastructure, Taiwan would have no way to unload cargo containers or oil tankers, causing its economy to grind to a halt.

China would hope that Taiwan would quickly concede, but history suggests a PLA blockade would need to last several weeks, if not months or years, to force Taiwan to capitulate. The reason is that modern states typically adapt to supply shortages, and civilian populations are usually willing to hold out under harsh conditions to defy a foreign enemy. For example, the most comprehensive blockade in history was the US blockade of Japan in the early 1940s (code-named Operation Starvation), which slashed Japan's imports by 97 percent. Japan, however, surrendered only after US forces decimated the Japanese military, firebombed its major cities, and dropped atomic bombs on Hiroshima and Nagasaki.[15]

Moreover, if China maintained a blockade for an extended period, it would be vulnerable to sanctions, attacks, and counterblockades from other powers. Historically, anti-submarine warfare forces have been able to disrupt blockades. Germany's attempted blockade of Allied shipping in World War II, for example, became increasingly porous once the Allies launched a dedicated anti-submarine warfare campaign, and Iran's and Iraq's attempts to blockade each other in the 1980s mostly failed because neither side could maintain sea control. The US blockade of Japan in World War II, by contrast, was enforced only after the United States dominated the waters around Japan.

Offshore Island Seizure. Another option for China is to seize one of Taiwan's offshore islands to test Chinese capabilities, assess American resolve, undermine Taiwanese confidence, or use the island as a jumping-off point for annexing Taiwan itself.

To conduct an amphibious assault on Taiwan proper, experts estimate that at least one to two million PLA combat troops would have to cross the Taiwan Strait.[16] Thousands of ships, ferries, fishing boats, container carriers, and cargo ships would need to carry PLA troops across the strait. Some believe that the PLA Navy does not currently have the necessary number of warships since the PLA would have to simultaneously protect shipping lanes, support operations against Taiwan, and land PLA forces on Taiwan.[17] Furthermore, mobilizing so many people and resources could make detection easier, thus eliminating the element of surprise.

It might therefore be more attractive for Chinese forces to practice such an invasion against a real opponent by seizing one of Taiwan's outlying islands. This would send a political signal about Beijing's seriousness without risking the failure that could come with invading Taiwan. Taiwan could make such a seizure painful for China, bleeding the PLA and sapping its strength, hopefully long enough to preclude a move on the main island. But defending these outlying features is likely to be nearly impossible, even for the United States, given the geographic closeness of some of the islands to China.

For decades, studies have suggested that China could conduct a phased invasion of Taiwan by seizing Quemoy.[18] Although Quemoy is heavily fortified with tunnel and bunker complexes, it has at most 50,000 defenders. If China seizes Quemoy quickly, Taiwan would have to decide whether to accept a fait accompli. If the Chinese can succeed in taking Quemoy, the next logical step would be an invasion of the Pescadores Islands, which are only 30 miles from the main island of Taiwan.

Another option would be for China to seize Pratas Island, which is situated 275 miles from Taiwan's main island. Taiwan has deployed hundreds of soldiers there, recognizing that Chinese seizure of Pratas, despite its small size, would have broader implications. For instance, it could be a way for China to test the waters ahead of a more aggressive campaign, such as seizing Quemoy, the Pescadores, and Taiwan's main island.

Defending some of Taiwan's offshore islands from falling under China's control is close to impossible. Fortifying them with anti-access and area-denial platforms could, however, make the costs of conquering them unpalatable. Furthermore, the seizure of offshore islands would give the United States, Taiwan, and the rest of the international community warning that a full-scale invasion of Taiwan proper is likely next, providing time and incentive to prepare. For all these reasons, Chinese leaders may think twice about seizing Taiwan's offshore islands, as they could pay a high cost to gain hold of them.

Amphibious Invasion. An amphibious invasion is the most difficult mission in warfare. An attacker must first achieve air superiority, then land forces in a place where they outnumber the defender and surge reinforcements to the landing zone faster than the defender does. In the successful amphibious invasions of World War II and the Korean War, the United States and its allies enjoyed all these advantages yet still suffered huge losses.

Assuming that China already has air superiority, it would need to land enough troops on Taiwan's shores to secure a beachhead and then reinforce that position faster than Taiwan's defenders could converge on the landing site. China has roughly 100 amphibious ships. If they all survived the daylong trip across the Taiwan Strait, they could land roughly 30,000 troops and 800 armored vehicles on Taiwan's shores. China could supplement these amphibious ships with hundreds of repurposed ferries and fishing vessels and dozens of coast guard ships. Most of these vessels, however, cannot hold large numbers of armored vehicles or landing craft, so most troops ferried by them would have to disembark and trudge ashore on foot. In addition, Chinese civilian ships lack heavy armor and defensive weapons, so they would be vulnerable to attack from Taiwanese coastal artillery.

Another difficulty China would face is that only 10 percent of Taiwan's coastline is suitable for amphibious landing. The east coast consists of steep cliffs, and PLA landing craft would have to sail many hours around Taiwan to reach it—a journey during which they might encounter high sea states, which are common in those waters, and attacks from any surviving Taiwanese ships, aircraft, or shore-based missile launchers. On the other hand, the west coast consists mostly of mudflats that extend miles out to sea. To avoid getting stuck in the mud, PLA units would have to land at high tide at one of a few suitable locations. Taiwan's defenders know those locations well and have defenses prepared on them and forces based near them.

Having made an initial landing, Chinese forces would need to reinforce the initial assault faster than Taiwan could strengthen its defenses at the point of attack. By some estimates, the PLA could ferry roughly 25,000 troops per day to the landing zone using its amphibious ships, assuming none are destroyed or broken down, and more if it uses fishing, coast guard, and civilian transport vessels. It also could supplement its invasion with an airlift of several brigades. These numbers, however, do not account for attrition, which would depend in part on the size and skill of Taiwan's defending force.

Taiwan's military still has a long list of shortcomings. As part of its ongoing transition to an all-volunteer military, Taiwan has reduced the length of conscription from one year to four months. Recruits receive only a few weeks of basic training, and reservists are called up for just a few days each year. Many Taiwanese soldiers lack basic tactical knowledge, have rarely practiced firing their weapons, and suffer low morale. Taiwan also has underfunded its logistics force. In some cases, soldiers have avoided training with their weapons for fear of accidents or wasting precious ammunition.

Yet even a small and weak Taiwanese force could complicate a Chinese invasion. Unless China destroys all of Taiwan's anti-ship missile launchers, Taiwan could strike PLA amphibious ships as they load in Chinese ports or transit the Taiwan Strait. Taiwan also could bombard PLA landing craft with short-range artillery fire as they make their final 20-minute run into the beach.

Past operations suggest the PLA could lose many ships. For example, during the 1982 Falklands War, the United Kingdom carried out the only major amphibious assault in the past 40 years against an Argentine military with fewer than 100 combat aircraft, five anti-ship cruise missiles, and some World War II–era "dumb" bombs. Yet the Argentines managed to sink 15 percent of Britain's naval task force (five ships out of 33) and damage an additional 35 percent, even though British ships never came within 400 miles of Argentina's coast. China's ships, by contrast, would be operating within 100 miles of Taiwan from the moment they left Chinese ports and be targeted by much more numerous and advanced forces armed with precision-guided munitions. Attrition rates would almost surely be higher than what Britain suffered in the Falklands War.

Once PLA ships land on Taiwan's shores, Chinese troops would need to run up the beaches and attack Taiwanese defenses. During the D-Day assault of 1944, the United States lost roughly 10 percent of its troops on the beaches while attacking a severely overstretched German army (most German units were in Eastern Europe, fighting the Soviet Union), in many cases defending hastily dug positions on foreign soil with mortars, cannons, and small arms. If the PLA invaded Taiwan today, it would be attacking massed forces defending home soil with precision-guided munitions, attack helicopters, tanks, and smart mines. PLA losses during each wave, therefore, could be much higher than 10 percent.

Based on an analysis of these four potential contingencies, we conclude that Chinese leaders can only control Taiwan through an inherently risky full-scale invasion. Therefore, though we address these other options, none would likely result in Beijing forcing Taipei into submission. The only way for China to gain sovereignty over Taiwan is likely by outright physical occupation of its main island, which should, as a result, ultimately be the top focus for US defense planning. This means accepting some risk that missile strikes, a blockade, or outlying-island seizure could occur, but we assert that these scenarios should not be seen as the pacing contingency when evaluating the viability of US plans for a Taiwan Strait contingency. If US planners are able to satisfy the needs of the amphibious-invasion scenario, then they should turn to the other three conflict scenarios.

Four US Defense Choices

Given China's development of anti-access and area-denial capabilities and its proximity to the likely zones of conflict, it will not be possible for the United States to establish sea or air control within several hundred miles of China's territory early in a conflict, in contrast to the situation of the past 70 years. Fortunately, the United States does not need to control the seas and skies within the first island chain to stop a cross-Strait invasion; it only needs to be able to deny China's sea and air control. Therefore, the United States should shift to a denial strategy to prevent China from controlling waters and airspace along and within the first island chain. This section looks at four areas in which the United States should consider altering its approach to better deter a Taiwan Strait contingency: readiness, modernization, force structure, and force posture.

Readiness. The slew of recent US Navy ship collisions underscores that crucial air and naval forces are being overstretched by a combination of high operational tempo and lack of investment in maintenance and training. American forces are everywhere at once; they conduct a seemingly endless number of missions around the world, limiting their ability to focus on and prepare for a potential Chinese assault on Taiwan.

Several steps could be taken to free up resources for readiness. First, the US could reduce certain missions outside Asia, which tie up forces and wear down the military's most in-demand combat units. Second, it could shift more investment to denial systems, such as cruise missiles, that would be crucial in a war with China. In many cases, the constant presence of denial systems could provide more consistent combat capability than a rotational deployment of large and vulnerable systems. Third, the US could reduce the size and readiness of its heavy ground forces, both active and reserve, protecting funding to keep conventional missile forces, advanced aircraft, and maritime assets in a high-readiness state.

Modernization. To change the status quo in maritime Asia—vis-à-vis Taiwan, in particular—China has to cross a large body of water with substantial numbers of forces. The United States will remain vulnerable to a Chinese first strike, given it has a limited number of bases in the region.

But US forces can deny China's power-projection efforts and thereby deter revisionism by developing robust sea-denial capabilities. Washington should also encourage US allies and partners to build similar capabilities by providing them with loans, arms, training, and intelligence.

The United States should develop and deploy conventional missile forces and lethal drones for these purposes. It should also train and equip ground forces to conduct expeditionary long-range precision fires. Where possible, the US should pre-position these forces on allied territory in potential conflict zones. This would help turn East Asia into a sensor-rich environment by massively increasing the production and deployment of unmanned sensors, radars, and reconnaissance vehicles. The United States can also build additional undersea systems, such as towed payload modules that can be deployed in the region ahead of a conflict, and install missile launchers on barges to ensure it can strike both Chinese surface ships and land targets at the outset of a conflict.

Force Structure. Asia is largely a maritime theater, so the US Army has a limited role in most China scenarios. To the extent that funding constrains US force structure, elements of the active Army can be cut substantially, with some force structure shifting to the National Guard. A portion of the Army should also follow the Marine Corps's lead in shifting resources away from heavy units toward long-range, land-based missile forces for cross-domain operations. Savings from the Army could be used to invest in the Navy, Marine Corps, and Air Force.

This reprioritization should focus on winning a long-range salvo competition. To do so, the Navy should de-emphasize aircraft carriers, unless it can protect them in the modern threat environment. Meanwhile, it should invest in additional undersea capabilities and missile capacity. The Air Force should de-emphasize purchases of short-range fighters and instead increase bomber numbers, including autonomous or teamed aircraft. The Marine Corps should continue developing a stand-in force that can operate inside the threat ring within the East Asian littoral.

Force Posture. The United States should forward deploy more air-, sea-, and ground-based missile forces in Asia. It must prioritize areas near the first island chain—including Japan and the Philippines—and Australia, the

Pacific Islands, and other locations. This would help reduce US reliance on Guam by developing other regional access points, thereby decreasing the possibility that China might launch a first strike against US forces at the outset of a conflict.

Doing so might require more reliance on an offshore-balancing strategy in the Middle East, limiting the US peacetime presence there to a skeletal base structure and Special Operations Forces. New spending should be devoted to increasing the number and resiliency of forward-operating sites in maritime East Asia. Spending should include hardening existing bases on Okinawa and Guam and developing additional ports, airfields, and missile batteries, with particular emphasis on building new facilities on the Marianas and securing access to facilities in the Philippines.

Conclusion

Deterring coercion and conflict across the Taiwan Strait is no simple task, given the political, strategic, technical, and cultural challenges involved. But as Chairman of the Joint Chiefs of Staff Gen. Mark Milley noted in congressional testimony, the difficulty of an invasion of Taiwan is still a major barrier for China.[19] The United States can use geographic and technological advantages to raise the costs to China. This might not prevent missile strikes, a maritime blockade, or the seizure of outlying islands, but it could deter a full-scale invasion of Taiwan.

Notes

1. Lonnie Henley, "PLA Operational Concepts and Centers of Gravity in a Taiwan Conflict," testimony before the US-China Economic and Security Review Commission, February 18, 2021, https://www.uscc.gov/sites/default/files/2021-02/Lonnie_Henley_Testimony.pdf.

2. US Department of Defense, Office of the Secretary of Defense, *Military and Security Developments Involving the People's Republic of China: Annual Report to Congress*, November 3, 2021, https://media.defense.gov/2021/Nov/03/2002885874/-1/-1/0/2021-CMPR-FINAL.PDF.

3. Michael A. Hunzeker, "The Cross-Strait Military Balance," statement before the US-China Economic and Security Review Commission, February 18, 2021, https://www.uscc.gov/sites/default/files/2021-02/Michael_Hunzeker_Testimony.pdf.

4. Country Reports, "Taiwan Geography," https://www.countryreports.org/country/Taiwan/geography.htm.

5. Central Intelligence Agency, World Factbook, "Taiwan," March 17, 2022, https://www.cia.gov/the-world-factbook/countries/taiwan.

6. Terrence K. Kelly, David C. Gompert, and Duncan Long, *Exploiting U.S. Advantages to Prevent Aggression*, RAND Corporation, 2016, https://www.rand.org/content/dam/rand/pubs/research_reports/RR1300/RR1359/RAND_RR1359.pdf.

7. US Department of Defense, Office of the Secretary of Defense, *Military and Security Developments Involving the People's Republic of China*.

8. US Department of Defense, Office of the Secretary of Defense, *Military and Security Developments Involving the People's Republic of China*.

9. David Lague and Benjamin Kang Lim, *New Missile Gap Leaves U.S. Scrambling to Counter China*, Reuters, April 25, 2019, https://www.reuters.com/investigates/special-report/china-army-rockets.

10. Peter Suciu, "Taiwan Invests in Air Defense Systems to Counter China," *National Interest*, February 16, 2022, https://nationalinterest.org/blog/buzz/taiwan-invests-air-defense-systems-counter-china-200630; Michael J. Lostumbo et al., *Air Defense Options for Taiwan: An Assessment of Relative Costs and Operational Benefits*, RAND Corporation, 2016, 4, https://www.rand.org/pubs/research_reports/RR1051.html; and Ian Easton, *Able Archers: Taiwan Defense Strategy in an Age of Precision Strike*, Project 2049 Institute, 2014, 35–37, https://project2049.net/2014/09/22/able-archers-taiwan-defense-strategy-in-an-age-of-precision-strike.

11. International Institute for Strategic Studies, *The Military Balance 2022* (London: International Institute for Strategic Studies, 2022), 308–10; Easton, *Able Archers*, 35–45; and Ian Easton and Randall Schriver, *Standing Watch: Taiwan and Maritime Domain Awareness in the Western Pacific*, Project 2049 Institute, 2014, 9, https://project2049.net/2014/12/16/standing-watch-taiwan-and-maritime-domain-awareness-in-the-western-pacific.

12. Fang-Yu Chen et al., "What Do Taiwan's People Think About Their Relationship to China?," *Diplomat*, May 29, 2020, https://thediplomat.com/2020/05/what-do-taiwans-people-think-about-their-relationship-to-china.

13. John Mearsheimer, *The Tragedy of Great Power Politics* (New York: W. W. Norton, 2014), 99–110; and Robert A. Pape, *Bombing to Win: Air Power and Coercion in War* (Ithaca, NY: Cornell University Press, 1996).

14. Michael Beckley, *Unrivaled: Why America Will Remain the World's Sole Superpower* (Ithaca, NY: Cornell University Press, 2018), 83.

15. Michael A. Glosny, "Strangulation from the Sea? A PRC Submarine Blockade of Taiwan," *International Security* 28, no. 4 (Spring 2004): 145–46.

16. Ian Easton, "Hostile Harbors: Taiwan's Ports and PLA Invasion Plans," Project 2049 Institute, July 22, 2021, https://project2049.net/2021/07/22/hostile-harbors-taiwans-ports-and-pla-invasion-plans.

17. Michael A. McDevitt, *China as a Twenty-First-Century Naval Power: Theory, Practice, and Implications* (Annapolis, MD: Naval Institute Press, 2020), 72–117.

18. Piers M. Wood and Charles D. Ferguson, "How China Might Invade Taiwan," *Naval War College Review* 54, no. 4 (Autumn 2001), https://digital-commons.usnwc.edu/cgi/viewcontent.cgi?article=2535&context=nwc-review.

19. Sam LaGrone, "Milley: China Wants Capability to Take Taiwan by 2027, Sees No Near-Term Intent to Invade," US Naval Institute News, June 23, 2021, https://news.usni.org/2021/06/23/milley-china-wants-capability-to-take-taiwan-by-2027-sees-no-near-term-intent-to-invade.

Getting Ready for a Long War: Why a US-China Fight in the Western Pacific Won't End Quickly

HAL BRANDS AND MICHAEL BECKLEY

The United States is finally getting serious about the threat of war with China. The Pentagon has labeled China its "pacing challenge" and is crafting new deterrence concepts to hold the People's Liberation Army (PLA) at bay.[1] Civilian leaders have directed the US military to develop credible plans to defend Taiwan, the most likely site of a clash for geopolitical primacy in Asia.[2] President Joe Biden has strongly implied that America would not allow that island democracy to be conquered; other officials have stated it would be a terrible mistake if Beijing used force to alter the status quo.[3] Opinion polls show that a bare majority of Americans now favor defending Taiwan if it were attacked.[4] Keeping the US-China rivalry cold, it increasingly appears, will require deterring—by preparing to win—a hot war.[5]

Yet Washington may be preparing for the wrong kind of war. The Pentagon and many defense planners appear to be focused on winning a short, localized conflict in the Taiwan Strait. That would mean riding out an opening missile blitz, blunting a Chinese invasion, and thereby forcing Beijing to relent. Chinese leaders, for their part, seem to envision rapid, paralyzing strikes that break Taiwanese resistance and present the United States with a fait accompli. Both sides would prefer a splendid little war in the western Pacific, but that is not the sort of war they will get.

A war over Taiwan is likely to be long, not short; regional, not localized; and far more easily started than ended. It would expand and escalate as both countries look for paths to victory in a conflict they feel they cannot afford to lose. It would present severe war-termination dilemmas and involve far higher risks of going nuclear than many Americans realize. If

Washington doesn't start preparing to wage, and then end, a protracted conflict now, it could face catastrophe once the shooting starts.

This chapter proceeds in four parts. First, we explain why a US-China war is likely to turn into a protracted slugfest, almost regardless of what happens in its opening phases. Second, we offer an analysis, informed by history, of how great-power wars evolve and expand as the fighting drags on—and how a US-China war could follow the historical pattern. Third, we explain why nuclear weapons won't necessarily impede a major US-China war and outline three plausible paths to nuclear escalation. Finally, we discuss the requirements of success in a long conflict.[6]

The Logic of Protraction

A US-China war over Taiwan would begin with a bang.[7] China's military doctrine emphasizes coordinated operations to "paralyze the enemy in one stroke."[8]

In the most worrying scenario, Beijing would launch a surprise missile attack, hammering not only Taiwan's defenses but also the American naval and air forces concentrated at a few large bases in the western Pacific. Simultaneous Chinese cyberattacks and anti-satellite operations would sow chaos and hinder any effective US or Taiwanese response. And the PLA would race through the window of opportunity, staging amphibious and airborne assaults that would overwhelm Taiwanese resistance. By the time the United States was ready to fight, the war might effectively be over.[9]

The Pentagon's planning increasingly revolves around preventing this scenario. It aims to harden and disperse the US military presence in Asia and develop the ability to blunt the PLA's offensive capabilities and sink an invasion fleet.[10] The United States also seeks to encourage Taiwan to field asymmetric capabilities—including road-mobile anti-ship missile launchers, mines, and small missile-armed ships—that can inflict a severe toll on Chinese attackers. This planning is predicated on the assumption that the early weeks, if not days, of fighting would determine whether a free Taiwan survives.

Yet whatever happens at the outset, a conflict almost certainly wouldn't end quickly. Most great-power wars since the Industrial Revolution have lasted longer than expected, because modern states have the resources to fight on even when they suffer heavy losses. Moreover, in hegemonic wars—clashes for dominance between the world's strongest states—the stakes are high because the future of the international system is at issue, and the price of defeat may seem prohibitive.

During the 19th and 20th centuries, wars between leading powers—the Napoleonic Wars, the Crimean War, and the World Wars—were protracted slugfests. Although not technically a great-power conflict, the US Civil War was also a long, bloody slog.[11] And the last time America and China fought a major war, in Korea, the conflict was one of unrelenting attrition rather than rapid annihilation. A modern US-China war would likely follow this pattern.

If the United States managed to beat back a Chinese assault against Taiwan, Beijing wouldn't simply give up. Starting a war over Taiwan would be an existential political gamble for the Chinese Communist Party (CCP). The nationalist narrative that the CCP has sold to the Chinese people emphasizes the party's commitment to make China "whole" again by taking back territories lost during the "century of humiliation" (1839–1949).

President Xi Jinping has declared explicitly that the Taiwan problem cannot be passed down generation to generation. In 2017, he announced that "reunification" is an inevitable requirement for "achiev[ing] the great rejuvenation of the Chinese nation."[12] Admitting defeat to what Xi deems Taiwanese renegades and American imperialists would therefore jeopardize the regime's legitimacy and Xi's hold on power—perhaps even his life.

A heavy defeat that wiped out a significant chunk of China's air and naval forces would leave China more vulnerable to its rivals, whether advocates of Taiwanese independence or countries such as India, Japan, and Vietnam. It would destroy China's dreams of regional primacy for years to come. Continuing a hard fight against the United States would be a nasty prospect, but quitting while China was behind would seem even worse. So Xi's government would have every incentive to gamble for resurrection, doubling down on its efforts to win the conflict rather than accepting a politically fatal defeat.

Washington would also be inclined to fight on if the war were not going well. Washington, like Beijing, would view a war over Taiwan—the fulcrum of the balance of power in the western Pacific—as a fight for dominance of a crucial region. The fact that such a war would probably begin with a Pearl Harbor–style missile attack on US bases would make it even harder for an outraged American populace and its leaders to accept a quick defeat. Even if the United States failed to prevent Chinese forces from seizing Taiwan, it couldn't easily bow out of the war. Quitting without first severely damaging Chinese air and naval power in Asia would badly weaken Washington's reputation and its ability to defend remaining allies in the region. The United States might well fear that admitting defeat would mean the end of its influence in the world's most economically dynamic region.

Protraction isn't simply a matter of will, of course; it is also a matter of ability. And both sides, in fact, would have the capacity to keep fighting. The United States could take advantage of its overall military primacy, summoning ships, planes, and submarines from other theaters to make up for initial losses. It could use its command of the Pacific beyond the first island chain—which runs from Japan in the north through Taiwan and the Philippines to the south—to conduct sustained attacks on Chinese forces while remaining out of range of Beijing's most formidable defenses. It could deploy relatively invulnerable assets, such as attack submarines and stealth aircraft, to keep the pressure on and pound Chinese forces relentlessly.

For its part, China could dispatch its surviving air, naval, and missile forces for a second and third assault on Taiwan and press its maritime militia of coast guard and fishing vessels into service. China could also use the strategic depth of the mainland as a giant base from which to operate in a long war. Both the United States and China would emerge from these initial clashes bloodied but not exhausted, increasing the likelihood of a long, ugly war.

What Happens Next

When great-power wars drag on, they get bigger, messier, and more intractable. In a US-China conflict, expect to see four dangerous dynamics.

First, long wars become more economically consuming as time goes on, with all the societal effects that follow. After the initial salvos, the combatants would race to rearm by replenishing stocks of vital weapons and, if necessary, manpower. (This was, for instance, the dynamic that played out after the initial offensives failed to decide World War I in the summer and fall of 1914.) This massive mobilization effort compels them to retool their economies and whip up patriotic fervor in their populations.

A Sino-American war would see hurried efforts to replace munitions, ships, submarines, and aircraft expended or lost in the early fighting. This arms race would place immense strain on both countries' industrial bases, demand the reorientation of their domestic economies, and evoke nationalist appeals—or the use of government compulsion—to mobilize the people for the long and grinding struggle ahead.

Second, long wars expand and escalate as the combatants look for new sources of leverage and new ways of forcing each other to concede. Belligerents open new fronts, in hopes of outflanking their opponent; they rope additional allies into the fight, in hopes of decisively shifting the balance of forces in their favor. They expand their range of targets and worry less about civilian casualties. Sometimes they explicitly target civilians, whether by bombing cities or torpedoing civilian ships. And they use naval blockades, sanctions, and embargoes to starve the enemy into submission.

The World Wars followed this logic. They ultimately dragged in countries on every inhabited continent and repeatedly crossed new thresholds of violence, coercion, and terror. To bring Japan to its knees, for example, the United States firebombed most of Japan's major cities, imposed a blockade code-named "Operation Starvation" that cut Japan off from 97 percent of its imports, and dropped atomic bombs on Hiroshima and Nagasaki.[13] In a war today, if China and the United States unload on each other with nearly every tool at their disposal, as they almost surely would do, a local war would quickly turn into a whole-of-society brawl that spans multiple regions.

Third, as wars get bigger and longer, war aims become more grandiose. The greater the sacrifices required to win the war, the better the peace must be to justify those sacrifices. Indeed, one of the ways governments try to rally their populaces is by promising that victory will deliver vast rewards and lasting security. What begins as a US campaign to defend Taiwan could easily turn into an effort to render China incapable of new aggression by totally destroying its navy, air force, and offensive missile forces. Conversely, as the Pentagon inflicts more damage on China and its military, Beijing's war aims could grow from conquering Taiwan to pushing Washington out of the western Pacific entirely.

These dynamics lead to a final problem: War termination becomes devilishly difficult. Expanding war aims narrow, and perhaps eliminate, the diplomatic space for a settlement. Protracted bloodshed intensifies hatred and mistrust. Allies may stand in the way of a peace that prejudices their own objectives.

This pattern has played out many times in the past. World War I became exhausting for the combatants long before most of them were willing to call it quits. In the Korean War, the front lines stabilized in early 1951, but the fighting dragged on for two more years amid inconclusive peace talks. In other words, even when US and Chinese leaders begin to sense that further fighting is undesirable, they may not be able to find a mutually acceptable peace settlement to bring the bloodshed to an end.

The Path to Armageddon

A war between China and the United States would differ from previous hegemonic wars in one fundamental respect: Both sides have nuclear weapons. On first glance, one might assume that a situation of mutually assured destruction would prevent a US-China war from escalating. Both sides might cap their war aims short of the enemy's complete defeat and humiliation, because they understand that the decisive outcomes and total conquests that marked the World Wars are unachievable in the 21st century, even as the logic of mobilization pushes them to enlarge their ambitions. But it is a mistake to think that nuclear weapons will eliminate the dangers inherent in a long war; they could, in fact, compound them.

For starters, both sides may feel free to unload the full weight of their conventional arsenals on each other under the assumption that their nuclear arsenals shield them from massive retaliation. Scholars call this the stability-instability paradox, a situation in which blind faith in nuclear deterrence unleashes a massive conventional war.

China and the United States aren't immune to this trap. To the contrary, Chinese military writings often suggest that the PLA could wipe out US bases in East Asia and sink American aircraft carriers, killing thousands in the process, while China's nuclear arsenal deters the United States from attacking targets on the Chinese mainland. Meanwhile, some American strategists have called for striking Chinese mainland bases early and hard in a war while assuming that US nuclear superiority would deter China from responding in kind.[14] Far from preventing a major US-China war, nuclear weapons could catalyze it.

Once that war is underway, it could escalate to nuclear use in at least one of three ways. First, whichever side is losing would be tempted to use tactical nuclear weapons—low-yield warheads that could destroy specific military targets without obliterating the recipient's homeland—to turn the tide of battle. That was how the United States planned to halt a Soviet invasion of Central Europe during the Cold War. It was what Israel considered doing during the 1973 Yom Kippur War with Egypt, and it is what North Korea, Pakistan, and Russia have suggested they would do if they were losing a war today. If China crippled US conventional forces in East Asia and were poised to overrun Taiwan, the United States might make a desperate gamble to avoid defeat by using tactical nuclear weapons against Chinese ports, airfields, or invasion fleets. This is no fantasy: The US military is already developing nuclear-tipped, submarine-launched cruise missiles that could be used for such purposes.

China would be even more likely than the United States to use nuclear weapons to try to snatch victory from the jaws of defeat. Beijing has long claimed it would never use nuclear weapons first in a war. Yet the words and deeds of its military suggest otherwise: The PLA has recently embarked on an unprecedented expansion of its nuclear arsenal, including the development of tactical nuclear options, and PLA officers have written that China could use nuclear weapons if a conventional war threatened the survival of its government or nuclear arsenal—which would almost surely be the case if China appeared to be losing a protracted war over Taiwan.[15]

Perhaps these unofficial claims are bluffs. Yet it is not hard to imagine that, in the heat of battle and when facing the annihilation of its navy and the prospect of a humiliating defeat that permanently separates Taiwan from the mainland, China would fire off a nuclear weapon (perhaps at or near America's huge military base on Guam) to regain tactical advantage or shock the United States into a cease-fire. Indeed, a "demonstration shot"—the use of one or a small number of nuclear weapons over the ocean or in ways that do not cause massive destruction and casualties—might be especially appealing as a means of signaling that even more intense escalation will follow absent a resolution of the conflict on China's terms.

As the conflict drags on, either side could also use the ultimate weapon to end a grinding war of attrition. During the Korean War, American leaders repeatedly contemplated dropping nuclear bombs on China to force it to accept a cease-fire or simply gain a decisive edge on the battlefield. It was the lack of suitable targets, as much as any moral consideration, that ultimately precluded this coercive nuclear use.[16] Today, the United States and China are the world's two largest economies and are full of appealing targets for nuclear attack. Both countries would thus have the option of using limited nuclear strikes to compel a stubborn opponent to concede. In fact, the incentives to do so could be strong, given that whichever side pulls the nuclear trigger first might gain a major and perhaps irreversible advantage.

A final route to nuclear war is inadvertent escalation. Each side, knowing that escalation is a risk, may try to limit the other's nuclear options. The United States could, for instance, try to sink China's ballistic-missile submarines before they hide in the deep waters beyond the first island chain. Yet such an attack could put China in a "use it or lose it" situation with regard to its nuclear forces, especially if the United States also struck China's land-based missiles and communication systems, which intermingle conventional and nuclear forces.[17]

Even if the United States tried to avoid threatening China's nuclear arsenal, any US attack on Chinese mainland bases, missile forces, and command centers could be misinterpreted as an attempt to cripple China's nuclear forces. In this scenario, China's leaders might use their nuclear weapons rather than risk losing that option altogether.[18] The risk of inadvertent escalation may recede over time, because China has ambitious plans to quadruple the size of its nuclear arsenal and diversify its forces into an indestructible triad of ground-, air-, and submarine-launched missiles.[19] But for now, its arsenal is relatively small and vulnerable, which could make the prospect of losing its nuclear capabilities loom larger.

To be clear, we don't really know how nuclear escalation would unfold in a US-China conflict, because such a war has never occurred. It could be, for instance, that officials on both sides conclude that any nuclear exchange is unlikely to remain limited, which restrains them from using nuclear weapons in the first place.[20] Or it could be that the same conclusion pushes one side to use nuclear weapons more dramatically, for fear of losing a significant first-mover advantage. We will be in uncharted territory if two nuclear powers come to blows. The only certainty is that a long conflict will introduce unprecedented dangers.

Preparing for a Long War

There is no easy way to prepare for a long war with an inherently unpredictable course and dynamics. Yet the United States and its allies can do four things to get ready for whatever comes—and, hopefully, prevent the worst from happening.

First, Washington can win the race to reload. China will be much less likely to go to war if it knows it will be outgunned as the conflict drags on. Washington and Taipei should therefore aggressively stockpile ammunition and supplies. For the United States, the crucial assets are missiles capable of sinking China's most valuable ships and aircraft from afar. For Taiwan, the key weapons are short-range missiles, mortars, mines, and rocket launchers that can decimate invasion fleets. Both nations also need to be ready to churn out new weapons in wartime.[21] Taiwanese factories will be obvious targets for Chinese missiles, so the United States should enlist the industrial might of other allies. Japan's shipbuilding capacity, for example, could be retooled to produce simple missile barges rapidly and on a massive scale.

Second, Washington should demonstrate the ability to hang tough. The United States and Taiwan need to be ready to ride out a protracted Chinese punishment campaign. In a long war, China could try to strangle Taiwan with a blockade, bombard it into submission, or take down US and Taiwanese electrical grids and telecommunications networks with cyberattacks. It could use conventionally armed, hypersonic missiles to attack targets in the American homeland. Preventing such coercion from succeeding will require defensive preparations, such as securing critical networks, expanding Taiwan's system of civilian shelters, and enlarging its stockpiles of fuel, food, and medical supplies. It also will require preparing both the

US and Taiwanese populations psychologically for what could be a long and bloody conflict.

Breaking a Chinese campaign of coercion also requires threatening Beijing with painful retaliation. A third objective, therefore, is to own the escalation ladder. By preparing to blockade Chinese commerce and cut Beijing off from markets and technology in wartime, America and its allies can threaten to turn an extended conflict into an economic catastrophe for China. Beijing imports nearly 75 percent of its oil and 45 percent of its natural gas. Most of this is shipped through narrow choke points, such as the Strait of Malacca, far from Chinese mainland bases. The US military, with its unparalleled power-projection capabilities and network of allies and partners, could demonstrate its ability to close off those choke points with peacetime military exercises.[22]

In addition, by preparing to sink Chinese naval vessels anywhere in the western Pacific and destroy Chinese military infrastructure in other regions, the United States can threaten a generation's worth of Chinese military modernization. By bringing additional allies, whether located in the western Pacific or elsewhere, into the fight, the United States can drive up the long-term strategic cost to Beijing for continuing the war.[23] And by developing the means to hit Chinese ports, airfields, and armadas with tactical nuclear weapons, the United States can deter China from initiating limited nuclear attacks. Washington should confront Beijing with a basic proposition: The longer a war lasts, the more devastation China will suffer.

Because controlling escalation will be essential, the United States also needs options that allow it to dial up the punishment without necessarily dialing up the violence. By subtly demonstrating it has the cyber capabilities to cripple China's critical infrastructure and domestic security system, for example, the United States can threaten to bring the war home to Beijing. Similarly, by improving its ability to suppress Chinese air defenses near Taiwan with cyberattacks, electronic warfare, and directed energy weapons, the United States can increase its freedom of action—and help Taiwan break or simply survive a sustained Chinese blockade—while limiting the amount of physical destruction it wreaks on the mainland.[24]

All of these steps will ratchet up the intensity of the conflict. So, as a final preparation, Washington needs to counteract that effect by defining victory down. A war between nuclear-armed great powers won't end with regime change or one side occupying the other's capital. It will end with a negotiated compromise.

The simplest settlement would be a return to the status quo ante: China stops attacking Taiwan in exchange for a pledge that the island would not declare, and America would not endorse, formal independence. To sweeten the deal, the United States could offer to keep its forces off Taiwan and out of the Taiwan Strait. Xi would be able to tell the Chinese people that he had taught Taiwan and the United States a lesson, just as Deng Xiaoping justified a sloppy invasion of Vietnam in 1979 as a "punitive" expedition. The United States would have saved a vibrant and strategically positioned democracy. Both sides would save some face and live to see another day.

That may not be a fully satisfying end to a hard-fought conflict. It certainly wouldn't bring an end to the larger Sino-American rivalry: The United States would be wise to view any such settlement as a cease-fire rather than a lasting peace. But in a long war between great powers, protecting America's vital interests while avoiding outright catastrophe might have to be good enough.

Notes

1. Jim Garamone, "China's Capabilities Growth Shows Why U.S. Sees Nation as Pacing Challenge," US Department of Defense, October 27, 2021, https://www.defense.gov/News/News-Stories/Article/Article/2824060/chinas-capabilities-growth-shows-why-us-sees-nation-as-pacing-challenge.

2. White House, "U.S. Strategic Framework for the Indo-Pacific," January 2021, https://trumpwhitehouse.archives.gov/wp-content/uploads/2021/01/IPS-Final-Declass.pdf.

3. Doina Chiacu, "Blinken Warns of China's 'Increasingly Aggressive Actions' Against Taiwan," Reuters, April 11, 2021, https://www.reuters.com/world/china/blinken-warns-chinas-increasingly-aggressive-actions-against-taiwan-2021-04-11; and BBC, "Biden Says U.S. Will Defend Taiwan If China Attacks," October 22, 2021, https://www.bbc.com/news/world-asia-59005300.

4. Dina Smeltz and Craig Kafura, "For First Time, Half of Americans Favor Defending Taiwan If China Invades," Chicago Council on Global Affairs and Lester Crown Center on US Foreign Policy, August 26, 2021, https://www.thechicagocouncil.org/sites/default/files/2021-08/2021%20Taiwan%20Brief.pdf.

5. An earlier version of this chapter was published as Hal Brands and Michael Beckley, "Washington Is Preparing for the Wrong War with China: A Conflict Would Be Long and Messy," *Foreign Affairs*, December 16, 2021, https://www.foreignaffairs.com/

articles/china/2021-12-16/washington-preparing-wrong-war-china. See also Hal Brands, "Win or Lose, U.S. War Against China or Russia Won't Be Short," Bloomberg Opinion, June 14, 2021, https://www.bloomberg.com/opinion/articles/2021-06-14/win-or-lose-war-against-china-or-russia-won-t-be-short. The present version of the chapter has been considerably revised and expanded from the original.

6. For other works on protracted great-power war in the US-China context, see Joshua Rovner, "A Long War in the East: Doctrine, Diplomacy, and Prospects for a Protracted Sino-American Conflict," *Diplomacy & Statecraft* 29, no. 1 (2018); and Andrew Krepinevich, "Protracted Great-Power War: A Preliminary Assessment," Center for a New American Security, February 5, 2020, https://www.cnas.org/publications/reports/protracted-great-power-war.

7. Thomas Shugart and Javier Gonzalez, *First Strike: China's Missile Threat to U.S. Bases in Asia*, Center for a New American Security, June 2017, https://css.ethz.ch/content/dam/ethz/special-interest/gess/cis/center-for-securities-studies/resources/docs/CNAS-First%20Strike,%20China's%20Missile%20Threat%20to%20US%20Bases%20in%20Asia.pdf.

8. Joshua Rovner, "Two Kinds of Catastrophe: Nuclear Escalation and Protracted War in Asia," *Journal of Strategic Studies* 40, no. 5 (2017): 697; Jeffrey Engstrom, *Systems Confrontation and System Destruction Warfare: How the Chinese People's Liberation Army Seeks to Wage Modern Warfare*, RAND Corporation, 2018, https://www.rand.org/content/dam/rand/pubs/research_reports/RR1700/RR1708/RAND_RR1708.pdf; and Alison A. Kaufman and Daniel M. Hartnett, *Managing Conflict: Examining Recent PLA Writings on Escalation Control*, Center for Naval Analyses, February 2016, 68, https://apps.dtic.mil/sti/pdfs/AD1005033.pdf. For an example, see Guangqian Peng and Youzhi Yao, eds., *The Science of Military Strategy* (Beijing, China: Military Science Publishing House, 2005), 327.

9. Hal Brands and Michael Beckley, *Danger Zone: The Coming Conflict with China* (New York: W. W. Norton, 2022).

10. David Ochmanek and Michael O'Hanlon, "Here's the Strategy to Prevent China from Taking Taiwan," *Hill*, December 8, 2021, https://thehill.com/opinion/national-security/584370-heres-the-strategy-to-prevent-china-from-taking-taiwan.

11. Williamson Murray, "Strategies of Annihilation and Strategies of Attrition," in *Makers of Modern Strategy*, ed. Hal Brands, 3rd ed. (Princeton, NJ: Princeton University Press, forthcoming).

12. Xi Jinping, "Secure a Decisive Victory in Building a Moderately Prosperous Society in All Respects and Strive for the Great Success of Socialism with Chinese Characteristics for a New Era" (speech, 19th National Congress of the Communist Party of China, Beijing, China, October 18, 2017), http://www.chinadaily.com.cn/china/19thcpcnationalcongress/2017-11/04/content_34115212.htm.

13. Michael A. Glosny, "Strangulation from the Sea? A PRC Submarine Blockade of Taiwan," *International Security* 28, no. 4 (Spring 2004): 145–46, https://direct.mit.edu/isec/article-abstract/28/4/125/11794/Strangulation-from-the-Sea-A-PRC-Submarine.

14. Jan van Tol et al., *AirSea Battle: A Point-of-Departure Operational Concept*, Center for Strategic and Budgetary Assessments, May 2010, https://csbaonline.org/research/publications/airsea-battle-concept/publication/1.

15. Caitlin Talmadge, "Would China Go Nuclear? Assessing the Risk of Chinese Nuclear Escalation in a Conventional War with the United States," *International Security* 41, no. 4 (Spring 2017): 50–92, https://direct.mit.edu/isec/article-abstract/41/4/50/12156/Would-China-Go-Nuclear-Assessing-the-Risk-of.

16. Rosemary Foot, *The Wrong War: American Policy and the Dimensions of the Korean Conflict, 1950–1953* (Ithaca, NY: Cornell University Press, 1985).

17. Tong Zhao and Li Bin, "The Underappreciated Risks of Entanglement: A Chinese Perspective," in *Entanglement: Russian and Chinese Perspectives on Non-Nuclear Weapons and Nuclear Risks*, ed. James Acton (Washington, DC: Carnegie Endowment for International Peace, 2017), https://carnegieendowment.org/files/Entanglement_interior_FNL.pdf.

18. Talmadge, "Would China Go Nuclear?"

19. The foremost analysis on the risk of inadvertent nuclear escalation is Barry R. Posen, *Inadvertent Escalation: Conventional War and Nuclear Risks* (Ithaca, NY: Cornell University Press, 1992).

20. During the 1950s, for instance, fear that nuclear war would escalate explosively drove the United States to formulate plans for the massive use of nuclear weapons at the outset of a conflict. See Marc Trachtenberg, *A Constructed Peace: The Making of the European Settlement, 1945–1963* (Princeton, NJ: Princeton University Press, 1999).

21. R. Robinson Harris et al., "Converting Merchant Ships to Missile Ships for the Win," *Proceedings* 145, no. 1 (January 2019), https://www.usni.org/magazines/proceedings/2019/january/converting-merchant-ships-missile-ships-win.

22. Sean Mirski, "Stranglehold: The Context, Conduct and Consequences of an American Naval Blockade of China," *Journal of Strategic Studies* 36, no. 3 (2013), https://carnegieendowment.org/2013/02/12/stranglehold-context-conduct-and-consequences-of-american-naval-blockade-of-china-pub-51135.

23. It seems likely, purely for operational reasons, that Japan would be involved in a US-China war over Taiwan from the outset, simply because China cannot cripple US military power in the western Pacific without hitting bases and other targets on Japanese soil. It is less certain whether other key countries, such as Australia, India, the Philippines, and South Korea, to say nothing of European powers such as France and the United Kingdom, would join the fray.

24. Lonnie Henley, "PLA Operational Concepts and Centers of Gravity in a Taiwan Conflict," testimony before the US-China Economic and Security Review Commission, February 18, 2021, https://www.uscc.gov/sites/default/files/2021-02/Lonnie_Henley_Testimony.pdf.

Bigger Might Be Better

GISELLE DONNELLY

"Whenever I run into a problem I can't solve, I always make it bigger."

This quote, often attributed to Dwight D. Eisenhower and said to be a favorite of the late Defense Secretary Donald Rumsfeld, deserves consideration in shaping any US military response to a Chinese attack on Taiwan. Looked at as merely a cross-Strait problem, the defense of a tiny island within minutes' range of Chinese missile barrage and air attack and at the extreme limit of American power projection is, if not insoluble, a very difficult problem.

The Chinese People's Liberation Army (PLA) has spent decades building a Taiwan-centric force—a giant stick that is already intimidating to Taipei, Washington, and much of maritime East Asia—capable of inflicting immediate, widespread, and severe damage on the island. And although "great-power competition" and a "Pacific pivot" have become accepted US strategy and military doctrine, no administration has taken concrete steps or made serious investments to give much reality to this rhetoric.

While the first order of business in the event of an attack by Beijing is to ensure there's still a Taiwan left to defend—and one that is independent, de jure and de facto—it is imperative that the United States aim for more than a simple cessation of hostilities and return to the status quo ante. That's more easily said than done, but the Cold War literature on horizontal escalation may offer an eye to today's near-blind presidents and generals. Ike's aphorism has a certain Sun Tzu–esque ring that resonates in the context of the current China conundrum.

What Is Horizontal Escalation?

The mainstream understanding of all forms of escalation in warfare has been shaped by two factors, beginning with political scientists' studies of nuclear weapons' effects during the Cold War and treatments of the prelude to and early phases of World War I. The classic example of the former is Bernard Brodie's 1965 *Escalation and the Nuclear Option*, a RAND Corporation monograph and later a full-length book.[1] And probably the most broadly influential rendering of the latter is Barbara Tuchman's Pulitzer Prize winner, *The Guns of August*, published in 1962, also the year of the Cuban missile crisis.[2] Fear of runaway nuclear arms races was an essential element of the geopolitical zeitgeist of the time.

Yet the focus on the logic of new and poorly understood weaponry has tended to obscure a deeper and more historically resonant understanding of escalation: Truly revolutionary developments in military technology have been predicted far more often than they have been realized. Conflict, particularly among rival great powers, is perhaps more likely to expand in scope than intensity, a phenomenon especially prevalent during the Cold War and in the presence of nuclear weapons.

Secondly, escalation, like deterrence, is best understood subjectively, through the eyes of the contestants—that is, escalation must "cross [a] threshold considered significant by one or more of the participants."[3] In other words, strategic signaling counts.

Thus, the traditional metaphor of an escalation "ladder"—introduced in another seminal Cold War study, Herman Kahn's 1965 *On Escalation: Metaphors and Scenarios*, which identifies 44 "rungs"—has encouraged a too-narrow concept of what has most often been a far more complex and ambiguous way of war.[4] This vertical paradigm appears to be strongly at work in much of US military thinking about the defense of Taiwan and the larger deterrence of Chinese expansionism: If the PLA can attack Taiwan and US bases or ships at will using ballistic and cruise missiles, we must not only defend against them but also develop a broadly symmetric ability to rocket the mainland.

Responding in kind to the trends in Chinese military modernization is a military and strategic necessity but perhaps not sufficient to produce a satisfactory deterrent or outcome in the event of hostilities. Too little explored are the possibilities for horizontal escalation: expanding the geographical scope of conflict, even to multiple theaters.

Ironically, this approach was a strong influence on the late Cold War thinking of the Reagan administration. Not only was there an attempt to threaten Soviet outposts in Africa, the Caribbean, and East Asia, but even within western Europe, the centerpiece of the AirLand Battle doctrine was a powerful counterattack into Warsaw Pact states. This threatened to unravel the Soviets' Eastern European glacis, the strategic depth Moscow had won from World War II and for which it paid a terrible price. Both escalation and deterrence are best understood as multidimensional balances. The horizontal spaces—the boundaries of conflict, locations of targets and bases, elimination of sanctuaries, and even violations of neutrality—deserve more attention in the geostrategic competition with Beijing.

American Options

For decades, the United States has been the dominant power in East Asia and globally. This position of preeminence creates a wealth of opportunities for potential horizontal responses to Chinese actions against Taiwan.

Japan. Principal among them are the many facets of Japan, long a treaty ally and home to 50,000 US Forces Japan troops and an extensive network of logistics nodes and operational bases, including those on Okinawa, just 500 miles—tiny on a Pacific scale—from Taiwan. Indeed, the centrality of these facilities to the US Pacific military posture makes it a near certainty that the Chinese would target them in a serious conflict over Taiwan. It also would compel the United States to escalate horizontally from the outset.

Japan's public strategic posture is, like that of the United States, intentionally ambiguous, though increasingly antagonistic toward China. While in 1972 Japan recognized the Beijing regime as the "sole legal Government of China," Tokyo has not acknowledged China's claim to Taiwan.[5]

In the summer of 2021, as cross-Strait tensions rose and Chinese incursions into Taiwanese and Japanese air defense identification zones mounted, Taro Aso, a controversial and "gaffe-prone" 80-year-old politician but also deputy prime minister and a stalwart of Japan's ruling Liberal Democrats, described a Chinese attack on Taiwan as an "existential threat" to Japanese security interests. "If a major incident happened," Aso said, "it's safe to say it would be related to a situation threatening the survival [of Japan]. If that is the case, Japan and the U.S. must defend Taiwan together."[6]

While expert opinion is divided on Japan's willingness and ability to contribute to Taiwan's defense, Aso's statement reflects a powerful strategic logic: If Taiwan were to become a Chinese outpost, it would control the southern approaches to Japan and truly threaten Japan's commercial and military sea lines of communication. Aso's statement also reflects the historical enmity between China and Japan, embodied in the still-raw attitudes over Japan's killing of millions of Chinese during World War II and expressed in continuing disputes over the Senkaku (or Diaoyu, as they are known in China) islands in the East China Sea. In a 2016 poll, Pew researchers found that 81 percent of Chinese had unfavorable views of Japan, while a full 86 percent of Japanese had negative views of China.[7] This ingrained animosity has important consequences for a strategy of horizontal escalation: For China, the prospect of a war with Japan would evoke powerful and painful memories.

Moreover, Beijing has, since the end of World War II, relied on the United States to suppress the traditionally strong Japanese sense of racial superiority and aggressive nationalism. A successful Chinese conquest—or even a peaceful absorption—of Taiwan could well induce Tokyo to uncouple itself from its American alliance, taking, in the context of a changing and more threatening Asian balance of power, its security into its own hands. And one of the first likely Japanese responses in such a situation would be to acquire an independent nuclear capability, something well within Tokyo's rapid reach.

From Beijing's point of view, the only thing worse than having Japan as a nearby American outpost might be to have Japan as an independent and—if history is a guide—potentially anxiety-ridden actor. This unknown but potentially great risk might even outweigh the anticipated benefits of taking Taiwan.

The Japan Self-Defense Force (JSDF) is a small but serious military. Although Tokyo retains constitutional restrictions on the use of force, the previous prime minister, Shinzo Abe, pushed through a package of new defense laws in 2015 permitting the JSDF to cooperate with other militaries. And though Japan spends just 1 percent of gross domestic product on defense, that adds up to $51 billion per year, the eighth most in the world—enabling, for example, the purchase of at least 100 F-35 fighters.[8] And China, rather than North Korea, is regarded as the pacing threat for the JSDF.

Finally, the high probability of Japan's involvement in a Taiwan Strait conflict will shape any negotiations for a cease-fire or more durable cessation of hostilities. While it is impossible to predict precisely what Tokyo would want in such circumstances, China and the United States would have to take Japanese interests into account. Among those interests would be the continuity of American guarantees of Japanese security and sovereignty and the reliability of any renunciation by Beijing of territorial claims. In sum, any substantial Taiwan Strait conflict is almost certainly a three-way affair.

Korea. The Republic of Korea is a second "jewel in the crown" of America's East Asian military posture; no more in the 21st century than in 1950 can the United States avoid that the Korean Peninsula lies within its defensive perimeter. Indeed, the security of the first island chain—running from Japan through the Ryukyus and Taiwan to the Philippines—begins in Seoul, as Dean Acheson would be forced to admit.[9]

Although a formal end to the Korean War may or may not be on the horizon, and the strength of US Forces Korea has, for the first time since 1950, dipped below 30,000 troops, the US position on the peninsula remains crucial to America's military posture in the Pacific. As with Japan, it is highly questionable that a Taiwan conflict—which we can now see is inherently a war for maritime East Asia—could sidestep Korea or that South Korea could sidestep such a war, however a government in Seoul might wish. And the likelihood of a Korean connection would only increase were Japan involved in the conflict, given the historical connection between security on the peninsula and Japan's security.

While the United States has been most concerned about the danger North Korea poses to the peninsula, simple geography reveals the peninsula's operational importance in a Taiwan conflict. Much of the PLA is based in northern China, and its naval and air forces would have to pass through the Yellow Sea to operate farther south. At the very least, the potential of interception from US forces in Korea would tie down some Chinese forces. This is much of the purpose of horizontal escalation, and limiting the PLA's ability to bring second or third waves of attack to bear will be crucial to frustrating a campaign against Taiwan.

Southeast Asia. Similar uncertainty-creating and cost-imposing gambits might bear fruit in Southeast Asia. While Beijing has gone to great lengths to try to dominate the South China Sea region, its outposts there are inevitably vulnerable, open to US forces operating in the Philippines or Vietnam. This, in turn, suggests the degree to which Beijing suffers from what it calls the "Malacca Dilemma"—that is, the vulnerability of its sea lines of communication that are a pipeline for not only Chinese exports but also energy and other natural-resource imports from the Middle East and Africa.

India. A major Chinese move against Taiwan would also be viewed nervously in India. China and India share what has long been a contested border, and in recent years tensions have escalated, including, for the first time in five decades, fire exchanged across the Line of Actual Control in Ladakh, part of Kashmir. Delhi believes that Beijing is reprising the "salami slicing" strategy of small but constant land grabs that would, over time, tilt the regional balance of power in China's favor. Both sides have also engaged in extensive roadbuilding and other infrastructure construction that would allow for larger and more rapid troop movements. And in recent years, the Indian military has begun to develop plans and capabilities to challenge the extensive network of Chinese bases near the entire border region.

While India notoriously values its strategic independence, and any direct or overt support to US or other allied forces in a Taiwan crisis is doubtful, Delhi's commitment to the "Quad" with Australia, Japan, and the United States has been consistent since the Quad's inception in 2007. And the group's commitment to a "shared vision for a free and open Indo-Pacific . . . unconstrained by coercion," reaffirmed by the Biden administration in 2021, is based on fears of rising Chinese power and increased aggression.[10] If nothing else, India represents a "threat in being" that Beijing cannot ignore. Further, in the border region, the contest is a land-centric one at the other end of the operational spectrum from any Taiwan scenario. It demands that China retain a balance of military capabilities.

Thinking about India's role in the larger geopolitical competition with China is also useful in expanding American strategic horizons. It is a reminder that Beijing is the capital of a Eurasian empire whose first and principal concern has historically been the security of its western, continental frontiers.

China's position is not unlike that of Bourbon and Napoleonic France, whose maritime, colonial, and global ambitions were forever limited by the need to protect its land borders. Great Britain's classic "Whig" response to the French situation was to assemble balancing coalitions of European powers—including lavishing them with subsidies—to tie down French forces and deprive France of the resources needed for power projection abroad. The British also long cultivated ties to French Huguenots (a violently repressed Protestant minority in Catholic France), particularly those who lived near the Atlantic seaboard. The repression of Tibetans and Uyghurs—not to mention the desires of many Han Chinese for political and other forms of liberty—is a strategic weakness for the Chinese regime, a vulnerability that continues despite its crackdown on the Tiananmen protests or the socially repressive policies of Xi Jinping.

The View from Beijing

Arguably, Beijing has been quicker to realize that the prospects for horizontal escalation inherent in its desire to become a global great power would also frame a Taiwan conflict. As the Pentagon's recent annual reports on Chinese military power have observed, while Taiwan remains the azimuth-setting strategic direction for the PLA and the driver of its modernization efforts, a host of other missions have landed on the Chinese military's plate: deterring other regional rivals, from Japan to Vietnam to India; enforcing Beijing's territorial claims regarding not only Taiwan but also the islands of the East and South China Seas and China's land borders; protecting China's growing list of overseas strategic and economic concerns; and guaranteeing the Chinese Communist Party regime against domestic challengers.

A June 2020 report, *System Overload: Can China's Military Be Distracted in a War over Taiwan?* by Joel Wuthnow of the Center for the Study of Chinese Military Affairs at the National Defense University, well summarizes the view from Beijing as it comes to grips with the realities of great power in a globalized world. Further, the report offers a rich framework for assessing the prospects for devising a horizontal escalation strategy in response; one might argue that a paralyzing "system overload" would be the principal objective of such a strategy.[11] "Handling multiple problems remains a weakness for the PLA," writes Wuthnow.

> Specific deficiencies include difficulties setting priorities due to interservice bargaining, a weak force posture beyond the First Island Chain, a convoluted command structure for multitheater operations, and the lack of a rotational assignment system that would give officers exposure to multiple problem sets. Latent civil-military distrust could also reduce the confidence of civilian leaders that the system will work as intended in a war.[12]

These are problems well understood by Chinese strategists, who worry about "chain-reaction warfare," whereby the United States and Beijing's other antagonists could exploit a Taiwan conflict in ways and places that would put novel strains on military and political decision makers. While a complete summary of Wuthnow's work is beyond the scope of this chapter, several of its major analyses are worth reprising and should inform consideration of any strategy for horizontal escalation.

The first of these is to understand how Beijing's obsession with Taiwan has both enabled and distorted its decades-long program of military modernization. With the collapse of the Soviet Union and in the aftermath of the Taiwan crises of 1995 and 1996, the Chinese Central Military Commission—China's senior strategic decision-making body, led by the party's general secretary and including the PLA's senior generals—formally shifted China's main strategic direction away from its northwest land border with Russia to its southeast coastline. In Chinese doctrine, this designation subsumes not only operational planning but also force development, posture, and deployment.

The result has been, in Wuthnow's succinct formula, an operational focus on "joint firepower strikes on key targets, a blockade, or a full-scale island landing (which would be preceded by a missile bombardment and a blockade)." These concepts have driven the development of "short-range cruise and ballistic missiles, advanced fighters, amphibious units, and electronic and psychological warfare capabilities, many of which were initially deployed in the Nanjing Military Region (MR) opposite Taiwan."[13] These are the trends that have been foremost in the annual Pentagon reports of the past two decades.

However, the list of competing strategic demands has grown, especially under Xi's rule. The Chinese defense white papers of 2015 and 2019 reference a variety of potential conflict scenarios beyond Taiwanese independence: perceptions of strengthened US alliances in the region, instability on the Korean Peninsula, Uyghur and Tibetan independence movements, so-called Japanese militarization and infringements on East China Sea islands, other infringements in the South China Sea, and Australia's alliance building.

A further traditional concern, instability in Afghanistan and South Asia more generally, has been downplayed during the years of US involvement there, but recent Chinese actions and the American withdrawal from Afghanistan suggest this, too, might feature in future Chinese doctrinal and planning documents. Wuthnow also cites the 2013 edition of a main Chinese military journal, *Science of Strategy*, which concluded that the PLA's ability to respond to conflicts outside its main strategic direction had been historically weak and that current PLA planners needed to better account for "high-intensity military operations and even local wars that may occur in other directions."[14]

Indeed, it appears that Chinese leaders and strategists are struggling to adapt to the exigencies of global power, with a resulting loss of strategic focus and a force increasingly optimized for one kind of war—and now with service and procurement bureaucracies deeply invested in the primacy of the Taiwan scenario. And Xi's "China Dream" ambitions are only making matters more complex, as an article in the journal of the Central Party School suggests.

> Entering a new era, with the profound changes in the content of [our] national interests, various strategic directions may have security problems that infringe on national interests, which in turn cause serious harm and consequences to the overall development of the country. *This makes any strategic direction likely to be the main strategic direction.*[15] (Emphasis in the original.)

This paradox will sound all too familiar to American leaders and strategists of the post–World War II and, especially, the post-9/11 generations: The principal direction of strategy is determined by whatever direction you're already going in. And those defense reformers and strategic "realists" so frustrated by this fact will recognize the hopeless prescription the Chinese have set for themselves in the sentence following: "Only by scientifically coordinating the use of military forces can we effectively respond to security threats in all directions and ensure the balance and stability of the overall strategy."[16] When a nation's strategy suggests large doses of appetite suppressants for military commanders engaged in conflict, that nation is in trouble.

Rethinking the Scenario

The challenges of trying to successfully defend Taiwan against an overwhelming Chinese attack—a prospect that also shapes Beijing's efforts to bully and subvert Taipei into "peaceful" absorption into the Chinese empire—have done much to propel the long-postponed (and still anemic) project of US defense modernization in the post–Cold War era. If Taiwan is to survive a savage opening salvo, it will be up to the United States to intervene rapidly, effectively, and directly.

Yet were such a scenario to play out, it must be clear that these are the first shots in a long conflict and only part of an enduring great-power competition that will take decades to play out; the modern history of similar struggles—be they to contain Hapsburg Spain, Bourbon and Napoleonic France, Wilhelmine and Nazi Germany, or Tsarist Russia and the Soviet Union—strongly suggests so. As pressing and immediate as the cross-Strait danger is in itself, it is past time to begin thinking about and preparing for the longer-term defense of the world America made: the peaceful, prosperous, and still-free liberal international order.

No essay on strategy can be complete without a Carl von Clausewitz quote. In this case, it is relevant to recite that the "first, the supreme, the most far-reaching act of judgment that the statesman and commander have to make is to establish the kind of war on which they are embarking."[17] This exactly describes what the United States and its allies must do. Even the cursory analysis offered here should make plain that the canonical Taiwan scenario is inherently a larger contest than currently imagined and that horizontal escalation will be baked into the cake from the start.

This fact plays very much to an American advantage. This is true in not just the military and operational spheres highlighted by Wuthnow but the political spheres as well. Assessed globally, China is in a much weaker position than the US by all measures, and those nations with which China has nascent strategic partnerships are likely to be minuses rather than pluses. "If I get in trouble, Vladimir Putin's got my back" cannot inspire confidence in Beijing. Which domestic polities are most durable: an autocratic, repressive, centralized one-party state or a sprawling herd of liberal democracies? Which side has nine lives?

Notes

1. Bernard Brodie, *Escalation and the Nuclear Option*, RAND Corporation, June 1965, https://www.rand.org/content/dam/rand/pubs/research_memoranda/2006/RM4544.pdf.

2. Barbara W. Tuchman, *The Guns of August* (New York: MacMillan, 1962).

3. This definition is borrowed from Forrest E. Morgan et al., *Dangerous Thresholds: Managing Escalation in the 21st Century*, RAND Corporation, 2008, https://www.rand.org/pubs/monographs/MG614.html.

4. Herman Kahn, *On Escalation: Metaphors and Scenarios* (New York: Praeger, 1965).

5. Japanese Ministry of Foreign Affairs, "Joint Communique of the Government of Japan and the Government of the People's Republic of China," September 29, 1972, https://www.mofa.go.jp/region/asia-paci/china/joint72.html.

6. William Sposato, "Taro Aso's Taiwan Slip Was Likely Deliberate," *Foreign Policy*, July 12, 2021, https://foreignpolicy.com/2021/07/12/taro-aso-taiwan-japan-china-policy.

7. Bruce Stokes, "Hostile Neighbors: China vs. Japan," Pew Research Center, September 13, 2016, https://www.pewresearch.org/global/2016/09/13/hostile-neighbors-china-vs-japan.

8. See World Bank, "Military Expenditure (% of GDP)—Japan," https://data.world-bank.org/indicator/MS.MIL.XPND.GD.ZS?locations=JP.

9. National Archives, Harry S. Truman Presidential Library and Museum, "Remarks by Dean Acheson Before the National Press Club," January 12, 1950, https://www.trumanlibrary.gov/library/research-files/remarks-dean-acheson-national-press-club.

10. White House, "Quad Leaders' Joint Statement: 'The Spirit of the Quad,'" press release, March 12, 2021, https://www.whitehouse.gov/briefing-room/statements-releases/2021/03/12/quad-leaders-joint-statement-the-spirit-of-the-quad.

11. Joel Wuthnow, *System Overload: Can China's Military Be Distracted in a War over Taiwan?*, Institute for National Strategic Studies, Center for the Study of Chinese Military Affairs, June 2020, https://ndupress.ndu.edu/Portals/68/Documents/stratperspective/china/china-perspectives-15.pdf.

12. Wuthnow, *System Overload*, 1.

13. Wuthnow, *System Overload*, 7.

14. Wuthnow, *System Overload*, 9.

15. Quoted in Wuthnow, *System Overload*, 11.

16. Quoted in Wuthnow, *System Overload*, 11.

17. Carl von Clausewitz, *On War*, ed. and trans. Michael Eliot Howard and Peter Paret (Princeton, NJ: Princeton University Press, 1976), 88.

Clausewitzian Friends

OLIVIA GARARD

In *On War*, Carl von Clausewitz devotes the most attention to understanding the nature of the defensive form of warfare. His inquiry surveys the specifics of geography, the potential inherent in guerilla warfare, the integration of time and space, and the theoretical interplay between the defense as warding off a blow and the attack as acquisitive. Balancing the material, historical, and political aspects of war, Clausewitz weaves an analysis of the inherent potential strength of the defense. As we look to how the United States and its allies can best defend Taiwan, we should take heed of what Clausewitz has to say.

For this chapter, I will explore one of the lesser appreciated aspects of his analysis of defensive strength: allies and alliances. Unsurprising for those who consider defense and international relations outside the context of *On War*, allies and alliances are deeply integral to Clausewitz's entire work. Arguably, it is how he identified the connection between war and politics.[1] As the United States looks to best situate itself, politically and militarily, to defend Taiwan, a glance at the nuance Clausewitz detects inherent in defensive alliances is enlightening.

A philosophical account of friendship clarifies Clausewitz's distinction between ordinary and defensive allies, and the defense of Taiwan serves as a valuable case to see these distinctions in action. What does it mean to conceive of an alliance as a kind of friendship—or to see an ally as a friend? I first unpack Clausewitz's latent theory of international relations, presented mainly in *On War*. Next, I establish a preliminary sketch of a philosophical account of friendship by using the triptych of utility, pleasure, and complete friends, as laid out in Aristotle's *Nicomachean Ethics*. I then critique some, but not all, of Aristotle's account, as I follow Alexander Nehamas's *On Friendship* to a more robust understanding of friendship, the dynamics of which are found in Clausewitz's defensive alliances. I then

confront the question of the difference between comradery and friendship, before concluding with a final concern for the defense of Taiwan.

Clausewitz's Latent Theory of International Relations

Clausewitz, in *On War*'s Book VI, Chapter 6, "Extent of Means of the
Defense," enumerates the unique means available to the defender—the
means that proceed from the nature of the defensive form, to include
the landwehr, fortresses, the people, the arming of the people, and allies.
Specifically, allies are "the last support of the defensive."[2] They are "live
and reactive" means, and alliances are the "dynamic whereby [they]
. . . shift their means."[3] But these allies are not what Clausewitz calls
"ordinary," a distinction made to disqualify the allies an aggressor might
also have.[4] Defensive allies are *"essentially interested in maintaining* the
integrity of the country."[5] (Emphasis in original.) These allies are not
accidental to the circumstances; these allies arise from the nature of the
defensive form of war.

Clausewitz's description of allies morphs as one reads further into
his view of how states interact with one another. It is both antiquated
and prescient. It is antiquated because it is decidedly Eurocentric and
focuses on the fear of Europe consolidating into a universal monarchy.[6]
However narrow its scope, the dynamics he describes maintain today.
Clausewitz describes the relationship between states as myriad inter-
sections of "great and small States and interests of nations," which are
knotted and "interwoven with each other in a most diversified and
changeable manner."[7]

This is what W. B. Gallie, one of the few philosophers who explores
Clausewitz, identifies as one of Clausewitz's most innovative asser-
tions: States are states because of their relationship to other states.[8] This
can be seen in a physicalist sense, as in the actual border between the
United States and Mexico and how the United States government inter-
acts with Mexico over all manner of things. But greater still, Clausewitz
maintains that any movement by any actor cascades out to *all* the other
knots, such that "this general connection must be partially overturned by
every change."[9]

In an 1807 note, Clausewitz distinguishes between two kinds of balance of power. One emerges from "the mere rubbing of forces against each other," while the other is possible through reason. This "self-conscious balance of power" is maintained by "design and effort" at a time when "these alliances become a real necessity."[10] While he may have dismissed that Europe satisfied a deliberately constructed, "systematically regulated balance of power" at the time of his writing of *On War*, his earlier, emergent view still accounts for the underlying structure.[11] The knotted relations react and interact without demanding a particular sense of agency or direction of the whole, but they do not preclude one either. That motions can appear "in a whole with so little cohesion as an assemblage of great and little States is not to be wondered at, for we see the same in that marvelously organized whole, the natural world."[12] The open possibility of a "reasoned" order, whereby a power orchestrates and manages the whole, is exactly what the United States has been developing and fostering since the end of World War II.[13] The United States' hegemonic power and leadership role in the current international order is a direct manifestation of a particular set of interwoven, knotted interests.

Given that Clausewitz is writing in the wake of the Napoleonic Wars, he knows too well how these knotted relations can change and how such change can transpire because of a single actor. In his case, it was Napoleonic France; for today, it's the People's Republic of China. In an 1803 note, he observes how

> the balance of power *system* only reveals itself when the balance is in danger of being lost. As long as the natural weight of states is sufficient, without noticeable distortion or moral exertion, to keep everything in its place and the whole machine steady— that is, free of violent oscillations—there is no question of a balance of power *system*; the balance simply exists in itself.[14] (Emphasis in original.)

The increased ink spilled in recent years over the liberal international order indicates that the balance is in danger of being lost. But that does not mean it is or will be lost. A feature of the interwoven structure, let alone the one that the United States developed, is the underlying assumption that the status quo is preferable, all things being equal.[15] This conservatism is embodied, too, in the fact that the defensive is the stronger form of warfare, a strength for the political defensive. Clausewitz notes, "In this manner the whole relations of all States to each other serve rather to preserve the stability of the whole than to produce changes, that is to say, *this tendency* to stability exists in general."[16] (Emphasis in the original.) This preference does not exclude progress or evolution, especially if they are based on the consensus of the whole. The point is that seeking to deliberately change the knotted structure creates its own resistance.

Clausewitz reduces the question about how "to preserve the stability of the whole" into a question of efficiency. In some cases, there are "changes in the relations of single States to each other, which promote this efficiency of the whole, and others which obstruct it." Tendency toward efficiency is created by "universal interests" and the desire to seek to "perfect the political balance." Tendency away from efficiency of the system comes from "some single States, real maladies." Reflecting on history, Clausewitz sees that some rogue states succeeded while others failed, but neither type of case undermines the structure that he observes between states. No change is inevitable: "The effort towards an object is a different thing from the motion towards it."[17] It took seven coalitions to finally defeat Napoleon for good.

However perceptive Clausewitz's latent theory of international relations might be, it does not account for *why* a state would be *essentially interested* in the defense of another—that is, why such interest might be recognized as a structural benefit to the defender. The "collective interests of the whole" serve to maintain an equilibrium either at rest or tending toward change that was brought on by previous disturbances. Clausewitz expects that "each single State which has not against it a tension of the whole will have more interest in favor of its defense than opposition to it."[18] This is the closest he gets to fleshing out the idea of "essential interest," but the statement is wanting. The interwoven knots can account for why the United States is interested in Taiwan, for example, but not why the United States would be *essentially* so. What would make the United States a defensive ally and not just an ordinary one? What does such a difference entail? To answer these questions, we need to apply a philosophical notion of friendship to our notion of allies and alliances.

A Preliminary Sketch: Aristotelian Friendships as Alliances

Any philosophical account of friendship should start with Aristotle's *Nicomachean Ethics*. But such a start is even more apt because Aristotle invokes alliances in his discussion of friendship. He observes that, like friendships built on utility, "the alliances of states seem to aim at advantage."[19] Nehamas, whom I will follow later, observes how both Aristotle and Cicero "connected friendship and war."[20] Given that Aristotle has already gestured toward considering alliances in the terms of friendship, let's complete the movement.[21]

On Aristotle's account, there are three kinds of friendships: utility, pleasure, and complete. Utility friends are friends because of the *goods* they get for themselves from the other. These friendships are transactional. Pleasure friends are friends because of the *good* they get through, or by way of, interaction with the other. These friendships are contextual. Finally, complete friends are friends because of whom the other *is as the other*. Goods may arise from or in the pursuit of such friendship, but the primary good is the value of the other as other—what Aristotle calls "another self."[22] Comparing this to Clausewitz's allies, we can see that ordinary allies tend toward utility, which follows, too, from Aristotle's observation of Greek intuition. Defensive allies, as Clausewitz has sketched them, and in this Aristotelian framework, tend, then, toward complete friends.

Fortuitously, these alliance distinctions are captured in Rebecca Lissner and Mira Rapp-Hooper's recent book, *An Open World: How America Can Win the Contest for Twenty-First-Century Order*. Lissner and Rapp-Hooper advocate for a layered alliance structure for the United States that includes all three types of alliances: utility, pleasure, and complete. Their characterizations are helpful. First, they advocate for "a network of global partners in strategically vital regions," whose "partnerships will be more issue-specific and opportunistic, predicated on mutual interests [i.e., goods for *themselves*] rather than open-ended treaty commitments."[23] These are relationships built from utility. Next, they recommend that there should be "a category of relationships that are neither allies nor partners but rather alignments of convenience [i.e., pleasant to *themselves*] characterized by quiet and episodic cooperation."[24] These are relationships built from Aristotelian pleasure.[25] Finally, they want to reinforce more-traditional

American alliances "by insisting upon shared values."[26] This comportment leans toward the idea of Aristotle's complete friendships—"the friendship of men who are good and alike in excellence"—and by extension Clausewitz's sense of defensive allies, but such relationships are more exacting and extensive than just requiring "shared values."[27]

To what extent can we understand Clausewitz's defensive allies as complete friends? Recall how Clausewitz's defensive allies are *essentially interested in maintaining* the integrity of the country."[28] (Emphasis in the original.) The essential interest mirrors Aristotle's conception that complete friends build their friendship around neither the utility nor the pleasure they may get from the other but from the other in and of themselves—or, in Clausewitz's sense, the maintenance of the other country itself. The integrity that a defensive ally seeks to preserve is just like the integrity of the other as the other that makes the *good* of Aristotle's complete friend. The defensive ally's interest, to the extent that it can be seen as self-interest under this framing, is an interest in the other (country) as another self.

This is both a wider and narrower scope than just those who maintain shared values, as Lissner and Rapp-Hooper suggest. The scope is wider because more than just those who maintain shared values may satisfy the criterion of being a country that some state is essentially interested in. The scope is narrower because, as Aristotle notes, there are a limited number of complete friends one can have; complete friendships are hard, and few are good.[29] The criterion is not that the other (country) is worth preserving because of shared values but that the other country, as such, is worth preserving. In the case of Taiwan, the United States as a defensive ally is essentially interested in the maintenance of Taiwan not for the goods it receives as a result or by way of association but because the essential interest of the United States is *in Taiwan as Taiwan*. To the extent that shared values are involved, they are folded into what makes Taiwan Taiwan. Any Chinese invasion, subversion, or fait accompli is a threat to Taiwan *as such*.

Besides classifying kinds of friends, Aristotle's view on friendship reminds us that friendship is an activity. Clausewitz, too, sees alliances as dynamic.[30] Both take time to develop and take place over time. Second, friendships are not instantaneous; they develop with "time and familiarity."[31] A treaty may instigate an alliance, but the relationship must be a process of interaction.

Moreover, just as individuals vary, so too will friendships. No friendship is the same as any other. Friendship is a process of "living together" with the other.[32] It is a particular relationship that develops out of contingent circumstances. Aristotle even makes space for friendships under different power conditions, provided, of course, that the other is not a god.[33] All that is necessary is that a kind of justice is established—a fairness in reciprocity—for the friendship to maintain.[34]

Still, there is a limitation to a purely Aristotelian reading of friendship. Friendship is deeply tied to an individual's virtue, such that only good people (or entities) can be complete friends. Rather than seeking to account for virtue in defensive alliances, it is more fruitful to follow a modern account that emerges out of this Aristotelian view but then strips it of its moral necessity. Even as we eliminate the exacting requirement of Aristotle's virtue, Lissner and Rapp-Hooper's notion of shared values will be preserved, though the sense will modulate. Friendships will still be based on the values one sees in the other, but those values need not mirror an abstract kind of virtue. Friendships—and, for our argument, alliances—will move from a moral consideration to an aesthetic one.

A Refinement: The Aesthetics of Friendly Allies

Nehamas's *On Friendship* starts with Aristotle's triptych of utility, pleasure, and complete friends, but then he argues that Aristotle's view fails to account for our intuitive sense of friendship. Given the demands of virtue, the friends that we think we have will not count under Aristotle's view. And if few, if any, individuals satisfy these conditions, certainly no state will.

Nehamas's first concern is that utility and pleasure friends should not be considered friends because "what determines what I will or will not wish for you ultimately depends on my own interests."[35] While this is a valid critique for individual friendships, we can maintain these distinctions for Clausewitz's ordinary allies. As Clausewitz describes allies of the attacker, "They are only the result of special or accidental relations, not an assistance proceeding from the nature of the aggressive."[36] Ordinary allies can be of the utility or pleasure kind, but they only depend on contingent self-interest. Unlike defensive alliances, ordinary alliances are brittle.[37]

Nehamas's second critique of Aristotle is more helpful because it confronts the problem of complete friendships and the need for virtue. If only the virtuous can be friends, then on Aristotle's account, few, if any, are actually friends. Nehamas's contention is that if Aristotle's "virtue-*philia*," as he refers to complete friends, are to be like our notion of what makes close friends, then they do not require an objective moral foundation.[38] Nehamas contends,

> We are more likely to be friends not because we recognize in one another some independently acknowledged virtues but because we take the features we admire in one another, whatever they are, to be virtues, whether or not they are such in the abstract.[39]

This reversal is crucial because it means that "even the vicious have friends."[40] And for alliances, we need not concern ourselves with the question of whether a state is or can be morally virtuous.[41] That one sees value in the other, as such, is sufficient.

Next, Nehamas emphasizes the preference inherent in friendship. "Those to whom one pledged oneself were by necessity few and a vanishingly small segment of the world and were to be treated differently from everybody else."[42] The essence of the relationship is based in valuing differences and not commonalities. Whereas moral values prioritize the collective over the individual and find value in the commonality, aesthetic values emphasize the particular over the whole and find value in the difference.[43] In other words, it is *this* person, as opposed to *that* person, who is my friend. It is *this* state, as opposed to *that* state, that is my ally. Both are contingent, contextual, and deeply particular.

Nehamas quotes C. S. Lewis, who goes so far as to say that friendship is "a sort of secession, even a rebellion . . . a pocket of potential resistance."[44] Solidarity is specific, existential, and confrontational, qualities Clausewitz recognized in defensive allies. While at the individual level "the essential partiality of friendships is the most fundamental obstacle to modeling our social and political relationships," this element is inherent in the form of the political defensive.[45] At the level of war, Clausewitz identified that this obstacle *is* what enables the defense and the possibility of preservation and existential success.

While Nehamas's notion of close friends is not based on separate self-interest, such friends still maintain an interest in the other; one might even say they have an essential interest. (Still, "no friendship is completely *un*instrumental.")[46] (Emphasis in the original.) This is not interest in the virtue of the other, as Aristotle contends, but it is interest in what makes the other the other—*and* how that particularity makes them special to us. Nehamas reports,

> According to C. S. Lewis, Charles Lamb said somewhere that if one of three friends (A, B, and C) should die, B loses not only A but also "A's part in C", while C loses not only A but also "A's part in B."[47]

Friends are not fungible.[48] For instance, if Taiwan were lost, then the United States would lose not only its relationship to Taiwan as Taiwan but also the participation of Taiwan in all its relationships to other members of the international community, such as Lithuania.[49] While the individual parts are bilateral, the loss is collective; just like in Clausewitz's interwoven knots, all would be moved. What matters is the participation in the embodiment of the other, such that one is defined, in a way, by the other's existence.[50] Taiwan is worth defending not only because it is a democracy, a major trading partner, a manufacturer of semiconductor chips, and a strategically located country but also because, consisting of all these factors, among others, it is valued. The United States is *essentially interested* in Taiwan, composed as such.

The United States has been shaped militarily, diplomatically, bureaucratically, politically, and economically by its alliances since World War II. But this has taken time. Like Aristotle, Nehamas emphasizes the temporal element of friendship. Friendships require not only time to develop but, as Nehamas underscores, "a commitment to the future" such that "our place in each other's life will in some way make life for both of us better than it would be otherwise."[51]

This temporal commitment (i.e., permanent alliances) is exactly what George Washington objected to in his Farewell Address, but it is exactly what the United States constructed after World War II.[52] Such open-ended, future-oriented stances are inherently risky because one is entrusting a part of oneself, or one's capability and capacity, to another's hands. Nehamas concludes:

> Our friendships permeate our personality, they structure our perceptions of the world, and in many circumstances enable us to act in a particular way without a second thought: they are part of the background that allows us to perceive directly that we must do something for a friend that we wouldn't do for someone else.[53]

The same goes for defensive alliances.

A New Tension: Military Comradery or Political Friendship?

But if we are appealing to individual relationships to understand what makes a defensive ally and what makes a defensive ally separate and distinct from ordinary allies, then why would allies be friends and not comrades? Jesse Glenn Gray's *The Warriors: Reflections on Men in Battle* is the best philosophical complement to Clausewitz's *On War*. Whereas Clausewitz is primarily concerned with the macroelements of war and warfare and the militaries, communities, and governments that fight, Gray homes in on the individual fighting and existing in war and warfare. This is not to say that Clausewitz's work is not concerned, at times, with individuals, but his concern is either the excellence of the preeminent commander genius or the failure of the subordinates to maintain their cohesion, order, and discipline as a whole. Instead, Gray, clearly influenced by Friedrich Nietzsche, focuses on the interiority of the individual in war. Clausewitz's concern for the psychology of the soldier is at the highest level of military leadership, while Gray is concerned with the psychology of soldiers writ large. Consequently, in his investigation, Gray differentiates between comradery and friendships.

Gray says comradery is a "communal experience" and an "appeal of war."[54] Physical proximity is a minimal condition, and there must be "organization for a common goal."[55] Like Clausewitz, he thinks danger is necessary. Comradery entails individuals who have transcended their individual identity to recognize themselves in the group; "Comradeship at first develops through the consciousness of an obstacle to be overcome through common effort."[56] Gray identifies this intoxication and liberation in how the "'I' passes insensibly into a 'we', 'my' becomes 'our', and the individual fate loses its central importance."[57] Based on our understanding of friendship and alliances, this is deeply problematic if actioned at the political level. While Clausewitz sees an "essential interest in maintaining a country's integrity," it cannot be at the expense of one's own existence as such. Self-sacrifice may be noble, but it is rarely pragmatic and politically wise.[58] Yet in the context of warfare or the conduct of war, it is still a potent force. As Gray observes, "For the self that dies is little in comparison with that which survives and triumphs."[59] For defensive allies to actualize under a concept of friendship, they must be political friends, but to actualize the defensive alliance in war entails military comradery.

Comradery is unachievable among states politically, but it is necessary militarily. Clausewitz identifies this tension because "we never find that a State joining in the cause of another State takes it up with the same earnestness as its own." This holds, too, for friendships, unless the relationship has transcended, as Gray notes, into a communal space of comradeship in which the one *is* the other because they are both part of, and recognize themselves in, a larger whole. Clausewitz laments, mainly reflecting on the condition of alliances in the late 18th century, how allies do not "[hand] over entirely to the State engaged in War" their promised forces. Instead, the "force has its own Commander, who depends only on his own Government, and to whom it prescribes an object such as best suits the shilly-shally measures it has in view."[60] The problem, as Clausewitz sees it, is that states seek to maintain their own agency, even when it is disadvantageous from a purely military perspective. This is, as Gray explains, "the essential difference between comradeship and friendship," in the sense that there is "a heightened awareness of the self in friendship and in the suppression of self-awareness in comradeship."[61] Military action and coordination demand comradeship, but the politics of alliances demands friendship.

Ideally, as Clausewitz notes in 1805, "all the forces committed to the war [should be] under a *single* commander." But too often, he laments, "the ministers involved would use all their cunning" to prevent such consolidated command. Such unification, Clausewitz contends, would "increase the probability of victory." More important, however, is the existence of "a common strategic plan, based on the natural circumstances and advantages of each of the states involved."[62] Unfortunately, people

> hinder the uniform, harmonious operation of forces by bringing *conflicting points of view* into play and creating *divided interests*, and they seldom possess sufficient insight and skill to restore unity some other way, *through the proper deployment and coordination of these diverse elements.*[63] (Emphasis in the original.)

This adjudication between the assertion of the self as state and the deference to collective goals is best exemplified in NATO.[64] The institution can be seen as a compromise between the need for actualizing military comradery while preserving an individuated sense of the political self. Still, NATO considers an attack on one member to be an attack on all members. As Clausewitz reminds us: "People who complain about the ineffectiveness of coalitions do not know what they want; what better way is there to resist a stronger power?"[65]

Concluding Thoughts on Taiwan

Clausewitz's notion of defensive allies identifies them as potent means, and a philosophical account of friendship helps explain why. Alliances, like friendships, are nonmoral, particular, preferential relationships. Each is a knot that possesses a kind of inertia and inherent defensive potential, depending on how essential it is perceived to be in the integrated network of relations and interests. In the context of a potential conflict over Taiwan, the United States should cultivate its political friendship while encouraging and furthering military comradery. Both Aristotle and Nehamas underscore the inherent temporality of friendship and, thereby, alliances. This must be more than an act; it must be an activity.

The increased cooperation between the United States' Special Operations Forces and Taiwan's military revealed in 2021 is just such an activity. This is how the foundations for military comradery are laid. But the development of political friendship is more difficult, especially given Taiwan's complicated international status. If we imagine Clausewitz's knotted relations, Taiwan's knot is disputed. The People's Republic of China continues to coerce others to cease recognizing the existence of Taiwan's knot. In other words, the People's Republic of China seeks to subvert the potential for actualizing a defensive alliance by convincing the world that there is no such knot to defend, no such knot with which to be friends.

Under the Taiwan Relations Act, the United States operates with ambiguity. To what degree the vagueness of political friendship may be maintained while military comradery is promoted will depend on the relationship *over time* and how the United States—its people and institutions—chooses to recognize the value of Taiwan itself. Are we not a better nation for being friends with Taiwan? Nevertheless, should conflict commence, the United States, as a political friend and practiced in military comradery, provides the best means for the defense of Taiwan as Taiwan.

Notes

1. Olivia A. Garard, "Accounting for Alliances in Clausewitz's Theory of War," *Philosophical Journal of Conflict and Violence* 6, no. 1 (2022): 92–109, https://trivent-publishing.eu/img/cms/7-%20Olivia%20A-%20Garard_OA.pdf.

2. Carl von Clausewitz, *On War*, trans. J. J. Graham (New York: Barnes & Noble, 2004), 393.

3. Garard, "Accounting for Alliances in Clausewitz's Theory of War."

4. The word he uses is *gewöhnlich*. Clausewitz, *On War*, 393.

5. In the German: "*Welche bei der Erhaltung eines Landes* wesentlich beteiligt sind." (Emphasis in original.) Clausewitz, *On War*, 393.

6. See Jan Wilem Honig, "Clausewitz and the Politics of Early Modern Warfare," in *Clausewitz: The State and War*, ed. Andreas Herberg-Rothe, Jan Willem Honig, and Daniel Moran (Stuttgart, Germany: Franz Steiner Verlag, 2011), 31.

7. Clausewitz, *On War*, 393.

8. Walter Bryce Gallie, *Philosophers of Peace and War: Kant, Clausewitz, Marx, Engels and Tolstoy* (Cambridge, UK: Cambridge University Press, 1978), 61. See also Anders Palmgren, "Clausewitz's Interweaving of *Krieg* and *Politik*," in *Clausewitz: The State and War*, ed. Andreas Herberg-Rothe, Jan Willem Honig, and Daniel Moran (Stuttgart, Germany: Franz Steiner Verlag, 2011), 59.

9. Clausewitz, *On War*, 393.

10. Carl von Clausewitz, "Note of 1807," in *Historical and Political Writings*, ed. and trans. Peter Paret and Daniel Moran (Princeton, NJ: Princeton University Press, 1992), 247.

11. Clausewitz, *On War*, 393.

12. Clausewitz, *On War*, 394.

13. See Mira Rapp-Hooper, *Shields of the Republic: The Triumph and Peril of America's Alliances* (Cambridge, MA: Harvard University Press, 2020).

14. Clausewitz, "On Coalitions," in *Historical and Political Writings*, ed. and trans. Peter Paret and Daniel Moran (Princeton, NJ: Princeton University Press, 1992), 244.

15. Garard, "Accounting for Alliances in Clausewitz's Theory of War," 6.

16. Clausewitz, *On War*, 393–94.

17. Clausewitz, *On War*, 394.

18. Clausewitz, *On War*, 394.

19. Aristotle, "Nicomachean Ethics," trans. W. D. Ross, revised J. O. Urmson, ed. Johnathan Barnes, *The Complete Works of Aristotle: The Revised Oxford Translation* (Princeton, NJ: Princeton University Press, 1984), 2:1157a27–28.

20. Alexander Nehamas, *On Friendship* (New York: Basic Books, 2016), 42.

21. Friendship was "transformed from a public into a private good" around the 16th century. Now, I'm appealing from a private sense back to a public one. Nehamas, *On Friendship*, 42.

22. Aristotle, "Nicomachean Ethics," 1166a32.

23. Rebecca Lissner and Mira Rapp-Hooper, *An Open World: How America Can Win the Contest for Twenty-First-Century Order* (New Haven, CT: Yale University Press, 2020), 139; and Aristotle, "Nicomachean Ethics," 1156a15.

24. Lissner and Rapp-Hooper, *An Open World*, 139; and Aristotle, "Nicomachean Ethics," 1156a16.

25. Coalitions of the willing are another option.

26. Lissner and Rapp-Hooper, *An Open World*, 138.

27. Aristotle, "Nicomachean Ethics," 1156b8–9.

28. Clausewitz, *On War*, 393.

29. Aristotle, "Nicomachean Ethics," 1158a11–12.

30. Garard, "Accounting for Alliances in Clausewitz's Theory of War," 6.

31. Aristotle, "Nicomachean Ethics," 1156b26.

32. Aristotle, "Nicomachean Ethics," 1170b11.

33. Aristotle, "Nicomachean Ethics," 1159a5.

34. Aristotle, "Nicomachean Ethics," 1159b29–31. This is essential given the United States' status as a super- and nuclear power, among other powers that are neither or are only one. Consider this, too, as a reformulation of the 2 percent NATO defense spending argument.

35. Nehamas, *On Friendship*, 21.

36. Clausewitz, *On War*, 597.

37. This does not mean that ordinary allies cannot be successful; it just means that divergence is more likely. Once the transaction (utility) is over, or the episode (pleasure) is finished, there is nothing pulling the two together.

38. Nehamas, *On Friendship*, 25.

39. Nehamas, *On Friendship*, 28.

40. Nehamas, *On Friendship*, 29.

41. It may be important that Taiwan is a democracy, but that is a particular value for the United States. Taiwan *being a democracy* need not be conditioned as a universal good, even if the United States may think that it is so.

42. Nehamas, *On Friendship*, 30.

43. Nigel Warburton, "Alexander Nehamas on Friendship," October 26, 2008, in *Philosophy Bites*, MP3 audio, https://philosophybites.com/2008/10/alexander-neham.html. See also David Edmonds and Nigel Warburton, "Alexander Nehamas on Friendship," in *Philosophy Bites* (Oxford, UK: Oxford University Press, 2010), 38–46.

44. C. S. Lewis, *The Four Loves* (Orlando, FL: Harcourt, 1988), quoted in Nehamas, *On Friendship*, 51.

45. Nehamas, *On Friendship*, 51.

46. Nehamas, *On Friendship*, 112.

47. Nehamas, *On Friendship*, 138.

48. Nehamas, *On Friendship*, 125.

49. This secondary loss is significant, especially given that Taiwan is an exemplary democracy in a time when democratic backsliding is increasing.

50. See Kori Schake, *Safe Passage* (Cambridge, MA: Harvard University Press, 2017), 113. "America was unique as a foreign policy problem because choices about it could resonate back to Britain's own politics."

51. Nehamas, *On Friendship*, 134.

52. George Washington, Farewell Address, 1796, https://founders.archives.gov/documents/Washington/05-20-02-0440-0002; and Rapp-Hooper, *Shields of the Republic*, 5, 19.

53. Nehamas, *On Friendship*, 149.

54. Jesse Glenn Gray, *The Warriors: Reflections on Men in Battle* (Lincoln, NE: Bison Books, 1998), 39.

55. Gray, *The Warriors*, 41.

56. Gray, *The Warriors*, 43.

57. Gray, *The Warriors*, 45.

58. See Aristotle, "Nicomachean Ethics," 1169a18–26.

59. Gray, *The Warriors*, 47.

60. Clausewitz, *On War*, 696.

61. Gray, *The Warriors*, 90.

62. Clausewitz, "Note of 1805," 245.

63. Clausewitz, "Note of 1805," 246.

64. The command structure between the Republic of Korea and the United States is another deeply integrated actualization of military comradery.

65. Clausewitz, "On Coalitions," 242.

Asian Allies and Partners in a Taiwan Contingency: What Should the United States Expect?

ZACK COOPER AND SHEENA CHESTNUT GREITENS

How would American allies in Asia react to a major contingency between the United States and China, such as a crisis in the Taiwan Strait?[1] Although conflict over Taiwan is not the only crisis scenario in the Indo-Pacific that could implicate the United States and its allies, recent developments have heightened concern about Taiwan specifically.

Tensions over the Taiwan Strait have escalated. Increased numbers of Chinese military aircraft have flown through the southwest corner of the island's air defense identification zone (commonly referred to as an ADIZ), and Chinese state media explicitly frames the increase in military activity around the Strait as an "obvious countermeasure" to joint US-Japan military exercises near Taiwan.[2] In response, the American chargé d'affaires in Canberra, Australia, disclosed in 2021 that the United States and Australia had discussed contingency plans for a military crisis over Taiwan,[3] and Japanese media reported that the United States and Japan have established plans for joint operations under similar circumstances.[4] Meanwhile, the crisis precipitated by Russia's invasion of Ukraine has raised a host of questions about the options available for US and allied support to Taiwan under a similar conflict scenario in the Indo-Pacific.

Based on what we know today, would America's allies and partners provide support in the event of a military crisis over Taiwan? More importantly, *how* would they do so, and under what constraints or limitations would they do it? These are crucial questions for the United States and its allies and partners across the Indo-Pacific.

Xi Jinping's own statements have led some American analysts to speculate that a serious crisis is around the corner. While Xi has continued to use the language of "peaceful reunification," he has also tied unification more closely to the task of national rejuvenation, and he has said (in both 2013 and 2019) that the Taiwan problem cannot be handed down from generation to generation—implying a finite timetable, even if the deadline has never been clearly specified.[5] These circumstances have led American and allied defense planners to think about a range of scenarios that could emerge in the Taiwan Strait and how America's alliances and security partnerships would apply in these different contingencies.

Amid signs of increasing allied coordination, a number of analysts have warned American strategists and defense planners that they should be conservative in their assumptions about allied support and involvement. Former intelligence analyst John Culver, for example, expects "a chilling set of answers if you approached authoritative people in our treaty allies ... and [asked] them in the event that China attacks Taiwan, will you back our military alliance?"[6]

Answers from the region itself have not been consistent. For example, although former Australian Defence Minister Peter Dutton said that it was inconceivable Canberra would not back Washington to defend Taiwan in a conflict,[7] former Australian officials, such as retired Prime Minister Paul Keating, have pushed back, arguing that Taiwan is not a "vital interest" for Australia.[8] And at the subnational level, Japan's Okinawa prefecture has made clear that it opposes some aspects of the Japanese government's shift toward enhanced coordination with the United States on Taiwan.[9] These examples suggest that robust domestic political debates are ongoing in several allied countries.

Detailed thinking on this question is important—and overdue. With no sign that tensions over Taiwan will abate anytime soon, divergent expectations about allied involvement could not only threaten Washington's relationships with key allies but also undermine America's ability to deter a contingency with China in the first place.

Possible Contingency Scenarios

In a contingency over Taiwan, one can imagine at least four possible scenarios for conflict initiation, each of varying likelihood. In all four scenarios,

Beijing would probably make active efforts in the press and diplomatic forums to blame Taipei for the crisis or conflict, undermining domestic support among US allies in the region. Yet each scenario would create different political dynamics and implications for US allies, especially as the crisis extended over time.

- **Scenario 1.** China directly attacks Taiwan and US and allied forces and bases.

- **Scenario 2.** China directly attacks Taiwan but not US or allied forces and bases.

- **Scenario 3.** China directly attacks Taiwan and US forces but not those of US allies.

- **Scenario 4.** China coerces or pressures Taiwan but avoids targeting US or allied forces and bases.

In the first and most escalatory scenario, Beijing could attempt to invade Taiwan outright while launching first strikes against US forces in the region, including strikes on US bases in allied countries and potentially strikes on allied facilities, even if US forces are not present. Given the current basing locations of American forces in the region, this scenario would be most likely to result in Japan and perhaps the Philippines being forced immediately into an undesired contingency, but Australia, some Pacific islands, and South Korea could also be implicated.

Depending on the circumstances leading to the initiation of conflict, US allies may have little warning, meaning they could suddenly become participants in a contingency for which they are neither politically nor operationally prepared. Military and political responses would have to be carried out at rapid tempo under high pressure, as would any attempt at coordination with the United States or other international players.

In the second scenario, Beijing could attempt to invade Taiwan but avoid attacking both US forces and bases in the region and those of all US allies. This scenario presents Beijing with distinct military risks, as it leaves assets available closer to Taiwan for a US and allied response and diminishes the "tyranny of distance" that American planners often reference as a disadvantage in attempting to surge US forces across the western Pacific.

However, it also comes with political benefits for Beijing: Chinese leaders may well bank on the United States' and allied countries' reluctance to get dragged into a costly and potentially casualty-intensive shooting war—and on domestic politics to slow or constrain their provision of active military support while leaders and publics weigh various options for intervention. Depending on the time frame in which Beijing judges it could carry out an invasion, the political benefits of this approach might outweigh the military disadvantages in the minds of the Chinese leadership.

In the third scenario, Beijing could consider striking US forces or bases in the region but avoid hitting US allies directly, in an effort to split Washington from its key regional allies. (This is actually a spectrum of options in itself, because Beijing could strike US forces at sea or outside allied territory, or it could strike only US bases on allied territory but not the facilities of US allies themselves.) In this category of scenarios, America's allies would be deciding whether to intervene in a cross-Strait conflict that they have not yet been directly implicated in, rather than responding to a direct attack on their own forces and personnel. Whether US allies invoke US treaty commitments for their own defense, of course, could also shape the level and speed of Washington's response.

Under this scenario, we expect that Chinese media and diplomats would probably portray their restraint as an attempt to limit horizontal escalation of the conflict and shift blame solely to the United States and/or Taiwan. The effect of this shift could be to slow or complicate allied responses to the emergence of a crisis and to inhibit allied coordination in the early period of an unfolding contingency.

The fourth scenario, and perhaps the most likely, could be even more difficult from a coalition-building perspective. Beijing might seek to coerce Taiwan without invading—opting instead for some combination of an embargo, the seizure of remote islands, cyberattacks, and limited strikes short of a full invasion. In this case, the United States would have to calibrate its own actions while attempting to coordinate a regional response.

In this scenario, allied willingness to get involved would likely depend largely on perceptions of risk. If allied countries see more-limited applications of force by Beijing as signaling reduced commitment to the conflict on China's part and indicating a lower risk of casualties, that perception might make them more willing to participate. On the other hand, a more limited scenario might incline allies in the region to view their own contributions as less necessary; if there is disagreement among allies over the necessity of participation and basing permissions, then coordination could prove particularly challenging. The end result could leave the United States with a smaller regional coalition, fewer access points, and uncertain political footing in the Indo-Pacific during a conflict that might become protracted and economically damaging to all countries in the region.

Allied Perceptions of Contingencies and Planning

In the scenarios involving a direct invasion, the allies most likely to contribute forces would be Japan and Australia. They would likely desire more-defensive roles, acting as the alliance's shields rather than its spears.[10] They might allow US basing access, but this would be a politically fraught decision, particularly if US and allied forces were not targeted in an initial strike.

As noted at the beginning of this chapter, the United States has engaged in active discussions and contingency planning for a military crisis over Taiwan with counterparts in Australia and Japan,[11] and some recent articles have called for preparations around a Taiwan Strait conflict to become "a major priority for the U.S.-Japan alliance . . . driv[ing] force posture, procurement, and bilateral operational planning and exercises."[12] Although these discussions date back decades, in many senses they are still in the early stages, and publics in both the United States and allied countries are not yet familiar with likely contingencies and escalation possibilities.[13]

While the ground has undoubtedly shifted toward greater consultation on these issues, the United States must not overestimate the extent or stability of evolutions in thinking across the capitals of its allies and partners. Discussions of these issues are likely to remain difficult in both Tokyo and Canberra. Jeffrey Hornung notes that

> Japan expects that the United States will consult with it prior to conducting combat operations to obtain Japan's consent if the

United States is considering using its bases in Japan to engage
in armed conflict with another country when Japan itself is not
a party to that conflict.[14]

And while some experts see Japan's policy shifts on Taiwan as dra-
matic and far-reaching,[15] other analysts take a more conservative view
of these developments[16] or argue that growing alignment on Taiwan has
not removed underlying disagreements about how to respond in terms
of defense procurement and planning.[17] Meanwhile, despite strong statements of support from current Australian defense officials, other observers have pushed back, including Natasha Kassam and Richard McGregor,
who argue that "Australia has no interest, or indeed ability, to be a decisive
player in the Taiwan dispute."[18]

Other allies—namely the Philippines, South Korea, and Thailand—
would be even less likely to commit their forces to engage in an American-
led coalition. Although these countries—and partners such as Singapore—
might allow basing access under certain circumstances, this would likely
come with severe limitations.

For example, Seoul might be reluctant to do anything that could widen
the conflict or open a second contingency involving the Korean Peninsula.
Moreover, it would want to reserve its own forces for a peninsula-specific
contingency (either related to Taiwan itself or emerging from Pyong-
yang's willingness to take advantage of an unfolding crisis elsewhere in
the region).[19] The United States and South Korea would first have to agree
on whether it makes more sense for Seoul to pursue a substantial contri-
bution to allied efforts vis-à-vis Taiwan or whether South Korea's energy
would be best focused on securing the peninsula, freeing US forces to
focus elsewhere. Even if they agree on the latter option, discussions on
basing access and facilities use will still be necessary.

Seoul's peacetime willingness to engage in consultations with the
United States regarding Taiwan has been inhibited by South Korean leaders' fear of antagonizing Beijing and thereby undermining pursuit of unification on the Korean Peninsula.[20] One Korean analysis notes that a request
from Washington for Seoul to participate in a freedom of navigation operation or a military conflict with China would put South Korea in a "com-
promising position," in which Seoul will have to "reach an agreement with

Washington about strategic flexibility."[21] It remains to be seen whether this will change with Yoon Suk-yeol's election, given that he has promised a tougher stance on China.

Historical precedents are at work as well. After South Korea's Roh administration expressed concern that the George W. Bush administration's desire for "strategic flexibility" in the use of US forces based on the Korean Peninsula could drag South Korea into a US-China conflict, then–Secretary of State Condoleezza Rice promised to respect Seoul's position that it "shall not be involved in a regional conflict in Northeast Asia against the will of the Korean people."[22]

For these and other reasons, Jung Pak concludes, "Beijing perceives Seoul as the weakest link in the U.S. alliance network, given its perception of South Korea's deference and history of accommodating China's rise relative to other regional players."[23] All of these factors combine to limit Seoul's likely involvement in the case of a cross-Strait military crisis or conflict and make advance coordination and mutual understanding on these issues within the alliance more difficult.

The Philippines and Thailand might be similarly skeptical of basing access, particularly given recent tensions between US leaders and their counterparts in Manila and Bangkok. While outgoing Philippine President Rodrigo Duterte's skepticism of US reliability is well-known,[24] Duterte expresses in extreme fashion sentiments that appear among nontrivial segments of the Philippine public and policy elite. Newly elected president Bongbong Marcos has publicly downplayed the 2016 arbitration decision that ruled in Manila's favor against Beijing and floated instead the idea of striking a deal with Beijing to resolve disputes in the South China Sea.[25]

The Philippines's foreign policy has traditionally oscillated between seeking more accommodation with Beijing and relying more heavily on the US alliance. Given the structure of Philippine politics, which depends heavily on the foreign policy beliefs and preferences of whoever occupies the presidency, these personal views could have significant long-term alliance implications.[26] Marcos's early statements after winning the presidency suggest that he may focus on improving relations with China, so US basing access throughout the Philippine archipelago is far from guaranteed in a US-China crisis.

Table 1. Likely Ally and Partner Roles in a Taiwan Contingency

		Direct Military Engagement	
		Some	**None**
Basing Access	**Some**	Australia Japan	Philippines Singapore South Korea Thailand
	None	Taiwan	India Indonesia Malaysia Vietnam

Source: Authors.

Finally, an even larger group of countries—including many concerned about China's rise, such as Vietnam and India—would probably not contribute either forces or basing access. Many of these countries lack existing basing agreements with the United States, have limited experience operating jointly with US forces beyond basic training and exercises, and are likely to be worried about the economic fallout of actively opposing China in a crisis over something Beijing defines as a core interest. Joint operational concepts with these countries have not been tested, particularly the kinds of close coordination that would be needed in a major contingency. As shown in Table 1, the United States should not expect substantial force contributions or basing access from India, Indonesia, Malaysia, Vietnam, and most other regional players beyond those identified above.

Given the wide range of uncertainty on the specific timing and pathway into a possible future crisis, the United States must have a plan for a scenario in which political debates in any of these countries take center stage and potentially impede rapid and coordinated responses to a cross-Strait crisis. Therefore, in many (though not all) of these cases, the most realistic role the United States should expect from its allies and partners is the enhancing of their own defense capabilities, their security cooperation with the United States, and their security cooperation with each other, without a clear focus on a Taiwan contingency.

The United States should be clear-eyed about the fact that this kind of ally or partner role has ancillary benefits for broader American security interests, even when there is not explicit planning for involvement in a military crisis over Taiwan. Moreover, such activities do indirectly benefit preparations for a Taiwan contingency, as these developments around China's periphery would "[ramp] up the challenges the PLA Navy, Marines, and Air Force would have to counter outside the Taiwan Strait" and reduce the Chinese military's ability to prepare for a Taiwan contingency by "maximizing the range and complexity of challenges facing the PLA in other theaters."[27]

As Joel Wuthnow has noted, this type of medium- to long-term activity puts pressure on a People's Liberation Army organizational and command structure that is already designed for multiple smaller conflicts, not a single large one; distributes China's resources away from its Eastern Theater Command; and raises the likely difficulty of internal crisis coordination on the Chinese side.[28] In its regional diplomacy and messaging, therefore, the United States should make clear that it understands and values the contributions these partners make in the Indo-Pacific, even if they are not explicitly focused on Taiwan contingencies.

In short, despite the United States' large number of regional allies and partners, if a major contingency erupts between China and the United States over Taiwan, Washington should expect to find itself working actively with only a small handful of willing contributors. Furthermore, it should expect that even those contributors may avoid the use of their forces or significantly restrain US access to their bases. It is important that the United States understands which allies and partners are capable of playing which roles, so it can appropriately calibrate its long-term activities in the region and its crisis planning.

The above dynamics could sharpen, not subside, if a conflict becomes protracted. As American analysts of the People's Liberation Army have noted, a failed amphibious assault on Taiwan would not necessarily end the conflict. In an extended conflict, such as a blockade, Beijing would likely retain significant advantages over even the most robust US-led coalition,[29] and little is known about how US allies and partners in the region would contribute to Taiwan's ability to survive this kind of protracted scenario. For example, there has so far been almost no discussion about how America's regional allies and partners might view, let alone participate in, activities such as resupplying Taiwan in the face of a Chinese blockade or engaging in mine-clearing operations.

Casualty sensitivity is another major unknown in considering protracted conflict. It is difficult at present to gauge the United States' tolerance for casualties in a potential cross-Strait conflict,[30] unclear how casualty sensitivity might influence Taiwan's willingness to resist over a prolonged period, and hard to assess how strong Beijing's will would be to engage in a protracted attempt to take the island, especially if the PLA suffers heavy casualties during the initial fighting. The general rule that autocracies tolerate higher casualties than democracies depends somewhat on conscription rates, whether the conflict is a war of choice or a homegrown insurgency, and other factors, making the dynamics of an unfolding Taiwan-China conflict particularly difficult to predict in advance. Each decision, perhaps especially Taiwan's, could influence the decisions of regional actors.

Next Steps for Policymakers

What does this mean for how Washington should approach its allies and partners about Taiwan? First, the United States should lead a series of detailed discussions with key allies about their roles in different contingency scenarios involving China and Taiwan.[31] For some, these discussions should probably go hand in hand with consultation about other contingencies, such as possible flash points in the East China Sea or South China Sea.

These conversations should begin quietly, and many of the details can and should remain private and classified. However, if these discussions do not ultimately engage the publics in the United States and allied countries, then there will not be political support for participation in a contingency, and alliance coordination is likely to founder.

This will be especially important if part of Beijing's strategy in the early moments of a contingency is to split the United States from its allies and partners or in the event of a protracted conflict, in which divergences among alliance partners could emerge over time. Furthermore, the United

States and its allies must come to terms with the reality that the initial phases of conflict could produce high casualties that intensify domestic political debates and alliance disagreements.

These discussions must include a diplomatic and a military-operational component, as successful signaling could play a crucial role in preventing the above scenarios from occurring in the first place. One risk is that Beijing might not believe that key allies would fight in a contingency, increasing the possibility of China stumbling into an otherwise deterrable conflict; the other is that efforts at deterring conflict are misinterpreted as provocative, creating an unintended escalatory spiral. It is therefore crucial that the United States carefully balance the need to communicate a reliable deterrent with avoiding unnecessary provocations that could trigger a conflict.

The United States and its allies and partners should retain the high ground by clearly reiterating their commitment and openness to a peaceful resolution of cross-Strait tensions, however improbable one appears at present, while ensuring that deterrence signaling is clear and capabilities adequate. This is a delicate balance that will be easier to strike if Washington can come to an agreement with Canberra, Seoul, Tokyo, and other allies and partners *before* a crisis and if some baseline expectations about ally and partner responses can be clearly signaled in peacetime. Those discussions should include planning for how the United States and others would support countries against possible retaliation by China—not just military but also economic, and especially in protracted conflict scenarios.

What does all this mean for US military posture and the Biden administration's regional strategy? As it stands now, the United States will have to be prepared to not only "fight tonight" but also fight far from home with limited ally and partner support. In the future, administration officials should make efforts to avoid the kinds of tensions over basing arrangements that have taken up time and attention in the US alliances with both South Korea and the Philippines and try to focus on necessary, forward-looking conversations about regional contingencies that Washington should be having with its allies.[32] Continued US efforts to distribute forces throughout the region are wise, as they limit coalition vulnerability to changing domestic political conditions in any one ally or partner, but the United States must also be realistic that its dependence on Japan and Australia may increase for both basing and some key niche capabilities.

These discussions need to involve not only allied conventional capabilities but also US nuclear posture. The United States will also need to have difficult discussions with its allies and partners about the implications of potential nuclear threats or escalation from China, particularly given Beijing's recent modernization of its nuclear forces.[33] The recent discussion of escalation risks with allies in Europe following Russia's invasion of Ukraine highlights the urgency and relevance of such consultations.[34]

Finally, what does this mean for US force structure? American discussions with Taiwan about defense procurement and planning need to occur with the changing regional context in mind, while still being mindful of realistic expectations in a crisis. The contingencies described above require greater emphasis on a set of forces that can credibly deny Beijing the ability to take the island or prevail in a protracted coercive campaign, and they probably require a renewed discussion about the urgent need for Taiwan to rethink its approach to military manpower, especially reserve training and mobilization.[35]

They also require Washington to think about, and discuss with Taipei, the capabilities required to survive a protracted blockade after an initial invasion attempt fails. Shorter contingencies would put a premium on small and survivable systems on Taiwan combined with American undersea systems, long-range stealth aircraft, and ground-based missile forces. Longer contingencies would require mine clearing, survivable logistics, and deep munitions stockpiles sufficient for a protracted conflict.

The major bureaucratic losers in this construct would likely be large land units, short-range fighter aircraft, and less-survivable elements of the surface fleet. At present, however, Australia, Japan, and Taiwan have all invested significant sums in relatively expensive and vulnerable systems, meaning all three will need to consider more denial-focused postures, as Australia has recently done in its 2020 *Defence Strategic Update*.[36]

The United States should be talking with and pressing its allies to develop their own anti-access capabilities rather than replicating the power projection capabilities of US forces. Doing so would help ensure that the United States and its allies and partners have the capabilities needed to credibly deny Beijing the ability to invade or coerce Taiwan, which will be especially crucial if the United States can expect only limited basing access and force contributions from its regional allies and partners.

Notes

1. This chapter updates Zack Cooper and Sheena Chestnut Greitens, "What to Expect from Japan and Korea in a Taiwan Contingency," in *New Frontiers for Security Cooperation with Seoul and Tokyo*, ed. Henry D. Sokolski (Arlington, VA: Nonproliferation Policy Education Center, 2021), https://npolicy.org/article_file/2101_New_Frontiers_Occasional_Paper.pdf. The authors thank the Nonproliferation Policy Education Center for its support of the initial research and permitting publication of this updated version.

2. Liu Xuanzun, "PLA Holds Large-Scale Exercise near Taiwan 'to Counter US, Japanese Drills,'" *Global Times*, January 24, 2020, https://www.globaltimes.cn/page/202201/1246800.shtml; and *Global Times*, "Sheping: Jiefangjun junji zheng raozhe 'Taidu' bozi la xi sheng" [Editorial: PLA Military Planes Are Pulling Strings Around the Neck of "Taiwan Independence"], January 24, 2022, https://opinion.huanqiu.com/article/46XK3XhO2Uw.

3. Andrew Greene, "Australia Discussing 'Contingency' Plans with United States over Possible Taiwan Conflict," Australian Broadcasting Corporation, March 31, 2021, https://www.abc.net.au/news/2021-04-01/australia-discuss-contingency-plans-us-possible-conflict-taiwan/100043826.

4. Ellen Mitchell, "US, Japan Draw Up Joint Military Plan for Possible Taiwan Emergency: Report," *Hill*, December 23, 2021, https://thehill.com/policy/defense/587089-us-japan-draw-up-joint-military-plan-for-possible-taiwan-emergency-report.

5. In October 2021, Xi Jinping gave a speech saying, "The Taiwan issue arose out of national weakness and will be resolved with national rejuvenation." See Xi Jinping, "Taiwan wenti yin minzu ruo luan er chansheng, bijiang suizhe minzu fuxing er jiejue" [The Taiwan Issue Arose out of National Weakness and Chaos, and Will Surely Be Resolved with National Rejuvenation] (speech, Commemoration of the 110th Anniversary of the Revolution of 1911, Beijing, China, October 9, 2021), https://www.sohu.com/a/494178126_162522. For remarks from Taiwan experts in China, see also Taiwan Work Office of the Chinese Communist Party Central Committee and Taiwan Affairs Office of the People's Republic of China State Council, "Cucheng guojian wanquan tongyi shixian zhonghua minzu weida fuxing—quanwei zhuanjia tan xin shidai dang jiejue Taiwan wenti de zongti fanglue" [Promote the Complete Reunification of the Country and Realize the Great Rejuvenation of the Chinese Nation—Authoritative Experts Talk About the Party's Overall Strategy for Solving the Taiwan Issue in the New Era], December 22, 2021, http://www.gwytb.gov.cn/zt/djzt/jjddsjjlzqh/pljd/202112/t20211222_12397654.htm; and Wang Qi, "Xi Tackles Taiwan Question, Shows Steel-Like Determination and Confidence in Reunification," *Global Times*, July 1, 2021, https://

www.globaltimes.cn/page/202107/1227633.shtml. See also Richard C. Bush, "8 Key Things to Notice from Xi Jinping's New Year Speech on Taiwan," Brookings Institution, January 7, 2019, https://www.brookings.edu/blog/order-from-chaos/2019/01/07/8-key-things-to-notice-from-xi-jinpings-new-year-speech-on-taiwan; and Amber Wang, "'Only a Matter of Time' Before Taiwan Has No Allies, Chinese Vice Foreign Minister Says," *South China Morning Post*, January 18, 2022, https://www.scmp.com/news/china/diplomacy/article/3163815/only-matter-time-taiwan-has-no-allies-chinese-vice-foreign.

6. David Wertime, "Former Intel Officers: U.S. Must Update Its Thinking on Taiwan," *Politico*, October 8, 2020, https://politi.co/36LgfuS.

7. Reuters, "'Inconceivable' Australia Would Not Join U.S. to Defend Taiwan—Australian Defence Minister," November 12, 2021, https://www.reuters.com/world/asia-pacific/inconceivable-australia-would-not-join-us-defend-taiwan-australian-defence-2021-11-12.

8. Helen Davidson and Daniel Hurst, "Taiwan Hits Back After Paul Keating Says Its Status 'Not a Vital Australian Interest,'" *Guardian*, November 10, 2021, https://www.theguardian.com/australia-news/2021/nov/11/taiwan-hits-back-after-paul-keating-says-its-status-not-a-vital-australian-interest.

9. For background, see Hillary C. Dauer, "Increasing Support for U.S.-Japan Alliance in Okinawa Is Not a Pipedream," Tokyo Review, February 26, 2021, https://www.tokyoreview.net/2021/02/increasing-support-for-u-s-japan-alliance-in-okinawa-is-not-a-pipedream.

10. Ankit Panda, "US-Japan Alliance: Still 'Sword and Shield'?," *Diplomat*, November 5, 2014, https://thediplomat.com/2014/11/us-japan-alliance-still-sword-and-shield.

11. Greene, "Australia Discussing 'Contingency' Plans with United States over Possible Taiwan Conflict"; and Mitchell, "US, Japan Draw Up Joint Military Plan for Possible Taiwan Emergency."

12. David Sacks, "Enhancing U.S.-Japan Coordination for a Taiwan Conflict," Council on Foreign Relations, January 18, 2022, https://www.cfr.org/report/enhancing-us-japan-coordination-taiwan-conflict.

13. Sugio Takahashi, "Upgrading the Japan-U.S. Defense Guidelines: Toward a New Phase of Operational Coordination," Project 2049 Institute, June 2018, https://project2049.net/wp-content/uploads/2018/06/japan_us_defense_guidelines_takahashi.pdf.

14. Jeffrey W. Hornung, *Japan's Potential Contributions in an East China Sea Contingency*, RAND Corporation, 2020, 92, https://www.rand.org/pubs/research_reports/RRA314-1.html.

15. Ryan Ashley, "Japan's Revolution on Taiwan Affairs," November 23, 2021, https://warontherocks.com/2021/11/japans-revolution-on-taiwan-affairs.

16. Adam P. Liff, "Has Japan's Policy Toward the Taiwan Strait Changed?," *Washington Post*, August 18, 2021, https://www.washingtonpost.com/politics/2021/08/18/has-japans-policy-toward-taiwan-strait-changed; Yoshihiro Sakai, "How Kishida Is Inching Japan Toward a More China-Friendly Stance," *South China Morning Post*, January 20, 2022, https://www.scmp.com/comment/opinion/article/3163923/how-kishida-inching-japan-towards-more-china-friendly-stance; and Adam P. Liff and Ryan Hass, "Japan-Taiwan Relations: A Look Back on 2021 and Look Ahead to 2022," Brookings Institution,

January 20, 2022, https://www.brookings.edu/blog/order-from-chaos/2022/01/20/japan-taiwan-relations-a-look-back-on-2021-and-look-ahead-to-2022.

17. Daniel Sneider, "The Hidden GAP in American and Japanese Views on Defense," *Oriental Economist*, January 17, 2022, https://toyokeizai.net/articles/-/503647.

18. Natasha Kassam and Richard McGregor, "Taiwan's 2020 Elections," Lowy Institute, January 7, 2020, https://www.lowyinstitute.org/publications/taiwan-s-2020-elections.

19. Ki Suh Jung, "The Implications of Simultaneous Conflicts in South Korea and Taiwan," Center for International Maritime Security, November 2, 2021, https://cimsec.org/the-implications-of-simultaneous-conflicts-in-south-korea-and-taiwan.

20. Sungmin Cho, "South Korea's Taiwan Conundrum," War on the Rocks, December 31, 2021, https://warontherocks.com/2021/12/south-koreas-taiwan-conundrum.

21. Lee Dae Woo, "The Possibility of U.S.-China Military Conflict in the South China Sea," Sejong Institute, September 2, 2020, http://sejong.org/boad/22/egoread.php?bd=23&itm=0&txt=South+China+Sea&pg=1&seq=5497. The full Korean text is available at http://www.sejong.org/boad/1/egoread.php?bd=2&itm=&txt=&pg=1&seq=5482. For another perspective that emphasizes quiet alliance coordination and "promotion of joint operational awareness" to try to maintain stability in the western Pacific, see Institute of Foreign Affairs and National Security, "China's Naval Power Build Up and Military Competition," Korea National Diplomatic Academy, September 28, 2020, https://www.ifans.go.kr/knda/ifans/kor/act/ActivityAreaView.do?csrfPreventionSalt=null&sn=13638&boardSe=pbl&koreanEngSe=KOR&ctgrySe=12&menuCl=&searchCondition=searchAll&searchKeyword=%EC%A4%91%EA%B5%AD%EC%9D%98+%ED%95%B4%EA%B5%B0%EB%A0%A5+%EC%A6%9D%EA%B0%95%EA%B3%BC+%EB%AF%B8%EC%A4%91+%EA%B5%B0%EC%82%AC%EA%B2%BD%EC%9F%81&pageIndex=1.

22. Sean McCormack, "United States and the Republic of Korea Launch Strategic Consultation for Allied Partnership," US Department of State, January 19, 2006, https://2001-2009.state.gov/r/pa/prs/ps/2006/59447.htm.

23. Jung H. Pak, "Trying to Loosen the Linchpin: China's Approach to South Korea," Brookings Institution, July 2020, https://www.brookings.edu/research/trying-to-loosen-the-linchpin-chinas-approach-to-south-korea.

24. See, for example, Ben Blanchard, "Duterte Aligns Philippines with China, Says U.S. Has Lost," Reuters, October 20, 2016, https://www.reuters.com/article/us-china-philippines-idUSKCN12K0AS; BBC, "Philippines' Duterte Tells Obama to 'Go to Hell,'" October 4, 2016, https://www.bbc.com/news/world-asia-37548695; and Richard Javad Heydarian, "Duterte Bans Exercises with US in South China Sea," Asia Times, August 4, 2020, https://asiatimes.com/2020/08/duterte-bans-exercises-with-us-in-south-china-sea.

25. Sebastian Strangio, "Philippines' Marcos to Pursue Bilateral Deal with Beijing over South China Sea," *Diplomat*, January 28, 2022, https://thediplomat.com/2022/01/philippines-marcos-to-pursue-bilateral-deal-with-beijing-over-south-china-sea.

26. US forces' access to the Philippines occurs on a rotational basis because the 1987 Philippine constitution forbids permanent foreign military bases. See Sheena Chestnut Greitens, "The US-Philippine Alliance: Opportunities and Challenges," in

Strategic Asia 2014–15: Alliances and Partnerships at the Center of Global Power, ed. Ashley J. Tellis, Abraham M. Denmark, and Greg Chaffin (Washington, DC: National Bureau of Asian Research, 2014), http://www.sheenagreitens.com/uploads/1/2/1/1/121115641/ strategicasia2014_philippines.pdf.

27. Joel Wuthnow, "Defending Taiwan in an Expanded Competitive Space," *Joint Force Quarterly* 104 (December 2021), https://ndupress.ndu.edu/Media/News/News-Article-View/Article/2884395/defending-taiwan-in-an-expanded-competitivespace.

28. Wuthnow, "Defending Taiwan in an Expanded Competitive Space."

29. Lonnie Henley, "PLA Operational Concepts and Centers of Gravity in a Taiwan Conflict," testimony before the US-China Economic and Security Review Commission, Hearing on Cross-Strait Deterrence, February 18, 2021, https://www.uscc.gov/sites/ default/files/2021-02/Lonnie_Henley_Testimony.pdf.

30. Jacqueline Schneider, "Defending Taiwan Is a Worthy Goal. But Are We Ready for Heavy Casualties?," *Washington Post*, January 24, 2022, https://www.washingtonpost. com/outlook/2022/01/24/taiwan-defense-hawks-cost.

31. Jeffrey W. Hornung, "The United States and Japan Should Prepare for War with China," War on the Rocks, February 5, 2021, https://warontherocks.com/2021/02/ the-united-states-and-japan-should-prepare-for-war.

32. Yonhap, "US Committed to 'Mutually Acceptable' SMA Deal with S. Korea: State Dept.," *Korea Herald*, February 6, 2021, http://www.koreaherald.com/view. php?ud=20210206000029; and Reuters, "Philippines Extends Termination Process of U.S. Troop Deal, Eyes Long-Term Defence Pact," November 11, 2020, https://www. reuters.com/article/us-philippines-usa-defence/philippines-extends-termination-process-of-u-s-troop-deal-eyes-long-term-defence-pact-idUSKBN27R0RD.

33. Tsukasa Hadano, "China Eyes 'Armed Unification' with Taiwan by 2027: Key Academic," *Nikkei Asia*, January 31, 2022, https://asia.nikkei.com/Politics/International-relations/China-eyes-armed-unification-with-Taiwan-by-2027-key-academic?s=09.

34. Caitlin Talmadge, "What Putin's Nuclear Threats Mean for the U.S.," *Wall Street Journal*, March 3, 2022, https://www.wsj.com/articles/what-putins-nuclear-threats-mean-for-the-u-s-11646329125.

35. Michael A. Hunzeker, "Taiwan's Defense Plans Are Going off the Rails," War on the Rocks, November 18, 2021, https://warontherocks.com/2021/11/taiwans-defense-plans-are-going-off-the-rails.

36. Australian Department of Defence, *2020 Defence Strategic Update*, July 1, 2020, https://www1.defence.gov.au/strategy-policy/strategic-update-2020; and Australian Department of Defence, *2020 Force Structure Plan*, 2020, https://www.defence.gov.au/ about/publications/2020-force-structure-plan.

Reconciling Two Visions for the Defense of Taiwan: Reviving the Overall Defense Concept by Operationalizing the Taiwan Enhanced Resiliency Act

BLAKE HERZINGER

Taipei and Washington have markedly divergent views on how to best defend Taiwan against a hypothetical Chinese invasion. Taiwanese leadership has built up a modern war arsenal with expensive prestige platforms of the type fielded by the United States military. Meanwhile, the United States believes that a large arsenal of unmanned, cheap weaponry would best serve Taiwan in kinetic warfare with China.

The US is not bound by treaty to participate in Taiwan's defense; nevertheless, it is a reasonable assumption that Washington's lowest level of participation in a war between Taiwan and the People's Republic of China (PRC) would resemble the support provided to Ukraine in response to Russia's 2022 invasion, while the highest level may include American participation in combat operations. In either scenario, differing opinions about how to prosecute the war will inhibit effective operations and hobble the war effort. However, given the nature of US-Taiwan relations after 1979, the US has had little leverage to address the gap between its desires and Taiwan's defense plans.

The contemporary development of Taiwan's defense forces is a patchwork of platforms. Ranging from American hand-me-down Cold War–era ships and tanks to sophisticated domestically developed cruise missiles and a smattering of modern US platforms, Taiwan's acquisition strategy appears as a kludged-together Frankenstein's monster solution, ill-suited for either symmetrical or asymmetrical operations against a potential invasion.[1]

Factors contributing to this force confusion are many, but two stand out above the rest. First, Taiwan has long approached—arguably correctly—the

160

issue of Chinese sea and air incursions by countering with symmetrical responses. Fighters and bombers approaching Taiwanese airspace are intercepted by Taiwan's more advanced fighter aircraft. Taiwan's navy uses frigates and other surface ships to respond to maritime provocations. However, the high rate of employment of Taiwan's air and naval forces—China outnumbers its air force by around three to one—highlights several issues. Maintaining an effective response to a more numerous opponent will wear out aircraft faster than plans may allow for.[2] In a contingency, attempts to counter the People's Liberation Army Air Force conventionally will be prohibitively costly in platforms and, worse, trained pilots. While Taiwan's capabilities functionally serve peacetime deterrence and signaling requirements, said force will not be sufficient for Taiwan's wartime needs, which would be far better met by a mix of manned fighters augmented by more numerous, attritable, uncrewed systems.

Second, Taiwan's acquisitions have long trended toward so-called prestige platforms, such as large amphibious assault ships, Abrams tanks, and indigenously produced submarines. There is some element of logic to this, as Taipei has sought and obtained high-end military hardware from the United States to lend credibility to that relationship and burnish its own credentials at home. Some have argued that this boutique force is also a strategic gambit; purchasing a high-end force from Washington, though it admittedly cannot survive a head-to-head collision with the People's Liberation Army (PLA), might be designed to draw American forces into battle on Taiwan's behalf.[3] In reality, Taiwan's force structure is not one that will complement or enable US intervention. Taipei's relative underinvestment in key denial capabilities such as autonomous and uncrewed weapons and precision strike capabilities is starkly contrasted with Beijing's laser focus on counter-intervention capabilities and amphibious warfare.

The good news is that Taiwan already has a plan—the Overall Defense Concept (ODC)—on the shelf that could be used to bring the US and Taiwanese visions closer together, and the United States' fiscal year (FY) 2023 National Defense Authorization Act (NDAA) has created mechanisms to make it happen. Passage of the Taiwan Enhanced Resilience Act (TERA, formerly the Taiwan Policy Act) within the NDAA has created opportunities for arming and training Taiwan in ways that have not existed since 1979.

Shifting Strategy

Taiwan's active forces are outnumbered by China's at a 12-to-one ratio, and its defense investment is dwarfed by Beijing's. Taiwan cannot win a conventional war of attrition against the PRC. Despite this, Taiwan's defense forces are largely oriented around large, expensive, and conventional platforms.

Neutralizing the PLA's center of gravity—the element without which it cannot successfully take Taiwan—should be the objective of Taiwan's defense strategy. Rather than promoting continued investment in tools to fight a battle on Taiwan's territory, the ODC correctly identified the crossing of the Taiwan Strait as the most precarious and vulnerable moment for the PLA with naval, and specifically amphibious, forces as that center of gravity. A strategy that focuses on destroying those ships before the PLA's forces can hit the beach is the one that keeps Taiwan free.

Taiwan's ODC is a blueprint for a new kind of defense for the island nation. Developed in 2017 by then–Chief of the General Staff Adm. Lee Hsi-min, it represented an asymmetric vision for Taiwan's defense forces that revolved around preserving Taiwan's most irreplaceable resource—personnel—and keeping any fight for Taiwan far from its shores.[4] Rather than engaging an enemy on the beaches only a short drive from Taipei, the ODC called for investment in a robust stockpile of sea mines combined with uncrewed platforms and a deep magazine of cruise missiles. These weapons, along with a large force of cheaper, attritable platforms, would ensure that decisive battles took place at sea, rather than among Taiwan's towns and cities. For a wealthy, technologically advanced state with a relatively small population, this kind of strategy is ideal. Combined with the fact that Taiwan's natural geography makes it difficult to invade—with unruly seas for the majority of the year, few feasible landing beaches, and mountainous terrain—the ODC amplifies Taiwan's advantages and responsibly husbands its most precious assets.

For a brief moment, it seemed as if Taiwan's defense forces were aligned with their American partners, but after Lee's retirement, Taiwan's Ministry of National Defense reverted to the old way of doing business. High-dollar items won out over the ODC's asymmetrical approach, and references to the plan were dropped from Taiwan's defense strategy documents by 2021.[5]

Rather than concentrating on large numbers of counterinvasion tools, the military is sinking money into longer-range missiles that can hold the Chinese mainland at risk in an ill-considered attempt at deterrence.

While Taiwan's Ministry of National Defense has, for the moment, turned its back on the ODC, the 2023 NDAA offers incentives to return— or at least opportunities to enact—some of the strategy's core components. The TERA delivered invaluable policy mechanisms for providing equipment combined with mandated working groups and training that can enable key elements of the ODC—"force buildup" and its according "concept of operations."

Adm. Lee's vision for Taiwan's force buildup mentions three key areas— namely, force preservation, conventional capabilities, and asymmetric capabilities. The ODC makes the point addressed earlier: Taiwan requires conventional platforms for peacetime signaling. However, Taiwan's military structure has overweighted those at the expense of systems that would be of most use in the defense of Taiwan. Lee's strategy identifies these as "small, mobile, lethal, and numerous" or, more simply, "a large number of small things."[6]

Before the PRC's military modernization, Taiwan's defense model might have been likened to Israel's qualitative military edge, in that having a smaller number of high-tech platforms was sufficient to defeat a larger but unsophisticated PLA.[7] But now the PLA holds the technological and numerical advantage. This is the underlying logic to the ODC's concept of operations, which emphasizes *force protection, decisive battle in the littoral zone* and *destruction of the enemy at the landing beach.*[8] (Emphasis in original.) As mentioned, Taiwan's most irreplaceable resource is trained military personnel, which must be carefully stewarded. Survivability through deception, hardening, dispersal, mobility, and camouflage is paramount, and it will ensure that Taiwan's military survives the ferocious opening onslaught that would inevitably precede a large-scale invasion. The first step in launching a decisive counterblow to defeat a PRC invasion would be avoiding the knockout punch in the first round.

This asymmetric strategy is in line with a US vision for Taiwan's defense, primarily because it buys time and plays to Taiwan's not-inconsiderable defensive advantages as a mountainous island. Once Chinese forces establish a lodgment on Taiwan's beaches, the prospects for Taipei's survival dwindle rapidly, as do those for a successful intervention by Taiwan's partners. Keeping a Chinese invasion fleet bogged down in a heavily mined Taiwan Strait under steady attack from sea, shore, and air and then mopping up landing forces with reserves is a commonsense plan with strong bipartisan support in the US Congress. And Lee's views on civil defense offer multiple advantages and avenues for expanding cooperation beyond military engagements. Most importantly, his is an achievable strategy with increased US-Taiwan cooperation in not only the security sphere but also economic investment.

Force Buildup and US Assistance

Recent defense announcements are a mixed bag in Taiwan, with new military drones and minelayers featuring alongside bulk buys of Abrams main battle tanks, F-16 fighters, and an indigenous submarine program. To truly operationalize the ODC's force buildup vision, acquisition priorities need to be recalibrated toward smaller, cheaper, more numerous platforms that Taiwan can afford to expend or lose in larger numbers, without commensurate losses of manpower.

To this end, the TERA mandated that within six months of its passing, the US secretaries of state and defense, in consultation with the director of national intelligence, engage with the appropriate points of contact in Taiwan to establish a "joint consultative mechanism" with the intended outcome of producing a multiyear plan for Taiwan's defense. The operative phrase in Section 5506 is "appropriate defensive capabilities"—a clause that should be couched in those concepts presented in the ODC.[9]

The drawdown authority made available to Taiwan in the NDAA's Section 5505 will allow direct transfers of war stocks to Taiwan. This somewhat circumvents the creaking US defense industrial base, which is only now beginning to grapple with the growing pains of meeting wartime demand as a result of the war in Ukraine. While drawdown authority is usually limited to $100 million per fiscal year, the bill establishes a ceiling of $1 billion for defense articles and training for Taiwan per fiscal year, which should tightly focus on munitions and associated equipment. In comparison, making Taiwan an eligible recipient under the Excess Defense

Articles (EDA) authority presents additional opportunities for transfer of everything from meals and parts to uninhabited systems and aircraft that are no longer needed by US forces.

However, without an increase in output capacity, including Taiwan as eligible for drawdown authority and EDA will make real the hitherto false dichotomy between support for Ukraine and support for Taiwan. Taiwan's previous status as a foreign military sales (FMS) customer, before the advent of the TERA, meant that its acquisitions relied on defense production lines separate from EDA and US stocks. So to a certain degree, this well-intentioned move puts more pressure on US supplies required for national defense. But a superpower must be capable of managing competing priorities without abandoning less-urgent ones. The United States has a critical supply-chain problem that can be solved with investment, and it must pay for the industrial base it needs.

Perhaps most useful will be the provision, for the first time since Richard Nixon opened diplomatic relations with the PRC, of foreign military financing (FMF) to Taipei. This change moves Taiwan away from exclusive reliance on direct sales, in which Taiwan was paying cash on the barrelhead for specific equipment they wanted. While the previous arrangement has been preferable to no relationship at all, it provided few opportunities for Washington to influence Taipei's acquisitions and saw hundreds of millions of dollars thrown into platforms that do not necessarily fit within the ODC.

This arrangement has already changed to some degree under the Biden administration, with policymakers reportedly quietly informing both Taiwanese officials and arms manufacturers that requests to purchase large items in fewer numbers will be rejected.[10] To access the yet-to-be-appropriated $10 billion in FMF funds earmarked for them over the next five years, Taiwan's choices will be subject to not only congressional approval but also Department of Defense review, with regard to their underlying logic. The FMF process is designed around developing capabilities, rather than requesting specific platforms. So a not-so-theoretical Taiwanese requirement to deter or deny amphibious invasion would be evaluated in terms of which appropriate capabilities exist within the US defense enterprise, and then those capabilities would be offered to Taiwan to be acquired with grant assistance. In essence, FMF creates opportunities for more meaningful consultation between the two nations to arrive at the desirable mix for an asymmetric defense of Taiwan.

Missiles. Taiwan has a small existing supply of US-made Harpoon missiles and has developed sophisticated indigenous anti-ship cruise missiles that, in some ways, exceed the capabilities of those offered by the United States. Taiwan is also ramping up its domestic production, with a 2022 commitment to increase stocks of air-to-ground, anti-ship, and surface-to-surface cruise missiles significantly by 2028.[11] Within Taiwan's Sea-Air Combat Power Improvement Plan Purchase Special Regulation, announced in 2021, Taiwan's Chung-Shan Institute of Science and Technology will reportedly produce 70 Hsiung Feng III/IIIE supersonic cruise missiles[12] per year and 131 Hsiung Feng II[13] subsonic anti-ship cruise missiles and Hsiung Sheng land-attack missiles by developing a shared assembly line.[14]

But this is a five-year plan, and the promise of unbuilt missiles will not deter an invasion. To contribute to this key element of Taiwan's defense, US policymakers should leverage the NDAA's provisions to prioritize shipments of the 400 Harpoon missiles Taiwan has already ordered, along with the associated 100 mobile launch vehicles. The FY2023 NDAA's authorization for a multiyear purchase of 2,600 Harpoon missiles from Boeing should be exercised at the first opportunity, as should the provision for defense industrial base investment, to encourage Boeing to expand its production capability.[15]

Another area for emphasis is Taiwan's force of US-built M142 High Mobility Artillery Rocket Systems (HIMARS), which has an invaluable, validated anti-ship capability.[16] While the range of Taiwan's Guided Multiple Launch Rocket System (GMLRS) might only have the range to reach targets at the narrowest part of the Taiwan Strait, the rocket artillery systems could be devastatingly effective against amphibious assault vessels, which must remain stationed well within the rockets' range to deploy their embarked assault force. The same goes for any troops landing on Taiwan's shores.[17] Furthermore, the producer of HIMARS, Lockheed Martin, has already floated the idea of mounting its AGM-184C Long-Range Anti-Ship Missile Surface Launched (LRASM-SL) on the HIMARS launch vehicle, extending its anti-ship range to 1,000 kilometers.[18]

Originally intended as a force of 11 launchers and 64 Army Tactical Missile System (ATACMS) missiles,[19] Taiwan later upped that purchase to 29 launchers, 84 ATACMS, and 864 precision-guided rockets as part of its momentous 2023 defense budget.[20] While these were purchased under the previous procurement method, future FMF and EDA grants could deliver more launch vehicles, spare parts, and munitions. As a reference, Ukraine has received thousands of GMLRS fired by the M142; fewer than 1,000 for Taiwan will simply not suffice.[21] Lockheed Martin is a rare producer of good news in the US defense industrial base, having increased its production of launchers and munitions considerably during the Ukraine war.[22] Although its combination of LRASM-SL and HIMARS was originally proposed to the Australian Defence Force, this might be an option worth investing in for Taiwan as well.

Mines. Defensive mining is rightly of considerable interest to Taiwan. Sea mines offer a cheap and effective method of denying the use of the sea for a potential invader. By using a mix of mines, including those moored to the sea floor and newer self-propelled weapons, a defender like Taiwan can hold up an invasion force at sea for extended periods while its opponent attempts to clear a path through the minefield. This delay would then give Taiwanese defense forces an opportunity to employ standoff weapons to attack and degrade the amphibious assault force. While sea mines are in no way new, they are a potent weapon that deserve a central role in the defense of Taiwan.

There are promising signs that a defensive mining strategy would be part of the island's defense strategy, to include dedicated minelaying vessels and several domestic programs for building advanced mines. But the minelaying vessels are few in number, and the majority of Taiwan's mine inventory is World War II–era US Mk VI weapons, while its more advanced domestic programs have yet to reach initial operational capability.

These mines still constitute a serious capability (for reference, since World War II, more US ships have been lost to similar mines than any other weapon), but the US could provide new capabilities to Taiwan under either drawdown or FMF authorities. The US-made Quickstrike air-delivered mines are essentially converted Mk 80 series high-explosive bombs with a fusing system that detonates the weapon when it detects a passing ship. With payloads ranging from 500 to 2,000 pounds, these mines pose a significant threat to ships. Some variants—the Quickstrike-J and Quickstrike-ER—include upgrades such as Joint Direct Attack Munition GPS guidance kits and a wing kit, respectively.

Taipei showed public interest in purchasing 500-pound Mk 62 Quickstrike mines as recently as 2018, but no sale was ever approved or notified.[23] Should such a capability be offered, the NDAA's training provisions under the FMF authority could be used to develop working groups between Taiwan's military and the US Navy's Mine Warfare Training Center to train Taiwanese mine forces and establish information-sharing mechanisms and the exchange of best practices. Deconfliction and combined understanding of mine areas would be a crucial area for cooperation, particularly in any scenario that saw US forces supporting Taiwan by maritime routes or undersea warfare.

Drones. Past FMS deals saw Taiwan ink contracts for small numbers of US drones—including four MQ-9B SeaGuardians approved in 2020.[24] But Taiwan has also invested in domestic fixed- and rotary-wing unmanned aerial vehicles.[25] Most useful to the ODC, however, are the Chien Hsiang loitering munitions unveiled by Taiwan's National Chung-Shan Institute of Science and Technology in 2022.[26] Designed to locate and destroy radar systems (or the platforms carrying them) on land and sea, weapons like the Chien Hsiang provided a similar asymmetric edge for Azerbaijan in its successful campaign against Armenia in 2020.[27] But initial announcements projected only about 100 units to be built by about 2025.[28] For a one-way drone, larger numbers would be advisable.

Encouraging as these developments are, Taiwan's military has been slow to adopt unmanned technologies. It will need support in developing effective and integrated concepts of operation for their use, which can be provided and paid for via FMF.

Ultimately, all these opportunities rest on a foundation of strategic and operational coordination that is relatively nascent. The NDAA-mandated talks between the US and Taiwan's defense institutions should be acutely focused on these conversations. It is not necessary, as some have suggested, to threaten punishing sanctions on Taiwan for not arming itself the way the US prefers, but it should continue to be clearly communicated that these developments are required if Taiwan intends to obtain military support from the United States. Hard conversations between partners are part of defense relationships, especially when one partner is a superpower, but they need not be acrimonious. To have any expectation of American support, Taiwan will need to accommodate Washington's vision as the senior partner and enthusiastically embrace suggested reforms.

The Concept for Operations and "Going Winchester"

The operational concept of the ODC only works if backed by the defense industrial bases in Taiwan and the United States, which are capable of rapidly producing the weapons the ODC requires. And at the time this chapter is being written, they are not backing it.

Production shortfalls in precision munitions, particularly anti-ship missiles, in the United States must be addressed in order to operationalize the ODC on a reasonable timeline. Multiyear munitions contracts and industrial base investment authorized in the FY23 NDAA are a step in the right direction, allowing Congress to commit funding over several years to encourage defense contractors to hire the skilled workers and sustain or expand hot production lines required to meet government needs.

The Australia-UK-US agreement announced in March 2023 might offer a mechanism for further incentivizing US industry to increase its production capacity. As part of the trilateral deal for bringing nuclear-powered submarines to Australia, the Albanese government agreed to invest $3 billion in the US submarine industry, which would help create needed capacity.[29] Encouraging Taiwan to invest similarly in US companies producing munitions and launch vehicles could perform a similar function—and highlight to the American public that Taiwan is investing seriously in its own defense and, by extension, the American economy.

Precise information regarding the depth of Taiwan's war stocks is rare, for good reason. But some insights can be drawn from public-facing policy announcements like that of Taiwan's defense ministry in 2022, which announced plans to increase domestic missile production from 207 to 497 per year.[30] Some reports put this number as high as 1,000 per year. As mentioned above, within Taiwan's Sea-Air Combat Power Improvement Plan

Purchase Special Regulation, Taiwan's Chung-Shan Institute of Science and Technology will reportedly produce 70 Hsiung Feng III/IIIE supersonic cruise missiles[31] per year and 131 Hsiung Feng II[32] subsonic anti-ship cruise missiles and Hsiung Sheng land-attack missiles by developing a shared assembly line.[33] These figures would also include Wan Chien air-to-ground missiles.

Taiwan's more sophisticated Hsiung Sheng land-attack cruise missile, an upgraded variant of the Hsiung Feng IIE cruise missile, is capable of hitting targets as far away as the Chinese cities of Wuhan and Qingdao. A production rate of around 500–1,000 missiles per year may sound like a reasonable number, but some wargaming expectations predict that Taiwan's missile forces would be either entirely expended ("Winchester" in military brevity code) or destroyed within two weeks of the outbreak of conflict. A Center for Strategic and International Studies wargame in 2023 saw US forces launch nearly 5,000 long-range missiles (10 years of Taiwan's total missile production) in three to four weeks of intense fighting, a rate that exhausted US inventories of some weapons within days.[34] While no wargame is necessarily predictive, these kinds of high expenditure rates are likely to hold true in a Taiwan scenario. With this in mind, Taiwan's domestic production rates are almost certainly insufficient to achieve its wartime aims, especially if conflict breaks out before the completion of the announced buildup.

The US defense industrial base is perhaps the most glaring weakness in making this plan a reality. Where Taiwan has made at least some effort to invest in the anti-invasion capabilities it needs, a creaking US defense industrial base is letting the side down. In September 2022, the US State Department announced its approval to sell Taiwan 60 Harpoon anti-ship missiles and 100 Sidewinder air-to-air missiles.[35] That announcement was predated by a 2020 approval to sell 400 missiles and 100 mobile launch platforms with radars and other associated equipment.[36]

But in the intervening two years, the delivery date for the arms identified had already begun to slide. What was intended to arrive in Taiwan by 2024 would only begin to arrive by 2025, with the balance of the order arriving by 2028.[37] The resultant backlog affects all US customers, but Taiwan in particular is waiting on delivery of $14 billion in equipment ranging from jet fighters to heavyweight torpedoes.[38] And at the end of the day, the quantities of ordered weapons do not seem aligned with the scale of the problem: 60 Harpoon missiles would likely be a slow Tuesday in a high-intensity war with Beijing, not a particularly meaningful supply of weapons.

Conclusion

Russia's brutal invasion of Ukraine in 2022 and the ensuing slog of long-range artillery and missile duels brought a cruel operational reality to the fore. High-end warfare burns through munitions at incredible rates, far beyond the present capability of peacetime production to replace. Within two months of the outbreak of war, the US had depleted its own stocks of key munitions, such as the Javelin anti-tank missile, by a third. Under the normal production rate at that time, those missiles would take US industry three to four years to replace.[39]

Whether a question of smart weapons like cruise missiles or the simplest of artillery shells, the war in Ukraine casts a grim pallor over the Taiwan Strait, where Beijing's magazines are exponentially deeper than Taiwan's. And in a crucial difference with the situation in Ukraine, little likelihood exists for Taiwan to be resupplied mid-conflict. Ukraine's size, or strategic depth, allowed resupply in the western reaches of the country relatively untouched by the war. But Taiwan would inevitably be surrounded by a blockading force, with the entirety of the nation within range of the world's largest missile force. With that in mind, both the US and Taiwan must assume that at the outset of any conflict with the PRC, Taiwan will fight exclusively with the weapons it has in its possession at that time.[40] Resupply and logistical support from the United States or its allies will not be immediately forthcoming. Cruise missile stores that may today only number in the hundreds are likely to be exhausted quickly through a combination of combat expenditure and targeting by Chinese strike weapons.

Taiwan's defense is of global significance. Neither Taipei nor Washington can afford unpreparedness, nor can they afford to continue down parallel paths. The ODC gave Taiwan a way forward that its most consequential security partner heartily endorsed but then failed to see it through, creating space between the partners where there should be a unified front.

Taiwan's defense leaders may prefer another path but should reconsider Adm. Lee's strategic legacy before committing themselves to a strategy that diverges from their partners in Washington.

With the eyes of the world increasingly focused on the Taiwan Strait, the FY23 NDAA and TERA have delivered tools to US policymakers to engage more granularly with Taiwan's needs and the underlying conceptual basis of the island's defense. Using those tools will require creative thinking and consultations on a level unseen between the two for over 40 years, but it is not hyperbolic to suggest that the long peace in Asia may depend on their success in doing so.

Notes

1. Drew Thompson, "Hope on the Horizon: Taiwan's Radical New Defense Concept," War on the Rocks, October 2, 2018, https://warontherocks.com/2018/10/hope-on-the-horizon-taiwans-radical-new-defense-concept.

2. Ben Blanchard and Michael Martina, "Taiwan Scrambles Jets to Warn Away Chinese Planes in Its Air Defence Zone," Reuters, June 21, 2022, https://www.reuters.com/world/asia-pacific/taiwan-scrambles-29-jets-warn-away-chinese-planes-its-air-defence-zone-2022-06-21.

3. Raymond Kuo, "The Counter-Intuitive Sensibility of Taiwan's New Defense Strategy," War on the Rocks, December 6, 2021, https://warontherocks.com/2021/12/the-counter-intuitive-sensibility-of-taiwans-new-defense-strategy.

4. Lee Hsi-min and Eric Lee, "Taiwan's Overall Defense Concept, Explained," Diplomat, November 3, 2020, https://thediplomat.com/2020/11/taiwans-overall-defense-concept-explained.

5. Michael A. Hunzeker, "Taiwan's Defense Plans Are Going Off the Rails," War on the Rocks, November 18, 2021, https://warontherocks.com/2021/11/taiwans-defense-plans-are-going-off-the-rails.

6. Lee and Lee, "Taiwan's Overall Defense Concept, Explained."

7. Taipei Times, "US-Israel Model Apt for Taiwan: Expert," November 22, 2021, https://www.taipeitimes.com/News/taiwan/archives/2021/11/22/2003768288.

8. Lee and Lee, "Taiwan's Overall Defense Concept, Explained."

9. James M. Inhofe National Defense Authorization Act for Fiscal Year 2023, H.R. 7776, 117th Cong., 2nd sess. (2022).

10. Edward Wong and John Ismay, "U.S. Aims to Turn Taiwan into Giant Weapons Depot," New York Times, October 5, 2022, https://www.nytimes.com/2022/10/05/us/politics/taiwan-biden-weapons-china.html.

11. Lo Tien-pin and Jonathan Chin, "Official Outlines Plan to Make More Than 1,000 Missiles," Taipei Times, August 14, 2022, https://www.taipeitimes.com/News/front/archives/2022/08/14/2003783486.

12. Center for Strategic and International Studies, Missile Defense Project, Missile Threat, "Hsiung Feng III," July 30, 2021, https://missilethreat.csis.org/missile/hsiung-feng-iii.

13. Center for Strategic and International Studies, Missile Defense Project, Missile Threat, "Hsiung Feng II," July 30, 2021, https://missilethreat.csis.org/missile/hsiung-feng-ii.

14 Lo and Chin, "Official Outlines Plan to Make More Than 1,000 Missiles."

15. James M. Inhofe National Defense Authorization Act for Fiscal Year 2023, H.R. 7776.

16. Peter Ong, "Black Sea Drill Again Validates HIMARS as an Anti-Ship Weapon System," Naval News, November 24, 2020, https://www.navalnews.com/naval-news/2020/11/black-sea-drill-again-validates-himars-as-an-anti-ship-weapon-system.

17. Frederick W. Kagan et al., "HIMARS: A Peek Inside AEI," AEIdeas, October 3, 2022, https://www.aei.org/foreign-and-defense-policy/himars-a-peek-inside-aei.

18. Benjamin Felton, "Lockheed Pitches LRASM Touting HIMARS to Australia," Naval News, October 4, 2022, https://www.navalnews.com/naval-news/2022/10/lockheed-pitches-lrasm-touting-himars-to-australia.

19. Department of Defense, Defense Security Cooperation Agency, "Taipei Economic and Cultural Representative Office in the United States (TECRO)—HIMARS, Support, and Equipment," press release, October 21, 2020, https://www.dsca.mil/press-media/major-arms-sales/taipei-economic-and-cultural-representative-office-united-states-15.

20. Republic of China (Taiwan) Overseas Community Affairs Council, "Taiwan Plans to Buy More HIMARS from U.S. After Ditching Paladin Plan," September 1, 2022, https://www.ocac.gov.tw/OCAC/Eng/Pages/Detail.aspx?nodeid=329&pid=44576357.

21. John Ismay, "The American Guided Rockets Helping Ukraine Destroy Russian Forces," New York Times, September 9, 2022, https://www.nytimes.com/2022/09/09/us/ukraine-weapons-rockets.html.

22. Lockheed Martin, "Mission Focused: Ramping Up Production Ahead of Evolving Threats," https://www.lockheedmartin.com/en-us/news/features/2023/mission-focused-ramping-up-production-ahead-of-evolving-threats.html.

23. Drew Thompson, "Winning the Fight Taiwan Cannot Afford to Lose," National Defense University, Institute for National Strategic Studies, October 2021, https://ndupress.ndu.edu/Portals/68/Documents/stratforum/SF-310.pdf.

24. Department of Defense, Defense Security Cooperation Agency, "Taipei Economic and Cultural Representative Office in the United States (TECRO)—MQ-9B Remotely Piloted Aircraft," press release, November 3, 2020, https://www.dsca.mil/press-media/major-arms-sales/taipei-economic-and-cultural-representative-office-united-states-18.

25. Yu Tai-lang and Kayleigh Madjar, "Indigenous Teng Yun 2 Drone Flies Long-Range Test," Taipei Times, May 18, 2022, https://www.taipeitimes.com/News/taiwan/archives/2022/05/18/2003778404.

26. Associated Press, "Amid Tensions with China, Taiwan Shows Off Military Drones," November 15, 2022, https://apnews.com/article/taiwan-technology-science-business-china-35b2b91bcf82de7f86e784388f0a0245.

27. Shaan Shaikh and Wes Rumbaugh, "The Air and Missile War in Nagorno-Karabakh: Lessons for the Future of Strike and Defense," Center for Strategic

and International Studies, December 8, 2020, https://www.csis.org/analysis/air-and-missile-war-nagorno-karabakh-lessons-future-strike-and-defense.

28. Keoni Everington, "Taiwan to Produce 104 Chien Hsiang Kamikaze Drones by 2025," Taiwan News, November 21, 2022, https://www.taiwannews.com.tw/en/news/4725375.

29. Daniel Hurst and Julian Borger, "Aukus: Nuclear Submarines Deal Will Cost Australia up to $368bn," *Guardian*, March 13, 2023, https://www.theguardian.com/world/2023/mar/14/aukus-nuclear-submarines-australia-commits-substantial-funds-into-expanding-us-shipbuilding-capacity.

30. Yimou Lee, "Taiwan to More Than Double Annual Missile Production Capacity Amid China Tension," Reuters, March 3, 2022, https://www.reuters.com/world/asia-pacific/taiwan-more-than-double-annual-missile-production-capacity-amid-china-tension-2022-03-03.

31. Center for Strategic and International Studies, Missile Defense Project, Missile Threat, "Hsiung Feng III."

32. Center for Strategic and International Studies, Missile Defense Project, Missile Threat, "Hsiung Feng II."

33. Lo and Chin, "Official Outlines Plan to Make More Than 1,000 Missiles."

34. Mark F. Cancian, Matthew Cancian, and Eric Heginbotham, *The First Battle of the Next War: Wargaming a Chinese Invasion of Taiwan*, Center for Strategic and International Studies, January 2023, 135, https://csis-website-prod.s3.amazonaws.com/s3fs-public/publication/230109_Cancian_FirstBattle_NextWar.pdf.

35. Department of Defense, Defense Security Cooperation Agency, "Taipei Economic and Cultural Representative Office in the United States—AGM-84L-1 Harpoon Block II Missiles," press release, September 2, 2022, https://www.dsca.mil/press-media/major-arms-sales/taipei-economic-and-cultural-representative-office-united-states-agm.

36. Department of Defense, Defense Security Cooperation Agency, "Taipei Economic and Cultural Representative Office in the United States (TECRO)—RGM-84L-4 Harpoon Surface Launched Block II Missiles," press release, October 26, 2020, https://www.dsca.mil/press-media/major-arms-sales/taipei-economic-and-cultural-representative-office-united-states-17.

37. Ryan White, "The U.S. Delays Delivery of Harpoon Coastal Defense System to Taiwan," Naval Post, March 9, 2021, https://navalpost.com/taiwan-harpoon-coastal-defense-system-delivery-delays.

38. Bryant Harris, "Document Reveals $14 Billion Backlog of US Defense Transfers to Taiwan," *Defense News*, April 14 2022, https://www.defensenews.com/pentagon/2022/04/14/pandemic-delays-spark-14-billion-backlog-of-us-defense-transfers-to-taiwan.

39. Mark Cancian, "Will the United States Run Out of Javelins Before Russia Runs Out of Tanks?," Center for Strategic and International Studies, April 12, 2022, https://www.csis.org/analysis/will-united-states-run-out-javelins-russia-runs-out-tanks.

40. Blake Herzinger, "Taiwan Needs Weapons for Day 1 of a Chinese Invasion," *Foreign Policy*, September 8, 2022, https://foreignpolicy.com/2022/09/08/taiwan-needs-weapons-for-day-1-of-a-chinese-invasion.

Is the United States Military Ready to Defend Taiwan?

ELAINE MCCUSKER AND EMILY COLETTA

As the debate intensifies on US policy related to the defense of Taiwan, it is useful to examine when and why the US would carry out such a mission, the military resources and capabilities required to do so, and the potential obstacles to a successful outcome. Is the US prioritizing national security in its resourcing and budgeting decisions? Is the US military on a path to success in modernizing its equipment, processes, and capabilities to maintain a competitive edge over China?

We may not have much time to align the answers to these questions.

China regards Taiwan—an island democracy with 23 million citizens—as a renegade province to be folded back under Beijing's control. The 1979 Taiwan Relations Act does not require the United States to defend Taiwan but ambiguously states Washington will maintain the capacity to do so.[1]

It is evident that Taiwan matters to the United States.[2] China's control of Taiwan would give the People's Republic of China (PRC) a forward base 150 miles off the mainland, bringing Chinese aircraft and missiles much closer to important US allies such as Australia and Japan and to vital trade routes. Control over Taiwan, which is China's fifth-most-important trading partner, would also provide Beijing with an important economic asset linked to a strong technology industry. And it would provide the PRC with semiconductor factories that are essential to microelectronics.

The US-China Economic and Security Review Commission's 2021 annual report to Congress, released in November 2021, finds that decades of improvements by China's armed forces "have fundamentally transformed the strategic environment" and weakened military deterrence across the Taiwan Strait, diminishing the position of the US. The commission states,

Today, the [People's Liberation Army] either has or is close to achieving an initial capability to invade Taiwan—one that remains under development but that China's leaders may employ at high risk—while deterring, delaying, or defeating U.S. military intervention.

The commission also recommends

Congress take urgent measures to strengthen the credibility of U.S. military deterrence in the near term and to maintain the ability of the United States to uphold its obligations established in the Taiwan Relations Act to resist any resort to force that would jeopardize the security of Taiwan.[3]

We must take these recommendations seriously in light of indications that the moment of maximum danger in a conflict with China over Taiwan may be only a few years away.[4]

Barriers to Success

If, as noted, Taiwan matters to the US, and China's capability to take action against Taiwan is improving while the timeline for potential action by China is shrinking, we must ask if the US is resourcing the military to defend Taiwan if called on to do so. Is the US military currently set up for success? The short answer is no.

The US military has four key barriers to success:

1. Defense is not a priority for the current administration, demonstrated by the fiscal year (FY) 2022 budget request and further emphasized with an FY23 budget proposal for defense that does not keep pace with rising inflation.

2. Delays in annual appropriations and authorizations reduce buying power, hinder readiness, and delay the pursuit of a competitive advantage.

3. The definition of defense has been expanded to allow for diversion of defense resources and diffusion of attention to nondefense priorities.

4. Institutional and statutory rules and processes do not promote speed and agility in testing, procuring, and integrating modern capabilities.

These barriers to success are inflicted by the administration, Congress, and the Department of Defense (DOD) itself. So they are also fixable.

Defense Is Not a Priority for the Current Administration. When the Office of Management and Budget released the FY22 discretionary toplines for defense and nondefense departments and agencies in early April 2021, defense was clearly not a priority.[5] The Office of Management and Budget press release on the subject did not even mention defense.[6] The discretionary totals contained a nearly 16 percent increase for domestic activities, while the proposed defense number would not have kept pace with inflation, which at the time was much lower than it is now.

Upon release of the FY22 president's budget request to Congress in late May 2021, the lack of attention to defense was further emphasized. The White House budget summary mentioned no actual military capabilities. Some of the investments discussed under "Confronting 21st Century Security Challenges" were COVID-19, foreign assistance, the World Health Organization, the United Nations Population Fund, and a Global Health Security Agenda. When the summary touched briefly on the China threat and the Pacific Deterrence Initiative, it noted the importance of cybersecurity but highlighted none of the myriad investments required to compete militarily with China or defend Taiwan. Rather, the document stated that the budget included significant resources to "strengthen and defend democracies throughout the world; advance human rights; fight corruption; and counter authoritarianism."[7]

The FY23 budget proposal continues to de-emphasize defense. "The Budget Message of the President" released with the most recent request does not use the words "defense" or "national security."[8] Any matters relating to national security do not appear until halfway through the letter, and the Russian invasion of Ukraine is mentioned only as a cause of the rising prices affecting Americans. Lastly, while competition with China is mentioned, no context is provided. As of February 2022, US inflation was the highest it had been in 40 years, at 7.9 percent.[9] As inflation skyrockets and the defense budget stalls, investments essential to the readiness of our national security apparatus are being cut.[10]

Instead of investing in military capability, the budget proposes to divest $2.7 billion in systems without buying replacements. Procurement would remain essentially flat, which would be a cut under inflation. The Navy fleet would shrink as ships are retired without sufficient procurement to replace them. In just 2023 alone, the president's budget request decommissions 24 ships while only procuring eight.[11] Similarly, the request would decrease the procurement quantity for the F-35A fighter aircraft to 33 aircraft, down from the 48 requested in FY2022.[12]

Why is this a problem?

Since 2000, the DOD has spent about twice as much of its expenditures on operations and maintenance (O&M) costs as it did to procure new capabilities.[13] As platforms age, their O&M costs skyrocket, and US equipment is rapidly aging. The average aircraft in the Air Force is 31 years old, and some fleets average 60 years old.[14] The majority of the Navy's classes of ships are no longer in production. Additionally, in 2020, maintenance, refueling, and complex overhaul led to less than half the carrier fleet being available for deployments.[15]

In contrast, the Pentagon recently reported that the People's Liberation Army and People's Liberation Army Navy had amassed the largest fleet in the world, cited the acceleration of Chinese nuclear-warfare development in its annual report to Congress on military developments involving China, and called a recent test firing of a Chinese hypersonic missile "a near-Sputnik moment."[16]

Solution One. The administration should support the National Defense Strategy Commission's recommendations by providing 3–5 percent real growth for defense spending—real defense spending that results in readiness and modern military capacity and capability.[17]

A highly divisive Democrat-led Congress even acknowledges the dangerous lack of attention paid to the national security budget. The FY22 National Defense Authorization Act (NDAA) increased the DOD budget by $25 billion, or 3 percent over the requested amount. The appropriators followed suit in the FY22 Consolidated Appropriations Act by providing $743 billion for DOD, nearly $30 billion above the request.[18] The increases provided by Congress are admittedly a bit of a mixed bag since Congress has been guilty for years of diffusing defense resources to nondefense spending, but the signal that increases in defense spending are necessary is clear.

Now, with the FY23 defense budget request also falling well short of the real increases necessary, Congress will need to take the lead again. Defense will require a topline of at least $814 billion just to keep pace with inflation, under which resources should be aligned to readiness of the current force—to include incrementally integrating new capabilities into that force—and procurement of new capabilities that should be emerging from research, development, test, and evaluation investments made over the past five to 10 years.[19]

Specifically, in its 2021 report to Congress, the US-China Economic and Security Review Commission recommends Congress authorize funding and deployment of "large numbers" of anti-ship cruise and ballistic missiles in the US Indo-Pacific Command (INDOPACOM) area of responsibility.[20] In addition, the commission suggests Congress fund INDOPACOM requests for hardening US bases in the region and "robust missile defense."[21]

The US should stockpile large numbers of precision munitions in the Indo-Pacific region, the panel recommends, and support programs that enable US forces to continue fighting in the event central command and control is disrupted. Lastly, the panel recommends Congress authorize and fund INDOPACOM requests for "better and more survivable intelligence, surveillance, and reconnaissance in the East and South China Seas."[22]

The NDAA also compels a briefing on the advisability and feasibility of increasing United States defense cooperation with Taiwan: It is important we help Taiwan improve its overall readiness and acquire asymmetric capabilities most likely to make the Chinese government question its ability to take the island by force.

Congress will need to prioritize these investments as it considers required increases to the FY23 budget submitted by the administration.

Delays in Annual Appropriations and Authorizations Reduce Buying Power. Once again, the DOD operated under a continuing resolution (CR) for a large portion of the fiscal year.[23] Before enactment of the FY22 Consolidated Appropriations Act on March 15, 2022, the government operated under three successive CRs.[24] CRs essentially extend last year's funding and priorities into the new year to avoid a lapse in appropriations and government shutdown when Congress can't agree on regular annual spending. When the CRs for 2022 ended, DOD had operated under temporary funding extensions like this one for over 1,400 days during the past 12 years.[25]

CRs are expensive and damaging to national security.[26] The longer the CR, the more the damage.[27] For example, as the National Defense Industrial Association (NDIA) points out, a yearlong CR for FY22 would have meant "a $36 billion reduction from Congressional intent."[28] In this way, CRs compound the harm already done by insufficient toplines.

Secretary of Defense Lloyd Austin explained in a statement that a full-year CR for FY22 "would cause enormous, if not irreparable, damage for a wide range of bipartisan priorities." He said,

> The Department's efforts to address innovation priorities such as cyber, artificial intelligence and hypersonics programs would be slowed. . . .
>
> . . . It would misalign billions of dollars in resources in a manner inconsistent with evolving threats and the national security landscape, which would erode the U.S. military advantage relative to China, impede our ability to innovate and modernize, degrade readiness, and hurt our people and their families. And it would offer comfort to our enemies, disquiet to our allies, and unnecessary stress to our workforce.[29]

Comptroller Michael J. McCord reiterated during the briefing on President Biden's FY23 defense budget, "We were unable to move out as quickly as we would have liked to in F.Y.'23 because we were under a continuing resolution for months and months and months, unable to undertake new activities."[30]

The under secretary for research and engineering likened the CR to a self-inflicted wound, saying it would put the US further behind its adversaries.[31]

During the December 2, 2021, floor debate on the CR, members of Congress repeatedly conveyed the importance of full-year funding and stated that passing annual appropriations is their "most basic constitutional responsibility."[32] Rep. Rosa DeLauro (D-CT) said, "Continuing resolutions are not the way to govern. They are a short-term patch that leaves the American people behind." Rep. Ken Calvert (R-CA) said,

> The most basic responsibility of this Congress is to fund the government, to ensure seniors and veterans receive their earned benefits on time. . . .
>
> We cannot continue to cripple our national security apparatus with CRs year after year. It is not only wasteful—this CR is going to cost the Department of Defense about $1.7 billion per month for nothing—but it allows our adversaries to continue gaining while we remain stagnant.

Rep. David Price (D-NC) said, "I also urge my Republican colleagues to meet Congress' most basic constitutional responsibility of funding our government and directing investments for the future by coming to the table." Rep. Lucille Roybal-Allard (D-CA) suggested "enacting a year-long CR . . . would effectively wash our hands of our constitutional duty." Sen. Patrick Leahy (D-VT) said,

> In fact, the only thing worse than running the government under a continuing resolution, a CR, is a government shutdown. . . .
>
> . . . A full-year CR would not only reduce defense spending instead of increasing it, it would reduce it by $37 billion compared to the levels set forth in the NDAA that they voted for unanimously.

Industry has also conveyed the destructive nature of CRs through letters that members included in the congressional record. The Aerospace Industries Association said,

Both "new starts" and rate increases [which are prohibited under the CR] are critical for our national defense because our defense posture and threats are always evolving. . . .

. . . We count on stable, reliable and adequate funding to support the critical capabilities that we provide for all Americans.

The NDIA said,

We cannot stress enough the importance of the defense appropriations bill to our national security and to a healthy defense industrial base. The limbo caused under CRs wastes precious time and money our nation cannot recover. . . . Our nation's competitors face no similar challenges putting us at a competitive disadvantage, particularly with emerging technologies, and place our supply chains at increasing risk, something we cannot afford after the nearly two years of pandemic impacts. . . .

. . . The ultimate price of this is paid by our warfighters who will lose out on innovations and new capabilities not delivered.

Despite clear comments on the cumulative, damaging nature of CRs to national security, the industrial base, uniform personnel, military competitiveness, and local communities across the country and the unambiguous acknowledgment of enacting annual appropriations as the primary constitutional responsibility of Congress, most of the recent debate in Congress was spent by its members blaming each other for not getting the job done.

Meanwhile, time ticks by, and the lack of sufficient and appropriately placed resources further inhibits military capability necessary to carry out the nation's strategy or defend Taiwan.[33]

Solution Two. Congress must start taking its responsibility to pass annual appropriations on time seriously instead of relying on CRs almost every fiscal year.[34] The administration and Congress should get together early and often until a budget agreement is reached that allows appropriators to act on the president's budget submission with established allocations before the end of the fiscal year.

Nondefense Spending in the Defense Budget Continues to Grow. At the same time defense budget requests are stagnant, definitions are expanded, and resources and management attention are diverted to nondefense priorities.

Public perception is that the DOD budget is growing exponentially and that it only pays for military capabilities and operations spending. This is misleading. The defense budget has included funding for programs and activities that do nothing to advance military capability or increase national security for years.

The Biden administration is redefining what is included in "national security," further increasing the amount of nondefense spending in the defense budget, compounding the problems associated with the declining defense topline and unreliable funding, and diffusing the US ability to successfully defend Taiwan.

Budget documents note that "at home, the Department will invest in American manufacturing, military families, and national disaster and pandemic response infrastructure, ensuring the Department's positive impacts are felt across America as we work together to build back better."[35] This ignores that defense spending has long been recognized as an economic engine, an engine that should focus on building warfighting capability and not be an easy button for any and all challenges the nation faces.

The secretary of defense's concept of "integrated deterrence," as foundational to the revised National Defense Strategy, furthers the subservience of hard power and military capability, which should be his primary function in backing foreign policy.[36] While the military can and should support diplomacy, and vice versa, there is no replacement for the United States retaining superior military systems, as hard power gives credibility to diplomatic efforts. The recent US diplomatic approach of "surrender first, then negotiate" will result in severe consequences if our military power continues to fall in resourcing priority.

Every time a new mission is assigned to the DOD, it must manage, plan, execute, assess, and report on the activity. This draws personnel, management focus, and resources—beyond those appropriated for the function—away from what should be its core mission: preparing for, fighting, and winning America's wars.

For example, the House Appropriations Committee expressed concern that the "nation lacks medical surge capacity beyond what is currently available" and added $14 million to the budget for the DOD to "initiate investment in a joint civilian-military modular surge facility."[37] While this may be a federal priority, is it really something that the DOD should lead?

Congress annually adds well over $1 billion to the defense budget for Congressionally Directed Medical Research Programs, many of which duplicate programs managed by the National Institutes of Health. In fact, the National Institutes of Health budget in 2021 was more than $275 billion, within which $21.5 billion was reserved for conditions and diseases the DOD also funded.[38]

The DOD spends more on the Defense Health Program than it does on new ships.[39] It spends almost $10 billion more on Medicare than on new tactical vehicles.[40] It spends more on environmental restoration and running schools than on microelectronics and space launch combined.[41]

Congress added more than $480 million to the environmental restoration accounts in FY22 plus funding to address drinking-water contamination while acknowledging there is currently no plan for the use of such funds.[42]

Solution Three. We must redefine national security, and therefore what belongs in the DOD budget, to focus on military capability. Removing lower-priority expenses or transitioning their funding to another more appropriate department or agency will make room in the budget for military readiness, modernization, and operations, including those essential to Taiwan efforts.

The DOD is used as an easy button to solve problems that are not part of its core mission and function. Some of these activities may seem small in the scheme of the overall budget, and many are worthy efforts; however, they artificially inflate the defense budget and distract from true defense priorities. For example, the DOD runs excellent schools, but should funding for this be considered "defense" in budget discussions? And should the DOD maintain an infrastructure for management and oversight of this activity, thereby pulling attention from its primary purpose and from the mission only the DOD can carry out?

This same strain occurs with energy, environmental, and medical priorities. The other federal agencies with much more expertise in these respective areas should be taking the lead on these efforts. Pushing these responsibilities on the DOD results in a misleading sense of what the nation is spending for its security and diffuses attention from military capabilities necessary to compete with China and defend Taiwan if called on to do so.

Institutional and Statutory Rules and Processes Hinder Modern Capabilities. The United States must compete with China and any other adversary that threatens US national security. With the small wiggle room the DOD has left after the obstacles discussed earlier have wreaked havoc on its budget, the department must spend its funding as economically as possible. Barriers to doing so come in many forms, including incentive structures that support bureaucracy and risk aversion over innovation, agility, and speed; legacy and diverse business systems that don't communicate; and general stagnation and opposition to creative change.

The National Security Commission on Artificial Intelligence said it well: "Unless the requirements, budgeting, and acquisition processes are aligned to permit faster and more targeted execution, the U.S. will fail to stay ahead of potential adversaries."[43]

The ability to integrate and operationalize new technologies will likely determine success on the future battlefield. While the DOD and the US government remain significant investors in research and development (R&D), defense spending made up about 75 percent of the R&D funding spent by the government in 1960.[44] In FY21, the DOD retained only 41.4 percent of federal R&D, forcing the DOD to use commercial technologies to retain its military edge.[45]

Unfortunately, technology companies find it difficult to work with the DOD. A recent NDIA letter noted that

> the tomes of regulations, burdensome business requirements, sometimes Kafkaesque contracting and oversight procedures, and compressed margins have combined to drive businesses out of the defense sector with a net outflow of well over 10,000 companies since 2011 and . . . a halving of new entrants to the sector between fiscal 2019 and fiscal 2020 alone.[46]

Many startup firms, with technology solutions ideal for defense adoption, either decline to enter or quickly exit the federal market. This is driven by different reasons, but long lead times for resourcing new requirements play a key role. The DOD needs to maintain access to these cutting-edge businesses to ensure that the warfighting capabilities it delivers are and remain relevant.

Transforming future concepts of operations into actionable programming guidance will require a new construct that abandons the legacy life-cycle funding model in which a technology slowly moves from research, development, test, and evaluation to procurement and concludes with O&M. Instead, the budgeting process needs to support timely movements of funding to capture technology solutions and move them quickly from concept to a fielded capability. This approach also forces a reevaluation of how the DOD conducts oversight and management.[47]

Solution Four. At a time when political consensus on anything can be hard to reach, there is general agreement that the United States military must modernize to fend off a rising China and an aggressive Russia and meet other national security needs. The seemingly immense changes necessary to modernize how the DOD operates can be made more manageable by adopting an acquisition approach built around evolutionary innovation. This will require leadership, cultural change, and funding lines that are flexible and responsive to rapid iterative development, testing, and fielding.

Evolutionary innovation follows a simple formula: Experiment with diverse options, select the most promising candidates, and scale the results. Currently, budget and acquisition processes estimate the life-cycle cost of a system upfront. This model was intended to foster careful consideration of important decisions and stabilize planning.

It is not as effective today. To seize the opportunities of an evolutionary approach to modernization, the Pentagon needs three things.

First, it needs stable lines of funding that can accommodate the open-ended nature of an evolutionary development. The department's newly proposed Rapid Defense Experimentation Reserve is a step in the right direction.[48] To do better than previous attempts, it would need to be structured to provide current-year funding for any type of appropriation aligned with joint and combatant command needs.

Second, it needs business systems that can track metrics for information-age military capability to keep up with the speed of continuous development and enable effective oversight. The Advancing Analytics capability, initially developed to support the department's full financial statement audit, could meet this need when fully implemented.[49]

Third, it needs congressional support to modernize the Planning, Programming, Budgeting, and Execution process to match acquisition reforms made over the past decade with agile, responsive, and transparent funding not tied to a specific stage in development or fiscal year. The recently enacted NDAA provision that requires a commission to look at this issue, if structured correctly, should help shed light on what works, what does not work, and specifically what changes will have the most positive impact.

Conclusion

Any planning for the defense of Taiwan must fix the four above barriers to succeed. Proper budgeting is essential in the success of all US military priorities. The defense budget must account for inflation, which increases the cost of must-pay bills, and it must support the modernization necessary to remain competitive.

Congress should prioritize and hold itself accountable for executing its fundamental constitutional responsibility of passing annual appropriations bills. We can't spend good intentions or political blame on defense priorities.

Defense should remain focused on its primary and core function: deterring, preparing for, and winning America's wars. Nondefense spending should be removed from the defense budget to make clear what the nation is really spending for its security and to support federal priorities in other agencies that have corresponding missions.

And finally, the department and Congress should shake off the chains of the past in the way they plan, program, budget, and execute the sustainment and advancement of the world's best fighting force.

With these four barriers solved, the United States exponentially increases its ability to succeed in all future endeavors, including defending Taiwan.

Notes

1. Taiwan Relations Act, H.R. 2479, 96th Cong., 1st sess. (1979), https://www.congress.gov/bill/96th-congress/house-bill/2479.

2. John Bolton and Derik R. Zitelman, "Why Taiwan Matters to the United States," *Diplomat*, August 23, 2021, https://thediplomat.com/2021/08/why-taiwan-matters-to-the-united-states.

3. US-China Economic and Security Review Commission, *2021 Report to Congress of the U.S.-China Economic and Security Review Commission*, November 2021, https://www.uscc.gov/sites/default/files/2021-11/2021_Annual_Report_to_Congress.pdf.

4. Michael Beckley and Hal Brands, "Competition with China Could Be Short and Sharp," *Foreign Affairs*, December 17, 2020, https://www.foreignaffairs.com/articles/united-states/2020-12-17/competition-china-could-be-short-and-sharp; and Mallory Shelbourne, "Davidson: China Could Try to Take Control of Taiwan in 'Next Six Years,'" USNI News, March 9, 2021, https://news.usni.org/2021/03/09/davidson-china-could-try-to-take-control-of-taiwan-in-next-six-years.

5. Elaine McCusker, "Defense Is Not a Priority for the Biden Administration," AEIdeas, May 28, 2021, https://www.aei.org/foreign-and-defense-policy/defense-is-not-a-priority-for-the-biden-administration; and Office of Management and Budget, "Summary of the President's Discretionary Funding Request," April 9, 2021, https://www.whitehouse.gov/wp-content/uploads/2021/04/FY2022-Discretionary-Request.pdf.

6. Office of Management and Budget, "Office of Management and Budget Releases the President's Fiscal Year 2022 Discretionary Funding Request," press release, April 9, 2021, https://www.whitehouse.gov/wp-content/uploads/2021/04/FY2022-Discretionary-Request-Press-Release.pdf.

7. Office of Management and Budget, "Budget of the U.S. Government: Fiscal Year 2022," 23, https://www.whitehouse.gov/wp-content/uploads/2021/05/budget_fy22.pdf.

8. Office of Management and Budget, "Budget of the U.S. Government: Fiscal Year 2023," March 2022, https://www.whitehouse.gov/wp-content/uploads/2022/03/budget_fy2023.pdf.

9. US Bureau of Labor Statistics, "Consumer Prices for Food up 7.9 Percent for Year Ended February 2022," March 15, 2022, https://www.bls.gov/opub/ted/2022/consumer-prices-for-food-up-7-9-percent-for-year-ended-february-2022.htm.

10. John G. Ferrari, "Surviving the Inflation Anaconda: Congress Must Invest More in Defense," Breaking Defense, July 26, 2021, https://breakingdefense.com/2021/07/surviving-the-inflation-anaconda-congress-must-invest-more-in-defense.

11. Secretary of the Navy, "Department of the Navy FY 2023 President's Budget" (PowerPoint presentation, March 28, 2022), https://www.secnav.navy.mil/fmc/fmb/Documents/23pres/DON_Press_Brief.pdf; and Justin Katz, "Navy's Shipbuilding Request May Be 'Violation of Law,' Inhofe Warns," Breaking Defense, March 29, 2022, https://breakingdefense.com/2022/03/navys-shipbuilding-request-may-be-violation-of-law-inhofe-warns.

12. Gina Ortiz Jones and James Peccia, "Department of the Air Force FY 2023 Budget Overview" (PowerPoint presentation, US Air Force and US Space Force, March 18, 2022), https://www.saffm.hq.af.mil/Portals/84/documents/FY23/SUPPORT_/FY23%

20PB%20Rollout%20Brief_FINAL_wout_%20Scriptv5%2029%20Mar_22_1318.pdf.

13. Mackenzie Eaglen, *The 2020s Tri-Service Modernization Crunch*, American Enterprise Institute, March 2021, https://www.aei.org/wp-content/uploads/2021/03/The-2020s-Tri-Service-Modernization-Crunch-1.pdf.

14. Dakota L. Wood, ed., *2022 Index of U.S. Military Strength*, Heritage Foundation, 2022, https://www.heritage.org/sites/default/files/2021-09/a2022_IndexOfUSMilitary Strength.pdf.

15. Eaglen, *The 2020s Tri-Service Modernization Crunch*.

16. US Department of Defense, Office of the Secretary of Defense, *Military and Security Developments Involving the People's Republic of China*, 2021, https://media.defense.gov/2021/Nov/03/2002885874/-1/-1/0/2021-CMPR-FINAL.PDF; and David E. Sanger and William J. Broad, "China's Weapon Tests Close to a 'Sputnik Moment,' U.S. General Says," *New York Times*, October 27, 2021, https://www.nytimes.com/2021/10/27/us/politics/china-hypersonic-missile.html.

17. US Institute of Peace, *Providing for the Common Defense: The Assessment and Recommendations of the National Defense Strategy Commission*, November 13, 2018, https://www.usip.org/sites/default/files/2018-11/providing-for-the-common-defense.pdf.

18. US Department of Defense, Office of the Under Secretary of Defense (Comptroller)/Chief Financial Officer, *Defense Budget Overview*, May 2021, https://comptroller.defense.gov/Portals/45/Documents/defbudget/FY2022/FY2022_Budget_Request_Overview_Book.pdf.

19. John G. Ferrari and Elaine McCusker, "The Ukraine Invasion Shows Why America Needs to Get Its Defense Budget in Order," Breaking Defense, March 2, 2022, https://breakingdefense.com/2022/03/the-ukraine-invasion-shows-why-america-needs-to-get-its-defense-budget-in-order.

20. US-China Economic and Security Review Commission, *2021 Report to Congress of the U.S.-China Economic and Security Review Commission*.

21. US-China Economic and Security Review Commission, *2021 Report to Congress of the U.S.-China Economic and Security Review Commission*, 22.

22. US-China Economic and Security Review Commission, *2021 Report to Congress of the U.S.-China Economic and Security Review Commission*, 22.

23. Further Extending Government Funding Act, Pub. L. No. 117-70, https://www.congress.gov/117/plaws/publ70/PLAW-117publ70.pdf.

24. US Senate Committee on Appropriations, "FY22 Agreement Reached, Omnibus Appropriations Legislation Filed," press release, March 9, 2022, https://www.appropriations.senate.gov/news/y22-agreement-reached-omnibus-appropriations-legislation-filed.

25. Congressional Research Service, "Appropriations Status Tables: FY2021," https://crsreports.congress.gov/AppropriationsStatusTable?id=2021.

26. Elaine McCusker, "Continuing Resolutions Hurt National Security and Imperil Our Future," *Hill*, October 15, 2020, https://thehill.com/opinion/finance/521212-continuing-resolutions-hurt-national-security-and-imperil-our-future; and Elaine McCusker and Emily Coletta, "GAO's Review of the Impact of Continuing Resolutions Falls Short," *Hill*, September 27, 2021, https://thehill.com/opinion/finance/574013-gaos-review-of-the-impact-of-continuing-resolutions-falls-short.

27. Mackenzie Eaglen, "Congress' Spending Freeze Puts a Deep Chill on US Military Modernization," 19FortyFive.com, December 7, 2021, https://www.19fortyfive.com/2021/12/congress-spending-freeze-puts-a-deep-chill-on-us-military-modernization.

28. National Defense Industrial Association, *Risks to National Security: A Full-Year Continuing Resolution for 2022*, January 2022, 7, https://www.ndia.org/-/media/sites/policy-issues/continuing-resolution/cr_white_paper-3.pdf.

29. US Department of Defense, "Statement by Secretary of Defense Lloyd J. Austin III on the Impact of a Full-Year Continuing Resolution," press release, December 6, 2021, https://www.defense.gov/News/Releases/Release/Article/2862641/statement-by-secretary-of-defense-lloyd-j-austin-iii-on-the-impact-of-a-full-ye.

30. US Department of Defense, "Comptroller Michael J. McCord and Vice Adm. Ron Boxall Hold a News Briefing on President Biden's Fiscal 2023 Defense Budget," press release, March 28, 2022, https://www.defense.gov/News/Transcripts/Transcript/Article/2980711/comptroller-michael-j-mccord-and-vice-adm-ron-boxall-hold-a-news-briefing-on-pr.

31. Jaspreet Gill, "Continuing Resolution May Delay DOD's Rapid Technology Experimentation Plans," Inside Defense, December 6, 2021, https://insidedefense.com/daily-news/continuing-resolution-may-delay-dods-rapid-technology-experimentation-plans.

32. 167 Cong. Rec. H6875 (Dec. 2, 2021), https://www.congress.gov/117/crec/2021/12/02/167/208/CREC-2021-12-02.pdf.

33. Mackenzie Eaglen, "These Key Programs Face Real Delays from Continuing Resolution," Breaking Defense, October 27, 2021, https://breakingdefense.com/2021/10/these-key-programs-face-real-delays-from-continuing-resolution.

34. McCusker, "Continuing Resolutions Hurt National Security and Imperil Our Future."

35. US Department of Defense, Office of the Under Secretary of Defense (Comptroller)/Chief Financial Officer, *Defense Budget Overview*.

36. Thomas Spoehr, "Bad Idea: Relying on 'Integrated Deterrence' Instead of Building Sufficient U.S. Military Power," Center for Strategic and International Studies, December 3, 2021, https://defense360.csis.org/bad-idea-relying-on-integrated-deterrence-instead-of-building-sufficient-u-s-military-power.

37. Department of Defense Appropriations Bill, H. Rept. 117-88, 117th Cong., 1st sess., July 15, 2021, https://www.congress.gov/congressional-report/117th-congress/house-report/88/1?overview=closed.

38. National Institutes of Health, "Estimates of Funding for Various Research, Condition, and Disease Categories (RCDC)," https://report.nih.gov/funding/categorical-spending#.

39. US Department of Defense, Office of the Under Secretary of Defense (Comptroller)/Chief Financial Officer, *Defense Budget Overview*.

40. US Department of Defense, Office of the Under Secretary of Defense (Comptroller)/Chief Financial Officer, *Defense Budget Overview*; and US Department of Defense, Office of the Under Secretary of Defense (Comptroller)/Chief Financial Officer, *Program Acquisition Cost by Weapon System*, May 2021, https://comptroller.defense.gov/Portals/45/Documents/defbudget/FY2022/FY2022_Weapons.pdf.

41. US Department of Defense, Office of the Under Secretary of Defense (Comptroller)/Chief Financial Officer, *Defense Budget Overview*.

42. US House of Representatives Document Repository, "Division C—Department of Defense Appropriations Act, 2022," https://docs.house.gov/billsthisweek/20220307/BILLS-117RCP35-JES-DIVISION-C_Part1.pdf.

43. Eric Schmidt et al., *Final Report: National Security Commission on Artificial Intelligence*, 302, https://www.nscai.gov/wp-content/uploads/2021/03/Full-Report-Digital-1.pdf.

44. Aerospace Research Center, *Federal R&D Resources 1960–1973: Trends in Allocations*, May 1973, https://www.aia-aerospace.org/wp-content/uploads/2016/06/FEDERAL-RD-RESOURCES-1960-1973.pdf.

45. John F. Sargent Jr., *Federal Research and Development (R&D) Funding: FY2021*, Congressional Research Service, December 17, 2020, https://sgp.fas.org/crs/misc/R46341.pdf.

46. 167 Cong. Rec. H6875 (Dec. 2, 2021).

47. Day One Project, "Next-Generation Defense Budgeting Project," https://www.dayoneproject.org/defense-budget; and Defense Acquisition University, "Planning, Programming, Budgeting & Execution Process (PPBE)," https://www.dau.edu/acquipedia/pages/ArticleContent.aspx?itemid=154.

48. Sydney J. Freedberg Jr., "Hicks Seeks to Unify Service Experiments with New 'Raider' Fund," Breaking Defense, June 21, 2021, https://breakingdefense.com/2021/06/hicks-seeks-to-unify-service-experiments-with-new-raider-fund.

49. Elaine McCusker, "What Should You Know About the Defense Audit?," American Enterprise Institute, April 28, 2021, https://www.aei.org/research-products/report/what-should-you-know-about-the-defense-audit.

Conventional Deterrence and Taiwan's Independence: Necessary Investments

MACKENZIE EAGLEN AND JOHN G. FERRARI

> The greatest danger the United States and our allies face in the region is the erosion of conventional deterrence vis-à-vis the People's Republic of China.
>
> —Adm. Philip Davidson (ret.), US Navy commander, US Indo-Pacific Command, March 2021[1]

The United States no longer possesses the same military advantages over China in the Indo-Pacific region that it has enjoyed since the China-initiated Open Door policies in 1899. The Department of Defense's (DOD) 2020 and 2021 China military power reports have assessed just how rapidly the changes in Chinese military stature have been since the early 2000s.[2] These advances are a product of China's substantial investments in modernizing and expanding its armed forces, while the United States has focused on fielding the capabilities and capacity required for its wars in the Middle East and underfunded or delayed conventional defense modernization programs.[3]

Today, the Chinese Communist Party (CCP) is pushing a more aggressive and expansionist regional agenda in the western Pacific, particularly toward Taiwan, and the US military is struggling to field the conventional forces required to mount a forward defense in the theater—one capable of effectively deterring further Chinese aggression.[4] If China expects to achieve its geopolitical goals with a conventional attack on Taiwan at low cost because US forces will not be able to respond rapidly and effectively, the chances of China using its military to achieve these goals will only increase. Most wargames and Taiwan-crisis simulations today indicate China would successfully capture the island.

Importantly, the US military has not been completely idle in preparing for a potential invasion of Taiwan, even if it has not matched China's own military modernization and expansion efforts. In October 2021, Taiwanese leadership acknowledged for the first time the presence of US Special Operations Forces and Marines stationed on the island to train components of the Taiwanese military.[5] Still, the US military's capacity and capabilities must be expanded and improved simultaneously with continuing efforts to assist Taiwan as Taipei seeks to improve its own defenses.

Key solutions could decrease China's advantage, shoring up the strength of US conventional deterrence and improving the United States' ability to defend Taiwan against People's Liberation Army (PLA) forces. Core recommendations include:

1. Securing US Air Force air superiority across legacy and modernized systems, such as hypersonic missiles;

2. Increasing Army troop and funding levels, protecting both from budget sacrifices for the other services;

3. Expanding the US naval fleet and domestic production capacity; and

4. Ensuring Joint Force investments in regional posturing, air and missile defense, and intelligence, surveillance, and reconnaissance (ISR) are bolstered across services.

In June 2021, when outlining potential discrete moves of CCP aggression against Taiwan or in the East and South China Seas more broadly, Adm. Gary Roughead (ret.) explained that China's

> seizure of offshore islands, a blockade (complete cut off) of Taiwan or quarantine (denying the entry of commodities), missile strikes on the island, and ultimately a full-on invasion must be addressed. But more consideration must be given to more extensive and aggressive "grey zone operations," that activity between peace and war.[6]

In short, the advantages of the US military across each prominent Taiwan contingency are deteriorating.

This chapter focuses on potential US military investments in conventional capabilities that would provide an edge in a range of Taiwan deterrence and conflict scenarios. It contextualizes the evolving conventional Sino-American military balance and assesses capability gaps across the armed forces individually and Joint Force operations, listing key investments to bolster the services' and Taiwan's own conventional capabilities for the defense of the island.

Sino-American Military Balance

The Obama, Trump, and now Biden administrations have signaled a rebalance to Asia, but in bipartisan fashion, success has been minimal at best. America's regional posture in the Indo-Pacific remained relatively stagnant through the 2010s, partly as a result of inertia, competing priorities, and mismatched or insufficient defense investments. This stagnation has had clear consequences for the balance of conventional military power between the United States and China.[7]

Secretary of Defense Lloyd Austin III released high-level findings from the classified *Global Force Posture Review* in late 2021, emphasizing that posture requirements would be reduced in other theaters to support warfighting readiness and increased US military activities in the Indo-Pacific. Congress was generally unimpressed by the review's actual recommendations. One staffer familiar with the findings critiqued them for reflecting "no decisions, no changes, no sense of urgency, no creative thinking."[8] Pentagon officials also acknowledged that few shifts were made in the report, with one saying,

> There was a sense at the outset that there was a potential for some major force posture changes. . . . Then, as we got deeper and deeper into the work, we realized in aggregate that the force posture around the world was about right.[9]

While some analysts have cautioned that more shifts are likely in the future, particularly after the release of the 2022 National Defense and

Security Strategies, preliminary signs do not suggest the Biden administration's Pentagon is prepared for ambitious change.

Despite underwhelming progress from successive presidential administrations, there are plenty of road maps, frameworks, and defense programs that would bolster the US military's position in the Indo-Pacific. For the purposes of this chapter, the US military's Indo-Pacific posture requirements today and in the future are assessed in relation to US forces' ability to prevent China from capturing Taiwan or interfering with essential US trade and economic activity with the island.

Rather than discuss the multitude of deterrence strategies possible, this chapter remains acutely focused on direct investments that would allow US forces to succeed across a variety of scenarios. For the recommendations included, various cost estimates are based on fiscal year (FY) 2022 defense budget documents and can be found in the Defense Futures Simulator budget analysis software, developed by the American Enterprise Institute, the Center for Strategic and International Studies, and War on the Rocks.[10]

US Capability Gaps and Key Investments

Across the US Armed Forces and Joint Force, there are critical gaps in capability and crucial opportunities for investments that can shore up diminishing combat power.

Department of the Air Force. From hypersonic missile development to fighter distance capabilities, the US Air Force has various gaps to close and systems to maintain as new technologies progress.

Capability Gaps. US Air Force preparation to respond to a possible Chinese invasion of Taiwan is hampered by three factors: (1) ongoing congressional skepticism of hypersonic missiles, (2) the service's inability to move on from legacy programs, and (3) the "tyranny of distance" represented by the Pacific's size, which hampers the service's ability to be part of the fight.

For the first factor: At the time of writing, the House Appropriations Committee set a $44 million target cut from the Air Force's hypersonic missile program for FY22.[11] While these missiles are mostly still in development and testing, they are one of the most significant capability gaps the US faces in this arena, as China has also been testing its own advanced hypersonic capabilities. A scenario in which each side engages with hypersonic missiles is within reason in the foreseeable future; China has tested nuclear-capable hypersonic missiles that threaten Taiwan, US basing, and continental security.

The second problem, the maintenance of legacy platforms depleting funding allocations for modernization programs, is far from new. The Air Force has asked Congress to divest from the air- and ground-support purposed A-10 Warthog, F-15C/D and F-16C/D fighters, and KC-10 refueling tankers.[12] Domestic considerations occasionally complicate such requests; members of Congress are often hesitant to shift funding from programs based or built in their home states or trade existing platforms for those in development.

Undoubtedly, funding outdated and aging programs is preventing the service from investing in new aircraft and modernization. The Air Force wants to use funds freed from divestment to support its hypersonic missile programs and other long-range weapons.[13] The service also must grapple with how the F-35 program—the centerpiece of its modernization effort—will overcome the long distances in the Pacific to be relevant. So far, the shift of regional focus has not been met with a quick shift in investment to match changing priorities, which will undoubtedly make defending Taiwan more difficult.

Key Investments. In 2018 and 2019 Air Force wargames, the service lost disastrously in the South China Sea and Taiwan scenarios respectively.[14] In a late 2020 wargame, the Air Force reportedly successfully defeated a Chinese invasion of Taiwan by "relying on drones acting as a sensing grid, an advanced sixth-generation fighter jet . . . [and] cargo planes dropping pallets of guided munitions and other novel technologies yet unseen on the modern battlefield."[15] While the wargame victory reportedly depended on some technologies not in the current budget plan, the service made other decisions that, if implemented, could improve Air Force relevance in securing air superiority at the outset of a Taiwan crisis.

In the wargame, the Air Force reportedly disaggregated its command-and-control structure by making "investments to remote airfields across the Pacific region—fortifying and lengthening runways as well as pre-positioning repair equipment and fuel."[16] In addition to key posture adjustments, the Air Force should prioritize investments in fifth- and sixth-generation fighters, a mix of drones for a variety of purposes—including serving as long-range communications nodes, using bombers to penetrate contested air space, employing airlift assets in offensive roles, and securing aerial refueling to elongate fighter distance capability in the face of lengthy flight paths in a Taiwan conflict. The Air Force should also allocate funds above the current budget plan to the Next Generation Air Dominance fighter and its associated systems to accelerate the fielding of the program, and it should extend the service lives of the F-22s through the 2030s.[17]

While investing in new, relatively low-cost, and comparatively attritable drones such as the XQ-58A Valkyrie is important, the service should not prematurely cut legacy platforms when the assets can be used for new mission sets. Although the MQ-9 traditionally operated in uncontested battle spaces in the Middle East, with technological adjustments, the platform can support maritime and littoral domain awareness operations in the Pacific.[18] Finally, the service should accelerate investment in the new and still-developing B-21 Raider stealth bomber and replace its older tanker fleets.

Department of the Army. Rather than serve as the "bill payer" for the armed services, the Army could play various potential key roles in Taiwan's defense that are going underfunded and often overlooked.

Capability Gaps. The Army has been preparing for future budget cuts more than any other service has. According to Army Chief of Staff Gen. James McConville, without significant budget increases, the Army will be unable to increase its end strength.[19] Declining end strength will be met with declining influence and deterrence, and in the event of a conflict anywhere—such as the ongoing war in Ukraine—the United States cannot risk destabilization as a result of self-inflicted blows in force size and presence across the globe.

While some speculate the Army could play a smaller role in the defense of Taiwan than the other services would, it may be required to deploy troops to Taiwan to either deter or defend against Chinese troops.[20] In a late 2021 discussion regarding the Army's role in countering China, Secretary of the Army Christine Wormuth cited long-range precision fires as perhaps the most important of these but also emphasized that the service must work to answer many difficult questions about its role in a conflict with China, whether related to Taiwan or not.[21]

A scenario of failed deterrence followed by the United States being called on and deciding to restore Taiwan's territorial integrity, however, is largely under-discussed and particularly poignant for those who debate the US Army's future role in the Pacific; observers warn "these [restorative] roles are massive shifts for an insurgency-honed force, as well as expensive, bloody, and politically fraught."[22] Moreover, one of the biggest problems the Army faces is the pressure to become the bill payer for Navy and Air Force costs as the military shifts toward the Indo-Pacific.[23]

Secretary Wormuth detailed five key tasks for the Army, should a conflict begin.

1. The Army must establish, build up, secure, and protect staging areas and joint operating bases in-theater with integrated air and missile defense.

2. The Army must sustain the Joint Force with logistical support.

3. The Army must provide command and control at multiple operational levels.

4. The Army must provide ground-based, long-range fires as part of the Joint Force's strike capabilities.

5. If required, the Army should be ready to counterattack using maneuver forces such as infantry, Stryker elements, and combat aviation brigades.[24]

Key Investments. When discussing the role of US land power in response to a Taiwan contingency, it is helpful to consider the responsibilities of US forces before and after a conflict starts. Before an increase in hostilities between China and the United States over the independence of the island, the currently minimal footprint of US troops on Taiwan itself could be increased.[25]

The DOD could also choose to discretely or overtly conduct more security force assistance missions with Taiwan by means of the Army's 5th Security Force Assistance Brigade or dedicate two security force assistance brigades to the Indo-Pacific region, which includes raising and maintaining another brigade for the region over the next five years.[26] Recommendations to permanently station a full armored brigade combat team on Taiwan, however, would likely spell the end of US strategic ambiguity toward the island.[27]

Other frameworks short of a substantial land presence might involve dispersing smaller contingents of ground forces at key locations around the island, preserving Taiwan's ability to communicate in the event of an invasion. Further, independent from platform investments, personnel policies could support the development of critical language skills in the US military to support closer cooperation, if required in the future. At a minimum, the Army should resist end-strength reductions to its maneuver forces. More ambitiously and with more funding, the service could accelerate the fielding of new equipment, including, for example, investments in the future helicopter programs Future Attack Reconnaissance Aircraft and Future Long-Range Assault Aircraft.

Department of the Navy. Falling ship totals and maintenance declines call for bolstered support of the service and its procurement of naval and marine platforms, especially as China's navy breaks records in size and capability.

Capability Gaps. The United States' global advantage in anti-surface warfare has declined precipitously since 2015, negatively affecting the Taiwan scenario with China.[28] The Navy's 30-year shipbuilding plan released in 2020 acknowledges China's substantial improvements in naval capabilities, which have far surpassed US ship counts. Just two months before the release of the 30-year plan, the Navy acknowledged its aging surface fleet was becoming increasingly expensive and difficult to maintain.[29] The Aegis combat system's effectiveness is declining despite substantial upgrades to the systems. Hull lives are expiring across the fleet (perhaps most notably on cruisers), and maintenance standards are declining, which have all contributed to this problem.

The Navy's 500-ship-by-2045 mark has been met with some skepticism, though mostly for financial reasons. According to the Congressional Budget Office, meeting the deadlines in the plan would require an additional $20 billion in shipbuilding funds annually, with sustainment and personnel costs exceeding $300 billion.[30] With such severe conflicts between planning and budgeting, reversing course on China's increasing naval advantage in the Taiwan Strait seems like a distant possibility.

Key Investments. The US military should prioritize arresting the US Navy fleet's decline with targeted investments in platforms that would increase US undersea superiority, support more distributed operations, secure logistics, and procure more salvage-and-rescue ships that would be key in a conflict.[31]

The Navy could begin by buying one more amphibious transport docks (i.e., LPD Flight II) per year, to carry Marines to more remote operational areas and support larger amphibious operations. Of note, in a study on the future Navy fleet conducted in 2020, the Hudson Institute also recommended developing a light amphibious warship to support more littoral operations. The Navy could maximize production of the new Constellation-class frigate, buying nine ships above the current program of record over the next five years.

The service could also increase its production of Virginia-class attack submarines to three per year instead of two. Efforts such as the Navy's full spectrum undersea warfare project merit support, especially with its emphasis on subsea and seabed warfare technologies, key to enabling future undersea weapons systems. An additional six Navajo-class (T-ATs) salvage-and-rescue ships would markedly improve the fleet's ability to recover from damage sustained in a conflict.

Increasing the planned procurement of John Lewis–class oilers by six over the next five years will also advance the endurance and range of the Navy's existing ships, a crucial investment as the fleet operates with more regularity in the Indo-Pacific.[32] Overall, increased shipbuilding will prove exceedingly difficult without substantial concurrent investment in US shipyards to sustain a larger fleet. Recent efforts to this end in Congress include the introduction of the Supplying Help to Infrastructure in Ports, Yards, and America's Repair Docks (SHIPYARD) Act of 2021, which seeks to improve the infrastructure of public yards.[33]

The Navy should also think creatively about how it conducts a variety of mission sets. While SSN-class submarines and surface combatants are generally responsible for anti-submarine warfare, for example, this platform-intensive approach would be difficult to scale during a Taiwan contingency. Hudson Institute research in October 2020 recommended using torpedoes or depth bombs to suppress an adversary's submarine fleet, with investments in alternatives such as the Navy's new Very Lightweight Torpedo and its offensive version, the compact rapid attack weapon.[34]

Another investment route might involve increasing US procurement of maritime mines—and encouraging Taiwan to do the same—to be used as anti-surface ship or anti-submarine subsurface weapons. The US naval mining capability currently includes the Quickstrike family of mines, the MK 67 submarine-launched mobile mine, the MK 68 clandestine delivered mine, and the Hammerhead encapsulated effector.[35]

At a higher level, the Marine Corps's new "Stand-In Forces" warfighting concept will specifically enable the Marines to field and maintain the capabilities required to begin countering aggression below the level of armed conflict. For example, Stand-In Forces may be able to prevent Chinese militia from antagonizing vessels passing through the South China Sea—without the involvement of more-heavily armed US warships.[36]

The Navy would be well served by also investing in electronic warfare systems, the Rolling Airframe Missile Block 2, and the Evolved Sea Sparrow Missile Block 2—shorter-range systems that can be carried by ships at greater capacity. And the Navy should continue to invest in the Marine air defense integrated system for short-range air defense, which is intended to protect maneuver forces, installations, and other critical assets.[37]

The Navy should also sustain or increase investments in its ability to counter capable surface-to-air missiles from the PLA, including sustained spending on the Navy's advanced anti-radiation guided missile extended range and the procurement of 54 low-rate initial production missiles and associated equipment.[38] This capability supports the ability of US air forces to attack PLA integrated air defenses.[39]

The Joint Force. Many gaps stretch across the US Armed Forces and require a hybrid approach to strengthening US combat power.

Regional Posture. As the Air Force wargames found, improving US theater-based force posture and logistical capabilities is crucial for overcoming the tyranny of distance that characterizes the region, and it would allow US forces to jointly and rapidly respond to a variety of Taiwan scenarios. To this end, the recently established—and recently reformed—Pacific Deterrence Initiative serves as an instructive case study for where additional dollars might be well spent.

While the Pentagon's original request for the fund attempted to force through platform-centric investments, the reforms proposed by Congress in the FY22 National Defense Authorization Act redirected the fund's dollars to focus primarily on improving US regional posture. The American Enterprise Institute's Dustin Walker states that these reforms emphasize "'planning and design' activities that will be 'used to develop shovel-ready military construction projects to advance a distributed and resilient theater force posture.'"[40]

These changes will ensure military logisticians and troops have the supplies and plans they need to develop quick, usable access to a variety of critical operational sites, such as refueling centers and airstrips across the Indo-Pacific and potentially on the island itself. Even so, certain analyses caution that infrastructure investments in the initiative are still focused on large and centralized bases, not improvements to remote runways, for example, such as those proposed by the Air Force.[41]

At a minimum, substantially increasing current Pacific Deterrence Initiative program funding over the next five years would improve US basing in the Indo-Pacific. Simultaneously, the United States should be enhancing regional force survivability. Such investments include passive protection measures for forward bases, such as "expedient shelters, fuel bladders, [and] airfield damage repair equipment and materiel."[42]

Hybrid Air and Missile Defense. The US military must defend its bases and platforms against PLA attacks from the beginning of a conflict. As a case study, the Biden administration is focusing on securing the defense of Guam. The US territory provides support for Navy submarines operating in the Pacific, sustains Air Force strategic bombers, operates surveillance drones, and is simultaneously charged with developing point and area defense across the services. These capabilities are key to any Pacific conflict engaging US forces—especially in defense of Taiwan—because China is developing offensive weaponry that puts these critical operations at severe risk.

In mid-2021, Vice Adm. Jon Hill, director of the Missile Defense Agency, noted that US Indo-Pacific Command "has a clear requirement" to update the missile defense of Guam. He reported Guam's ballistic-missile defense as the combatant command's primary unfunded requirement for FY22, at $231.7 million.[43]

The Joint Force must develop a hybrid defense for Guam that incorporates the Navy's Aegis Ashore and the Army's Terminal High-Altitude and Area Defense systems. Developing an evolved missile defense architecture for Guam will grow in importance as advanced threats such as hypersonic missiles proliferate, and fully funding Guam's defense cannot and should not be underrated. Increases in the FY22 budget request for the Hypersonic Defense Program indicate DOD prioritization of the program and suggest further future investments.[44]

Of note, defense analysts have advocated investing in cost-effective passive defenses for US bases and platforms including "dispersing forces across multiple locations, spreading forces and equipment out on a base, hardening, redundancy, camouflage, concealment, deception, early warning systems, and recovery capabilities . . . to rapidly repair the damage."[45] Ultimately, the US military would most benefit from attention and investment in a combination of active *and* passive defenses.

Hybrid Long-Range Strike. Some commentators have warned that investments in long-range strike options across the Joint Force are needlessly repetitive in constrained budget environments. But should the United States commit to fully funding an ambitious defense agenda, long-range strike options across the services should be seen as important efforts to build useful redundancies across the US military. Not only is Taiwan interested in fielding long-range strike capabilities itself, but the United States' ability to deploy long-range precision missiles against Chinese land targets from surface and submarine systems will strengthen US deterrent capabilities and potential response in the event of a conflict. China is actively developing these technologies; US superiority in long-range precision munition deployment would serve Taiwan and US defenses well.

The Air Force is making substantial investments in joint air-to-surface standoff missiles and long-range air-to-surface missiles. The service is also investing in its most prominent hypersonic weapon, the Air-Launched Rapid Response Weapon (ARRW), with the hypersonic conventional strike weapon as an alternative, particularly as ARRW came under congressional scrutiny in 2021.[46] The Army is scheduled to field a prototype of its new long-range hypersonic weapon in 2023, while the service simultaneously endeavors to diversify its long-range strike portfolio with the development of the precision strike missile.

The Marine Corps is focused on fielding an anti-ship naval strike missile to undermine PLA Navy defenses, advancing its Navy Marine Expeditionary Ship Interdiction System.[47] The Navy intends to field its conventional prompt strike hypersonic missile on the Virginia-class submarines and Zumwalt-class destroyers.[48] If further funding is required for the new integration effort, Congress and the Navy should provide it.

ISR. If the United States cannot achieve an enhanced force posture in the region quickly, the advances in ISR that give US forces the warning they require to appropriately position themselves must be a priority. Broadly, more ISR assets that support US regional awareness would be money well spent. In particular, space-based warning platforms become more important in providing constant surveillance if the US posture cannot be rapidly adjusted. Accordingly, efforts such as the Space Development Agency's investments in developing beyond-line-of-sight targeting and advanced missile tracking merit sustained or increased funding where necessary.[49]

The US military could also accelerate investments in missile-sensing proliferated low Earth orbit satellites.[50] Accelerating the development and fielding of counterspace systems should also take priority.[51] Further, while the United States cannot depend on or force defense investments from allies and partners, fielding more geospatial intelligence capabilities, such as synthetic aperture radar, would be useful for supporting extended land surveillance and maritime awareness.[52]

Remotely crewed platforms such as the Navy's extra-large unmanned undersea vehicle, for example, would be useful for expanding the service's undersea ISR capacity. For the Air Force, a high-altitude, unmanned long-range reconnaissance system—like a larger RQ-180—is reportedly flying and operating.[53] If true, increasing the Air Force's inventory of the platform would also be a valuable investment.

Taiwan Defense Capabilities

In addition to US protection, Taiwan must also continue growing its investments in defense systems and personnel to deter aggression and be ready for potential conflict.

Support Taiwan's Defenses and Resiliency. Short of an outright assault, the CCP might pursue a range of potential methods to subjugate Taiwan, covering the full spectrum of conflict. The systems and investments detailed above would strengthen the US military's ability to mount an appropriate response in each scenario. But Taiwan must be able to do so as well. In May 2021, analysts identified a menu of defense investments that Taiwan should consider.

> If Taiwan acquires, over roughly the next five years, large numbers of additional anti-ship missiles, more extensive ground-based air defense capabilities, smart mines, better trained and more effective reserve forces, a significantly bolstered capacity for offensive cyber warfare, a large suite of unmanned intelligence, surveillance, and reconnaissance (ISR) and strike systems, and counterstrike capabilities able to hit coastal targets on the mainland, it will continually increase the price China will have to pay to win a war.[54]

The United States can do much to support Taiwan's development and acquisition of these capabilities. Most obviously, Washington could transfer relevant technologies to support the production of specific weapons, such as improved short-range (up to 1,000 kilometers or 539 nautical miles) missiles, particularly useful for advancing Taiwan's ability to "disrupt, degrade, and interdict Chinese command and control nodes, military airfields, supply depots and reinforcements in response to an attack."[55]

To bolster Taiwan's ability to counter Chinese aggression in the gray zone, the United States could assist Taiwan with developing its own resident cyber offense and defense capabilities and sustain other ongoing US efforts to train the Taiwanese armed forces. Enabling Taiwan to defend itself through resiliency against non-kinetic attacks, such as cyber and information operations, must be a key component of the assistance provided to it.

More broadly, Taiwan's defense ministry must also ensure its existing forces are capable of responding to a Taiwan Strait contingency.[56] Importantly, these asymmetric investments would mark a departure from Taiwan's current defense investment plans, which still focus on buying exquisite weapons systems from the United States—demonstrated by Taiwan's purchase of 66 F-16 fighters for an estimated $8 billion in 2019.[57]

First and foremost, the United States and Taiwan should determine how to maximize and rationalize their defense spending decisions and trade-offs.[58] The F-16 is a capable, highly maneuverable fighter that, while different from the F-35 in that it is more defensive than offensive in nature, would still provide advanced day-to-day operational airpower. Taiwan's decision to buy the Patriot Advanced Capability-3 Missile Segment Enhancement Missiles in early 2021 is a step in the right direction, even if deliveries will not begin until 2025.[59]

Smarter and More Ambitious Investments

Despite the grim outlook for the United States' ability to deter or defend against a Chinese invasion of Taiwan, this chapter provides concrete steps the US military and Congress can take to improve the outlook. While the options for conventional deterrence may be fading, an appropriate budget and the responsible allocation of funding will be key to restoring and maintaining American strength.

The Biden administration released the FY23 defense budget request following the initial drafting of this chapter. Regrettably, the concrete steps the US military needs to strengthen conventional deterrence are being scrapped even more rapidly than experts imagined. While the request rightly invests in hypersonic missile development and key cyber objectives, it cuts down troop-level goals for the services, decreases flight training for Air Force pilots, and decommissions more operational planes and ships over the next year and five-year period than it plans on replacing.

As the request essentially ignores today's record inflation, Joint Force procurement capabilities will deteriorate. Maintaining the readiness and capabilities of the warfighter are more or less deemed nonessential in comparison to shifting funds to what might be the conflict of the future. The assessment of senior military leaders quoted throughout this chapter is that a Taiwan conflict could most certainly occur in the near term; the FY23 budget request largely ignores investing in conventional deterrence capabilities and end strength that would not only deter but defend the island if need be.

None of the proposed investments in this chapter would immediately tip the balance in extreme favor of the United States should China decide to invade Taiwan. They are, however, solutions that lawmakers and defense officials can examine in the near term and begin to implement sooner rather than later. As Congress takes up the president's budget this year and begins planning future years' defense spending, it is crucial to invest heavily in forces that would imply combat power and that have deterred and defended for decades, alongside the modernization priorities of the DOD, which are also included in these recommendations.

While the United States might not have a role—or the same role—to play in every Taiwan scenario developed or wargamed, key investments listed throughout this chapter provide crucial capabilities that would allow the nation to play whatever role it assumes effectively and successfully. Closing capability gaps and securing American military superiority will only benefit the American and Taiwanese people, who jointly seek peace and freedom around the world.

Notes

1. Jim Garamone, "Erosion of U.S. Strength in Indo-Pacific Is Dangerous to All, Commander Says," US Department of Defense, March 9, 2021, https://www.defense.gov/News/News-Stories/Article/Article/2530733/erosion-of-us-strength-in-indo-pacific-is-dangerous-to-all-commander-says.

2. US Department of Defense, Office of the Secretary of Defense, *Military and Security Developments Involving the People's Republic of China 2021: Annual Report to Congress*, 2020, https://media.defense.gov/2021/Nov/03/2002885874/-1/-1/0/2021-CMPR-FINAL.PDF; and US Department of Defense, Office of the Secretary of Defense, *Military and Security Developments Involving the People's Republic of China 2020: Annual Report to Congress*, 2020, https://media.defense.gov/2020/Sep/01/2002488689/-1/-1/1/2020-DOD-CHINA-MILITARY-POWER-REPORT-FINAL.PDF.

3. Mackenzie Eaglen, "The 2020s Tri-Service Modernization Crunch," American Enterprise Institute, March 23, 2021, https://www.aei.org/research-products/report/2020s-tri-service-modernization-crunch.

4. Elbridge Colby and Walter Slocombe, "The State of (Deterrence by) Denial," War on the Rocks, March 22, 2021, https://warontherocks.com/2021/03/the-state-of-deterrence-by-denial.

5. Ben Blanchard and Yimou Lee, "Taiwan President Confirms U.S. Troops Training Soldiers on Island—CNN," Reuters, October 28, 2021, https://www.reuters.com/world/asia-pacific/taiwan-president-confirms-us-troops-training-soldiers-island-cnn-2021-10-28.

6. Gary Roughead, "Taiwan: Time for a Real Discussion," Strategika, June 30, 2021, https://www.hoover.org/research/taiwan-time-real-discussion.

7. US Department of State, *A Free and Open Indo-Pacific: Advancing a Shared Vison*, November 4, 2019, https://www.state.gov/wp-content/uploads/2019/11/Free-and-Open-Indo-Pacific-4Nov2019.pdf; Jonah Langan-Marmur and Phillip C. Saunders, "Absent Without Leave? Gauging US Commitment to the Indo-Pacific," *Diplomat*, May 6, 2020, https://thediplomat.com/2020/05/absent-without-leave-gauging-us-commitment-to-the-indo-pacific; Lindsey F. Ford, "Sustaining the Future of Indo-Pacific Defense Strategy," Brookings Institution, September 28, 2020, https://www.brookings.edu/articles/sustaining-the-future-of-indo-pacific-defense-strategy; and Mackenzie Eaglen, "Defense Budget Peaks in 2019, Underfunding the National Defense Strategy," American Enterprise Institute, May 17, 2018, https://www.aei.org/research-products/report/defense-budget-peaks-in-2019-underfunding-the-national-defense-strategy.

8. Tara Copp, "US Needs Indo-Pacific Force 'Enhancements,' Global Posture Review Finds," Defense One, November 29, 2021, https://www.defenseone.com/threats/2021/11/us-needs-indo-pacific-force-enhancements-global-posture-review-finds/187134. See also Jack Detsch, "'No Decisions, No Changes': Pentagon Fails to Stick Asia Pivot," *Foreign Policy*, November 29, 2021, https://foreignpolicy.com/2021/11/29/pentagon-china-biden-asia-pivot.

9. Gordon Lubold, "Pentagon Plans to Improve Airfields in Guam and Australia to Confront China," *Wall Street Journal*, November 29, 2021, https://www.wsj.com/articles/us-china-pentagon-middle-east-11638142162.

10. American Enterprise Institute, Center for Strategic and International Studies, and War on the Rocks, "Defense Futures Simulator," https://www.defensefutures.net.

11. Valerie Insinna, "House Appropriators Want to Shave $44M Off Air Force's Flagship Hypersonic Program," *Defense News*, July 12, 2021, https://www.defensenews.com/air/2021/07/12/house-appropriators-want-to-shave-44m-off-air-forces-flagship-hypersonic-program.

12. Valerie Insinna, "US Air Force to Mothball Dozens of A-10s, F-15s and F-16s in FY22 Budget," *Defense News*, May 28, 2021, https://www.defensenews.com/congress/budget/2021/05/28/us-air-force-to-mothball-dozens-of-a-10s-f-15s-and-f-16s-in-fy22-budget.

13. Frank Wolfe, "Kendall: 30-Year Old Aircraft an 'Anchor' Holding Back USAF Modernization," Defense Daily, December 6, 2021, https://www.defensedaily.com/kendall-30-year-old-aircraft-an-anchor-holding-back-usaf-modernization/air-force.

14. Valerie Insinna, "A US Air Force War Game Shows What the Service Needs to Hold Off—or Win Against—China in 2030," *Defense News*, April 12, 2021, https://www.defensenews.com/training-sim/2021/04/12/a-us-air-force-war-game-shows-what-the-service-needs-to-hold-off-or-win-against-china-in-2030.

15. Insinna, "A US Air Force War Game Shows What the Service Needs to Hold Off."

16. Insinna, "A US Air Force War Game Shows What the Service Needs to Hold Off."

17. Heater R. Penney, *The Future Fighter Force Our Nation Requires: Building a Bridge*, Mitchell Institute for Aerospace Studies, October 26, 2021, https://mitchellaerospacepower.org/the-future-fighter-force-our-nation-requires-building-a-bridge.

18. Lawrence A. Stutzriem, "Reimagining the MQ-9 Reaper," Mitchell Institute for Aerospace Studies, November 18, 2021, https://mitchellaerospacepower.org/reimagining-the-mq-9-reaper.

19. Jen Judson, "US Army Bracing for Budget Hit Next Year," *Defense News*, April 20, 2021, https://www.defensenews.com/land/2021/04/20/us-army-bracing-for-fy22-budget-hit.

20. Jacquelyn Schneider, "The Uncomfortable Reality of the U.S. Army's Role in a War over Taiwan," War on the Rocks, November 30, 2021, https://warontherocks.com/2021/11/the-uncomfortable-reality-of-the-u-s-armys-role-in-a-war-over-taiwan.

21. Tony Bertuca, "Wormuth: Army Must 'Ruthlessly Prioritize' to Avoid Becoming a 'Bill-Payer' for Other Services," Inside Defense, October 11, 2021, https://insidedefense.com/daily-news/wormuth-army-must-ruthlessly-prioritize-avoid-becoming-bill-payer-other-services.

22. Schneider, "The Uncomfortable Reality of the U.S. Army's Role in a War over Taiwan."

23. Schneider, "The Uncomfortable Reality of the U.S. Army's Role in a War over Taiwan."

24. Dontavian Harrison, "CSIS: China Power Conference 2021; Secretary of the Army's Opening Remarks," US Army, December 20, 2021, https://www.army.mil/article/252918/csis_china_power_conference_2021_secretary_of_the_armys_opening_remarks.

25. Jack Detsch, "Pentagon Quietly Puts More Troops in Taiwan," *Foreign Policy*, November 18, 2021, https://foreignpolicy.com/2021/11/18/pentagon-biden-troops-taiwan-china.

26. Joseph Trevithick, "American Forces Have Been Quietly Deployed to Taiwan with Increasing Regularity: Report," Drive, October 7, 2021, https://www.thedrive.com/the-war-zone/42658/american-forces-have-been-quietly-deployed-to-taiwan-with-increasing-regularity-report; and American Enterprise Institute, Center for Strategic and International Studies, and War on the Rocks, "Defense Futures Simulator," https://d3l1eb9zv1nxq7.cloudfront.net/hxxl4/dashboard/army/security-force-assistance-brigade/active.

27. Todd South, "An Army Brigade Posted to Taiwan, and Other Ways to Counter China Being Floated," *Army Times*, June 23, 2021, https://www.armytimes.com/news/your-army/2021/06/23/an-army-brigade-posted-to-taiwan-and-other-ways-to-counter-china-being-floated.

28. Eric Heginbotham et al., *The U.S.-China Military Scorecard: Forces, Geography, and the Evolving Balance of Power, 1996–2017*, RAND Corporation, 2015, https://www.rand.org/pubs/research_reports/RR392.html.

29. David B. Larter, "US Navy's Aging Surface Fleet Struggles to Keep Ships Up to Spec, Report Shows," *Defense News*, October 5, 2020, https://www.defensenews.com/naval/2020/10/05/the-us-navys-aging-surface-fleet-struggles-to-keep-ships-up-to-spec-report-shows.

30. John R. Kroger, "Esper's Fantasy Fleet," Defense One, October 13, 2020, https://www.defenseone.com/ideas/2020/10/espers-fantasy-fleet/169179.

31. Blake Herzinger, "The Budget (and Fleet) That Might Have Been," War on the Rocks, June 10, 2021, https://warontherocks.com/2021/06/the-budget-and-fleet-that-might-have-been.

32. American Enterprise Institute, Center for Strategic and International Studies, and War on the Rocks, "Defense Futures Simulator."

33. Lawmakers tried to introduce the $25 billion investment as an independent piece of legislation and as an amendment to the National Defense Authorization Act for Fiscal Year 2022. See Justin Katz, "Another $25B Boost, This Time for Shipyards, Proposed for NDAA," Breaking Defense, November 16, 2021, https://breakingdefense.com/2021/11/another-25b-boost-this-time-for-shipyards-proposed-for-ndaa; Supplying Help to Infrastructure in Ports, Yards, and America's Repair Docks Act of 2021, S. 1441, 117th Cong. (2021); and National Defense Authorization Act for Fiscal Year 2022, H.R. 4350, S.Amdt.4653 to S.Amdt.3867, 117th Cong. (2021), https://www.congress.gov/amendment/117th-congress/senate-amendment/4653/text?q=%7B%22search%22%3A%224653%22%7D&r=1&s=2.

34. Kyle Mizokami, "Here Comes the Navy's First New Torpedo in Decades," *Popular Mechanics*, January 1, 2021, https://www.popularmechanics.com/military/weapons/a35085267/navy-first-new-torpedo-in-decades.

35. US Department of Defense, Department of the Navy, *Fiscal Year (FY) 2022 Budget Estimates*, 1:375, https://www.secnav.navy.mil/fmc/fmb/Documents/22pres/WPN_Book.pdf.

36. Justin Katz, "Marines' New Warfighting Concept Focuses on Small, Agile Forces with an Eye on China," Breaking Defense, December 1, 2021, https://breakingdefense.com/2021/12/marines-new-warfighting-concept-focuses-on-small-agile-forces-with-eye-on-china.

37. US Department of Defense, Department of the Navy, *Fiscal Year (FY) 2022 Budget Estimates*, 1:67.

38. David Ochmanek, "Restoring U.S. Power Projection Capabilities: Responding to the 2018 National Defense Strategy," RAND Corporation, July 2018, https://www.rand.org/pubs/perspectives/PE260.html.

39. US Department of Defense, Department of the Navy, *Fiscal Year (FY) 2022 Budget Estimates*, 1:267, https://www.secnav.navy.mil/fmc/fmb/Documents/22pres/WPN_Book.pdf.

40. Dustin Walker, "Pacific Deterrence Initiative: A Look at Funding in the New Defense Bill, and What Must Happen Now," *Defense News*, December 15, 2021, https://www.defensenews.com/opinion/commentary/2021/12/15/pacific-deterrence-initiative-a-look-at-funding-in-the-new-defense-bill-and-what-must-happen-now.

41. Walker, "Pacific Deterrence Initiative: A Look at Funding in the New Defense Bill, and What Must Happen Now."

42. Ochmanek, "Restoring U.S. Power Projection Capabilities," 11.

43. John Grady, "MDA: US Has Several Options to Defend Guam from Missile Threats," US Naval Institute News, August 13, 2021, https://news.usni.org/2021/08/13/mda-u-s-has-several-options-to-defend-guam-from-missile-threats.

44. Wes Rumbaugh and Tom Karako, "Seeking Alignment: Missile Defense and Defeat in the 2022 Budget," Center for Strategic and International Studies, December 2021, 10, https://csis-website-prod.s3.amazonaws.com/s3fs-public/publication/211210_Rumbaugh_Seeking_Alignment_0.pdf.

45. Stacie L. Pettyjohn, "Spiking the Problem: Developing a Resilient Posture in the Indo-Pacific with Passive Defenses," War on the Rocks, January 10, 2022, https://warontherocks.com/2022/01/spiking-the-problem-developing-a-resilient-posture-in-the-indo-pacific-with-passive-defenses.

46. Rumbaugh and Karako, "Seeking Alignment," 4.

47. Mark F. Cancian, "U.S. Military Forces in FY 2022: Marine Corps," Center for Strategic and International Studies, November 2021, http://defense360.csis.org/wp-content/uploads/2021/11/211115_Cancian_MilitaryForcesFY2022_MarineCorps_v3.pdf; and Rumbaugh and Karako, "Seeking Alignment."

48. US Department of Defense, Department of the Navy, *Fiscal Year (FY) 2022 Budget Estimates*, 2:1455, https://www.secnav.navy.mil/fmc/fmb/Documents/22pres/RDTEN_BA4_Book.pdf.

49. US Department of Defense, Space Development Agency, *Department of Defense Fiscal Year (FY) 2022 Budget Estimates*, June 7, 2021, 5:19, https://comptroller.defense.gov/Portals/45/Documents/defbudget/fy2022/budget_justification/pdfs/03_RDT_and_E/SDA_PB2022_v2.pdf.

50. American Enterprise Institute, Center for Strategic and International Studies, and War on the Rocks, "Defense Futures Simulator," https://d3l1eb9zv1nxq7.cloudfront.net.

51. Ochmanek, "Restoring U.S. Power Projection Capabilities."

52. Jason Wang and Mark Matossian, "David vs Goliath: How Space-Based Assets Can Give Taiwan an Edge," *Diplomat*, March 27, 2021, https://thediplomat.com/2021/03/david-vs-goliath-how-space-based-assets-can-give-taiwan-an-edge.

53. David Axe, "America's New Stealth Drone Appears to Be Operational near China," *Forbes*, September 7, 2021, https://www.forbes.com/sites/davidaxe/2021/09/07/americas-new-stealth-drone-appears-to-be-operational-near-china; and Cancian, "U.S. Military Forces in FY 2022: Air Force," 18.

54. Patrick Porter and Michael Mazarr, *Countering China's Adventurism over Taiwan: A Third Way*, Lowy Institute, May 20, 2021, https://www.lowyinstitute.org/publications/countering-china-s-adventurism-over-taiwan-third-way#sec44786. See also US-China Economic and Security Review Commission, 2020 *Report to Congress of the US-China Economic and Security Review Commission*, December 2020, 467–68, https://www.uscc.gov/annual-report/2020-annual-report-congress. William Murray has offered one of the best summaries of how such an asymmetric strategy would look. Key elements of his proposed strategy include hardening and enhanced resilience for command and control and military facilities; a stronger and more redundant national power and communications infrastructure; a more professional volunteer force equipped with the most modern anti-invasion weapons; large numbers of decoys; use of smaller and more concealable systems, such as man-portable and small, truck-mounted anti-aircraft systems and anti-ship missiles; and stockpiles of essential materials to withstand a blockade for weeks or months. Such an approach, he argued, "would shift the responsibility for Taiwan's defence to Taiwan, rendering US intervention in a cross-strait battle a last resort instead of the first response." William S. Murray, "Revisiting Taiwan's Defence Strategy," *Naval War College Review* 61, no. 3 (2008): 13, 30–31.

55. Michael Hunzeker and Alexander Lanoszka, "Taiwan Wants More Missiles. That's Not a Bad Thing.," *Defense One*, March 24, 2021, https://www.defenseone.com/ideas/2021/03/taiwan-wants-more-missiles-s-not-bad-thing/172887.

56. Paul Huang, "Taiwan's Military Has Flashy American Weapons but No Ammo," *Foreign Policy*, August 20, 2020, https://foreignpolicy.com/2020/08/20/taiwan-military-flashy-american-weapons-no-ammo.

57. Ryan Browne, "Trump Admin Formally Approves Fighter Jet Sale to Taiwan amid China Trade Fight," CNN, August 20, 2019, https://www.cnn.com/2019/08/20/politics/taiwan-fighter-jet-sales/index.html.

58. Michael A. Hunzeker, "Taiwan's Defense Plans Are Going off the Rails," War on the Rocks, November 18, 2021, https://warontherocks.com/2021/11/taiwans-defense-plans-are-going-off-the-rails.

59. Yimou Lee, "Taiwan to Buy New U.S. Air Defence Missiles to Guard Against China," Reuters, March 31, 2021, https://www.reuters.com/article/us-taiwan-defence/taiwan-to-buy-new-u-s-air-defence-missiles-to-guard-against-china-idUSKBN2BN1AA.

Taking Taiwan Through Cyber

KLON KITCHEN

Xi Jinping, general secretary of the Chinese Communist Party (CCP) and the nation's head of state, is clear about his intentions for Taiwan: "The task of complete reunification of China must be achieved, and it will definitely be achieved." He continued, "Those who forget their heritage, betray their motherland and seek to split the country will come to no good."[1] Xi's timeline for "reunification" is unclear; however, there is growing concern that Beijing will take military action against Taipei in the next decade—not only imperiling the democratic government of Taiwan and the lives of its citizens but also potentially sparking a direct military confrontation between China and the United States, the first such war between two nuclear-armed nations.

If an operation against Taiwan takes place, it is likely to be novel in not only its relevance to nuclear arms but also how prominently it will feature cyber operations. This raises several questions: How does China strategically understand cyber operations? Who in the Chinese military would have primary responsibility for these actions? What goals would Beijing have for its cyber operations in a Taiwan scenario? What are China's cyber advantages and Taiwan's cyber vulnerabilities? Finally, what can be done to mitigate this threat? This chapter attempts to briefly address each question.

This task is daunting but necessary. If Xi is determined to attack Taiwan, this threat cannot be wished away. It must be seriously acknowledged, studied, and planned for. It is only by doing this that we can hope to prevent this conflagration or at least emerge victorious from it. And in so doing, we benefit from Chinese wisdom that teaches, "Plan for what is difficult while it is easy, do what is great while it is small."[2]

The Utility of Cyber Means

The forcible unification of Taiwan with China cannot be achieved exclusively via cyber means because, at some point, ground must be won and held, and that requires personnel and equipment. Chinese cyber capabilities will, however, play a crucial role in any scenario, because these capabilities are increasingly central to Chinese doctrine and strategy.

The People's Liberation Army (PLA) views cyber means as an elemental feature of "informatized" wars, in which information is both "a domain in which war occurs" and "the central means to wage military conflict."[3] Accordingly, Chinese doctrine locates cyber within the larger operational concept of information operations (IO), which also includes electronic, space, and psychological warfare. Chinese strategists say these are the key capabilities that must be coordinated as strategic weapons to "paralyze the enemy's operational system of systems" and "sabotage the enemy's war command system of systems."[4] In other words: The PLA believes information is *the* key resource on the modern battlefield and that victory is achieved by ensuring one's own access to this resource while denying it to the enemy. IO, then, is a broad operational concept centered on defending China's ability to collect, use, and share information while shaping its opponent's perceptions and ability to complete these same tasks. In the age of digitized data, cyber means are crucial to informatized war.

A review of PLA writings shows a strong preference for integrating cyber defense, offense, and reconnaissance into a single effort. White papers and other documents argue that cyber superiority must be seized early in a conflict and then used to deter or degrade an enemy's ability to attack. This is essential, they argue, for managing escalation and deterrence and demonstrating capabilities and resolve. Importantly, these lines of effort must be continually pursued, even in peacetime, if they are to have maximum effect. In the context of Taiwan, then, it is only safe to assume—and certainly there are many indicators—that China is actively laying the groundwork for information and cyber operations in support of unification and that the cyber realm will play a dominant role. But who is responsible for these actions?

The Strategic Support Force

The PLA's Strategic Support Force (SSF) was established in December 2015 as part of China's extensive military reforms. It is a theater command–level, leader-grade independent military force under the command of the Central Military Commission. The overall force structure and staffing of the SSF remains opaque, but we do have a basic sense of its operational organization (Figure 1). The SSF consists of two mission divisions—a Space Systems Department (SSD) and a Network Systems Department (NSD). The SSD has three unique missions: space launch; space telemetry, tracking, and command; and space command, control, communications, computers, intelligence, surveillance, and reconnaissance. The NSD also has three missions: cyber operations, electronic warfare, and psychological operations. Both the SSD and NSD share responsibility for counterspace and strategic intelligence missions.

Before this reform, the PLA had a discipline-centric structure in which individual cyber, electronic, space, and psychological warfare units were organized by mission (i.e., defensive, offensive, or reconnaissance). Under this old structure, defensive cyber was handled by the former Informatization Department, offensive cyber was conducted by the Fourth Department (known as 4PLA), and the Third Department (known as 3PLA) managed cyber espionage. The other warfare disciplines were similarly fractured.

As the PLA embraced new doctrines for modern warfare, it realized it must also modernize its force structure to effectively prosecute these wars. To this end, the SSF not only unifies these formally disparate elements but also is built around an imperative of "peacetime-wartime integration." Researchers Elsa B. Kania and John K. Costello elaborate on the importance of this evolution:

> The SSF has seemingly streamlined this process through organizing these units into operational groups as standard practice, optimized as a wartime structure. This concept of peacetime-wartime integration is particularly critical for the SSF's Network Systems Department and cyber mission. At a basic level, cyber operations require a persistent cycle of cyber

Figure 1. Structure and Missions of the Strategic Support Force

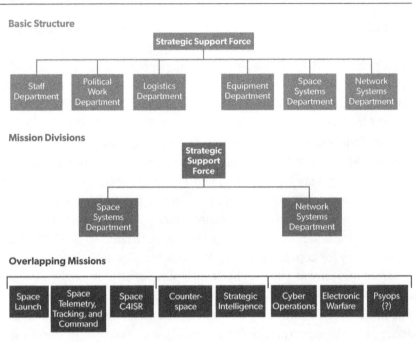

Note: C4ISR is composed of two abbreviations: command, control, communications, computers (C4) and intelligence, surveillance, and reconnaissance (ISR).
Source: John Costello and Joe McReynolds, "China's Strategic Support Force: A Force for a New Era," *China Strategic Perspectives* 13 (October 2018): 10, https://ndupress.ndu.edu/Portals/68/Documents/stratperspective/china/china-perspectives_13.pdf.

reconnaissance, capabilities development, and deployment to ensure cyber effects can be leveraged in a conflict. Given the functional integration of these peacetime and wartime activities—and the close relationship between reconnaissance and attack—in cyber operations, the integration of China's military cyber offense and espionage capabilities has become a functional necessity. This force structure is consistent with the PLA's recognition of the reality of blurred boundaries between peace and warfare in these domains, which is reflected in its notion of "military struggle" . . . in cyberspace, as confrontation occurring across a spectrum, of which the highest form is warfare.[5]

To summarize, China believes effective cyber warfare does not begin with the onset of official hostilities; it is instead an unending activity that must seamlessly transition between peacetime and wartime. Understanding this, we can discern the key objectives of Chinese cyber operations against Taiwan.

Chinese Cyber Activities Against Taiwan

As stated previously, Chinese planners believe it is essential to establish and maintain cyber superiority to enable the full spectrum of informatized warfare, deter opponents, and manage escalation. But this superiority, in the minds of PLA planners, is not something only sought in the early days of a conflict; it is an advantage that must be won and leveraged now. It is helpful, then, to think of PLA cyber objectives not as a list of tasks to be completed but as a collection of ceaseless activities only varying in intensity based on political requirements. The following form China's core cyber activities in support of unification with Taiwan.

Intelligence, Surveillance, and Reconnaissance. Intelligence, surveillance, and reconnaissance (ISR) is an SSF core mission and underpins all other cyber activities. Chinese hackers are constantly gaining access to Taiwan's information systems and networks to better understand China's targets. Mapping the island's critical infrastructure and political-military command-and-control networks are essential aims of these activities. Effective cyber ISR will synchronize and integrate assets, sensors, and processing, exploitation, and dissemination systems to develop a comprehensive understanding of Taiwan's political, military, economic, and social variables.

For example, in 2021 it was discovered that China had hacked Taiwan's popular Line messaging service to spy on high-level political officials, military personnel, and city leaders.[6] This had the tangible effect of giving the CCP crucial insight into these communities and the intangible, but still important, effect of undermining these communities' confidence in the security of their communications.

Operational Preparation of the Environment. The SSF is also tasked with operational preparation of the environment (OPE). OPE is formally a hallmark of American strategy and doctrine, but its defining features are also present in Chinese planning—particularly in the PLA's "three warfares": public opinion warfare, psychological warfare, and legal warfare. Cyber operations in support of Chinese OPE include pre-positioning tools and malicious code on vulnerable networks, the development of detailed intelligence and targets related to future military action, and operations intended to have specific effects on the attitudes and behaviors of Taiwan's citizens and government. All these actions are intended to create an environment that is favorable to China's objectives in peace and war.

For example, in 2019, SSF personnel manipulated Taiwanese social media in support of pro-Beijing Taiwanese politician Han Kuo-yu, fueling his surprise victory in the Kaohsiung mayoral race—historically, a stronghold of anti-CCP sentiment. Han later mounted a failed presidential bid with similar cyber support from China.[7]

Offensive Cyberattacks on Taiwan. China's hackers are also tasked with offensive cyberattacks on Taiwan—actions intended to manipulate, disrupt, or destroy networks, infrastructure, and daily life. During peacetime, these operations assume the form of distributed denial of service, ransomware, and the distribution of other malware.

For example, in 2020, Beijing used the ColdLock ransomware virus to target more than 10 critical infrastructure targets in Taiwan, including the state-owned CPC Corporation, which supplies more than 25 percent of the island's gas stations with petroleum, natural gas, and gasoline. This prevented gas stations across the country from accepting any form of electronic payment.[8] The ColdLock operation also reportedly affected two undisclosed companies in Taiwan's semiconductor industry.[9]

In wartime, these cyberattacks would be more aggressive. Chinese hackers would attempt to disrupt, degrade, or destroy everything from civilian telecommunications networks to military command-and-control systems. Air defense systems would go down, power grids would go dark, and essential government services would grind to a halt. These attacks would be precision strikes against key enemy targets aimed at sowing confusion, debilitating Taiwan's defenses, and maximizing Chinese operational freedom of movement. But, as noted in this chapter's introduction, military action against Taiwan would likely provoke a US response, so this challenge would also need to be engaged.

Deterring or Slowing the American Response. Deterring or slowing the American response in support of Taiwan is another key objective for the SSF. These operations would be extremely sensitive and highly influenced by the political context in which they occur. In many ways, Chinese informatized warfare doctrine is crafted specifically with the United States in view, and the SSF already has cyber plans for multiple scenarios. Whatever the scenario, the broad objective would be to undermine the United States' confidence in its ability to decisively intervene on behalf of Taipei and its capacity to do so.

Importantly, the SSF's NSD could be expected to work with its sister SSD to bring the full measure of space, cyber, electronic, and psychological warfare capabilities to this crucial task. This means the United States could face cyberattacks against naval ports to slow force deployments. Ransomware and other "signaling" attacks against critical industries and infrastructure would also be likely. As tensions rise, these operations could expand to anti-satellite and electronic warfare attacks intended to deteriorate American navigational, intelligence, reconnaissance, and targeting assets in the region. If things escalated further, we could expect large-scale cyberattacks intended to cripple the American economy, government, strategic nuclear missiles, and way of life. The Office of the Director of National Intelligence summarizes the threat as follows:

> We assess that China presents the broadest, most active, and persistent cyber espionage threat to U.S. Government and private sector networks. . . .
>
> China almost certainly is capable of launching cyber attacks that would disrupt critical infrastructure services within the United States, including against oil and gas pipelines and rail systems. . . .
>
> China's cyber-espionage operations have included compromising telecommunications firms, providers of managed

services and broadly used software, and other targets potentially rich in follow-on opportunities for intelligence collection, attack, or influence operations. . . .

Counterspace operations will be integral to potential military campaigns by the PLA, and China has counterspace weapons capabilities intended to target U.S. and allied satellites.[10]

While a direct military confrontation between the United States and China could escalate to the use of nuclear missiles, it would likely begin with the deployment of offensive cyberattacks.

Protecting China from Cyberattacks. Finally, CCP hackers are also focused on protecting China from cyberattacks. These defense measures include protecting CCP and PLA networks from disruptive enemy cyber operations and hardening the nation's critical infrastructure to withstand foreign infiltration. As Chinese society becomes ever more digitized, its digital "threat surface" expands and requires greater resources for its protection. And China certainly has its hands full.

The US Cyber Command (USCYBERCOM) employs a new concept of operations it calls "persistent engagement." In its strategic vision announcing the concept, USCYBERCOM explained:

Superiority through persistence seizes and maintains the initiative in cyberspace by continuously engaging and contesting adversaries and causing them uncertainty wherever they maneuver. It describes how we operate—maneuvering seamlessly between defense and offense across the interconnected battlespace. It describes where we operate—globally, as close as possible to adversaries and their operations. It describes when we operate—continuously, shaping the battlespace. It describes why we operate—to create operational advantage for us while denying the same to our adversaries.[11]

Put simply: In addition to its other actions, sizable portions of China's SSF are already consumed by cyber defense, and this operational toll will grow if Beijing takes coercive action against Taiwan. Having outlined these core cyber activities, we should now turn to a general assessment of the cyber situation.

An Assessment of the Situation

Taiwan is catastrophically vulnerable to Chinese cyber aggression. The island's critical infrastructure, government services, and key military capabilities already endure between 20 million and 40 million cyberattacks every month, with the vast majority of these coming from China. Chien Hung-wei, head of Taiwan's Department of Cyber Security, says he can defend against most of these attacks but admits "serious" breaches regularly occur. "The operation of our government highly relies on the internet," explains Chien. "Our critical infrastructure, such as gas, water and electricity are highly digitized, so we can easily fall victim if our network security is not robust enough."[12] This illustrates China's chief cyber advantage—scale.

Concrete personnel and budgetary numbers concerning Beijing's digital forces are not readily available in unclassified channels, but estimates range between 50,000 and 100,000 individuals, with hundreds of millions of dollars at their disposal. Whatever their actual workforce and funding, FBI Director Christopher Wray has stated that "here in the U.S., [Chinese hackers have] unleash[ed] a massive, sophisticated hacking program that is *bigger than those of every other major nation combined.*"[13] (Emphasis added.) It can be assumed, then, that similar economies of scale will be employed against one of Xi's most coveted aspirations—China's unification with Taiwan.

In early 2001, Taipei established the National Center for Cyber Security Technology (NCCST), tasked to "establish the cyber security protection mechanism and provide technical services to government agencies, including prior-incident security protection, during-incident early warning and responses, and post-incident recoveries and forensics."[14] While the NCCST has made notable progress, it is nowhere near the maturity, size, or strength required for its mission. Relatedly, Taiwan is only on the cusp of building the intragovernmental, industry, and international partnerships necessary for effectively engaging and rolling back the deluge of hostile Chinese efforts online. The aforementioned information operation behind the election of the pro-Beijing Taiwanese politician Han further demonstrates the island is seriously susceptible to cyber-enabled political warfare.

None of these critiques are aimed at Taipei's desires or political will. They are simply a recognition of a threat that even the United States, with its massive resources and capabilities, is utterly failing to mitigate. But hope is not lost, and meaningful improvements can be made in the near term that might dramatically shift the balance in favor of Taiwan.

What Can Be Done

First, the United States must continue to harden itself against Chinese cyberthreats to the American homeland and military forces. Taiwan has little to no chance of successfully deterring or preventing a Chinese military attack without American assistance. This assistance will be severely constrained if the United States does not make a systemic, comprehensive effort to close its own cybersecurity loopholes.

Looking beyond our borders, joint cyberwar exercises with Taiwan should be expanded in both frequency and scope. The first of these exercises was held in 2019, but it was hosted by the American Institute in Taiwan—which represents US interests on the island—not the US military. It is now time to synchronize our military cyber operations, because it would be precisely these capabilities that would count in a war with China. While Beijing would certainly protest these exercises, they would not constitute an act of war and likely would not substantively risk upsetting today's delicate political equilibrium in the Taiwan Strait. Even if they did, this risk of rising tensions is still preferable to Taipei remaining unable to protect itself against the legions of Chinese military hackers arrayed against it.

Another effective but admittedly controversial action would be for Taiwan to grant US cyber forces direct access to their systems for joint "active threat–hunting" operations. These would involve US and Taiwanese operators working side by side, crawling through the island's many networks to find and remove Chinese (and other) hostile actors. Certainly, Taipei could be forgiven for any hesitation about allowing such broad access to a foreign country, but China is already in these networks, and bringing US muscle to Taiwan's cyber defenses could be the difference between crumbling under a Chinese offensive and maintaining robust defensive capabilities. Aside from bolstering commitments to Taiwan, American forces would also gain indispensable experience in navigating the cyber conflicts of the future, particularly one in which its primary geostrategic rival is the aggressor. The only alternative—trying to hunt down network vulnerabilities at the onset of conflict—would be far too little, too late.

Finally, because artificial intelligence (AI) will be a key enabler of future cyber capabilities, the United States should require all American AI research to be pulled out of China. Housing the AI research labs of America's cutting-edge tech companies in authoritarian China was never a good idea. But given that the Chinese government uses foreign tech companies to help find and exploit security vulnerabilities and that it is claiming ever more control over tech companies' operations and data, this looks more objectionable than ever. AI is an increasingly crucial element of cybersecurity and hacking, and Xi's China has demonstrated repeatedly that China's high-tech sector serves the CCP, which sees AI technology as a core tool of its future autocratic rule.

Nonetheless, according to Georgetown University's Center for Security and Emerging Technology, 10 percent of the collective AI research labs of the leading US technology companies were housed in China in 2020.[15] Microsoft's Beijing-based Research Asia lab is the company's largest outside the US and is credited as being "the single most important institution in the birth and growth of the Chinese AI ecosystem over the past two decades."[16] In 2018, this same lab openly coauthored, with China's military-run National University of Defense Technology, research with clear applications to surveillance and censorship. Other companies have gone even further.

Since Cisco helped establish the "Great Firewall" in the early 1990s and Seagate built the first hard drive catered to surveillance for China's Hikvision in 2005, American companies laid the foundation for many of the systems powering China's technological authoritarianism.[17] Their contributions to Xinjiang's dystopia, such as the Intel chips likely being used to monitor forced labor and concentration camps and Thermo Fisher's DNA sequencing kits used to surveil Uyghurs, represent the grotesque culmination of this history.[18]

Given that American companies remain the gatekeepers of most of the more valuable insights in advanced AI computing, their research efforts in China are disproportionately valuable to the tech-hungry dictatorship and risky to a world chronically hacked by the Chinese. Under the auspices of international scientific collaboration, these research outposts grow the CCP's capacity to make its own high-tech tools—including for hacking—without having to resort to foreign companies to build out their capabilities.

The danger of China capitalizing on American AI research in its borders also has chilling military import, as our defense leaders know well. Even if the work of these research centers does not have direct application to areas of military concern, the dual-use nature of AI technologies makes secondary military application highly likely, in addition to growing China's military-pliant AI ecosystem more generally. Success in developing its AI capabilities will further grow China's leverage and aggression abroad—as if those were not already concerning enough.

Conclusion

Xi's desires for the forcible unification of Taiwan with China appear to be growing. But Taiwan cannot and will not be taken by cyber means alone. Chinese doctrine does, however, call for the expansive use of cyber means in the preparation, execution, and aftermath of military actions against the island. These operations are already underway and will grow in sophistication and aggression as tensions in the Taiwan Strait escalate—including the possible targeting of the US homeland. Presently, Taipei is not prepared for these attacks, but meaningful improvements can be made by shoring up American cyber defenses, expanding cyber cooperation between the United States and Taiwan, and removing US AI research from China. Finally, China's significant cyber capabilities and massive scale ensure that any defense of Taiwan will be difficult, and while no amount of preparation can ensure success, a failure to prepare in the manner discussed in this chapter will guarantee Taiwan's defeat.

Notes

1. Wayne Chang, Yong Xiong, and Ben Westcott, "Chinese President Xi Jinping Vows to Pursue 'Reunification' with Taiwan by Peaceful Means," CNN, October 9, 2021, https://www.cnn.com/2021/10/08/china/xi-jinping-taiwan-reunification-intl-hnk/index.html. An earlier version of this chapter was published as Klon Kitchen, "Informatized Wars: How China Thinks About Cyber," Dispatch, April 21, 2021, https://current.thedispatch.com/p/informatized-wars-how-china-thinks?s=r.

2. Sun Tzu, *The Art of War* (Oxford, UK: Clarendon Press, 1964).

3. Edmund J. Burke et al., "People's Liberation Army Operational Concepts," RAND Corporation, 2020, 1, https://www.rand.org/pubs/research_reports/RRA394-1.html.

4. Department of Defense, Office of the Secretary of Defense, *Military and Security Developments Involving the People's Republic of China*, November 3, 2021, 88, https://media.defense.gov/2021/Nov/03/2002885874/-1/-1/0/2021-CMPR-FINAL.PDF.

5. Elsa B. Kania and John K. Costello, "The Strategic Support Force and the Future of Chinese Information Operations," *Cyber Defense Review* 3, no. 1 (Spring 2018): 104–21, https://cyberdefensereview.army.mil/Portals/6/Documents/CDR%20Journal%20Articles/The%20Strategic%20Support%20Force_Kania_Costello.pdf.

6. Huang Tzu-ti, "Mass Hacking of Taiwan Politicians' LINE Accounts Sparks National Security Concerns," Taiwan News, July 28, 2021, https://www.taiwannews.com.tw/en/news/4259770.

7. Paul Huang, "Chinese Cyber-Operatives Boosted Taiwan's Insurgent Candidate," *Foreign Policy*, June 26, 2019, https://foreignpolicy.com/2019/06/26/chinese-cyber-operatives-boosted-taiwans-insurgent-candidate.

8. CyCraft Technology Corp, "China-Linked Threat Group Targets Taiwan Critical Infrastructure, Smokescreen Ransomware," June 1, 2021, https://medium.com/cycraft/china-linked-threat-group-targets-taiwan-critical-infrastructure-smokescreen-ransomware-c2a155aa53d5.

9. Cyberint, "Targeted Ransomware Attacks in Taiwan," May 14, 2020, https://cyberint.com/blog/research/targeted-ransomware-attacks-in-taiwan.

10. US Office of the Director of National Intelligence, *Annual Threat Assessment of the U.S. Intelligence Community*, February 2022, https://www.dni.gov/files/ODNI/documents/assessments/ATA-2022-Unclassified-Report.pdf.

11. US Cyber Command, "Achieve and Maintain Cyberspace Superiority," April 2018, https://www.cybercom.mil/Portals/56/Documents/USCYBERCOM%20Vision%20April%202018.pdf.

12. Eric Cheung, Will Ripley, and Gladys Tsai, "How Taiwan Is Trying to Defend Against a Cyber 'World War III,'" CNN, July 23, 2021, https://www.cnn.com/2021/07/23/tech/taiwan-china-cybersecurity-intl-hnk/index.html.

13. Christopher Wray, "Countering Threats Posed by the Chinese Government Inside the US" (speech, Ronald Reagan Presidential Library and Museum, Simi Valley, CA, January 31, 2022), https://www.fbi.gov/news/speeches/countering-threats-posed-by-the-chinese-government-inside-the-us-wray-013122.

14. Taiwan National Center for Cyber Security Technology, "About NCCST," April 21, 2021, https://www.nccst.nat.gov.tw/About?lang=en.

15. Roxanne Heston and Remco Zwetsloot, *Mapping US Multinationals' Global AI R&D Activity*, Georgetown University, Center for Security and Emerging Technology, December 2020, https://cset.georgetown.edu/wp-content/uploads/CSET-Mapping-U.S.-Multinationals-Global-AI-RD-Activity-1.pdf.

16. Matt Sheehan, "Who Benefits from American AI Research in China?," Macro Polo, October 21, 2019, https://macropolo.org/china-ai-research-resnet/?rp=e. See also Microsoft, "Microsoft Research Lab—Asia," https://www.microsoft.com/en-us/research/lab/microsoft-research-asia.

17. Hettie O'Brien, "Here's Looking at You—How China Built Its Great Firewall," *New Statesman*, September 6, 2019, https://www.newstatesman.com/culture/books/2019/09/the-great-firewall-of-china-james-griffiths-review; and Liza Lin and Josh Chin, "U.S. Tech Companies Prop Up China's Vast Surveillance Network," *Wall Street Journal*, November 26, 2019, https://www.wsj.com/articles/u-s-tech-companies-prop-up-chinas-vast-surveillance-network-11574786846.

18. Paul Mozur and Don Clark, "China's Surveillance State Sucks Up Data. US Tech Is Key to Sorting It.," *New York Times*, November 22, 2020, https://www.nytimes.com/2020/11/22/technology/china-intel-nvidia-xinjiang.html; and Sophie Richardson, "Thermo Fisher's Necessary, but Insufficient, Step in China," Human Rights Watch, February 22, 2019, https://www.hrw.org/news/2019/02/22/thermo-fishers-necessary-insufficient-step-china#.

Deterring War over Taiwan:
Some Lessons from Korea and Ukraine

PAUL WOLFOWITZ

The Korean War would never have happened if the Soviet dictator Joseph Stalin had believed the United States would intervene to oppose the North Korean invasion. That war was particularly terrible, and it was no less terrible for being comparatively short. Although most of the fighting ended with an armistice after three years, Xi Jinping would do well to use the Korean War to remember that once you unleash the dogs of war, you unleash havoc—and no one can predict the consequences.

Russia's present difficulties in Ukraine provide a useful reminder as well. As officials in China are reportedly meeting behind closed doors to study a Chinese Communist Party–produced documentary that extols Russian President Vladimir Putin as a hero, the chances of preventing another terrible war in East Asia would be greatly improved if the heroic Ukrainians can be enabled to demonstrate that the Chinese Communist Party's Russian "hero" has clay feet.[1]

Perhaps because it happened almost 70 years ago and didn't go on for 20 years like the post-9/11 wars in Afghanistan and Iraq, many Americans are surprised to learn that in many respects, the Korean War was far worse than either of those more recent two. In those three years, 36,574 Americans died fighting in Korea; in other words, 15 times as many American lives were lost in three years as were lost in Afghanistan in 20, and eight times as many were killed in Korea as in Iraq during the previous 18 years, up until July 2021.[2] Taken together, more than five times as many Americans died in Korea in just three years as in the roughly 20 years of those two more recent wars combined.

Broader measures of the costs of that terrible war only paint an even grimmer picture. Our South Korean allies lost more than 160,000 soldiers killed or missing, and estimates of North Korean losses range from 215,000 to 406,000, although as historian Guenter Lewy notes, "The only hard statistic" for Korean War losses is that of American military deaths.[3] At a ceremony in October 2014 marking the anniversary of China's "volunteers" entering the war, a Chinese official confirmed that there were 197,653 "martyrs of the War to Resist U.S. Aggression and Aid Korea."[4]

Unsurprisingly, however, as so often happens, the civilians suffered the most. As a result of fighting that left "almost every major city in North and South Korea in ruins," Lewy also notes that civilian deaths are estimated at between two and three million, adding up to almost one million military deaths and a possible 2.5 million civilians who were killed or died as a result of what he calls "this extremely destructive conflict."[5]

The geopolitical impact was also earthshaking. The Soviet-backed aggression in Korea, combined with the first Soviet test of a nuclear weapon, raised fears halfway around the world, in Europe, of larger threats backed by Soviet military power. Those fears hastened the completion of a process that had already been underway to create a permanent NATO military organization, based in Europe and commanded by an American general—the Supreme Allied Commander Europe. The first to hold that position, Gen. Dwight Eisenhower, was appointed in December 1950, six months after North Korea's invasion of the South.[6] The war also put in train negotiations about German rearmament, culminating in the Paris Agreements of October 1954 and West Germany joining NATO the following year.[7]

Perhaps most significant was the North Korean invasion's impact on American defense plans and programs. Americans were shocked at being nearly driven off the Korean Peninsula by a poorly equipped military just five years after building their own military into the strongest in world history and defeating the combined strength of the Axis powers. President Harry Truman dismissed Defense Secretary Louis Johnson, who had made himself the target of public anger over the hasty post–World War II dismantling of American military power.[8] The United States Objectives and Programs for National Security (more commonly referred to as NSC-68), the document that became known—with some exaggeration—as the blueprint for US participation in the Cold War, went from being a piece of paper in Secretary of State Dean Acheson's desk to becoming the nation's security strategy.[9] US defense spending shot up from $133 billion in 1950 to $402 billion in 1954 and remained above $300 billion for most of that decade.[10] The Korean War was the true beginning of the Cold War.

Stalin likely did not envision any of those developments when he gave North Korean dictator Kim Il Sung a green light to invade the South.[11] Nor were they likely to have pleased him.

North Korea's invasion also had large consequences in East Asia. It led to a strengthening of ties between the US and Taiwan, with the latter still calling itself the Republic of China (ROC) and claiming to be the legitimate government of all of China. That strengthened relationship was even formalized with the signing of the US-ROC Mutual Defense Treaty in December 1954.[12] The net result was to put US relations with the mainland-based People's Republic of China (PRC) into a kind of deep freeze for almost 20 years, until President Richard Nixon's historic visit to China in 1972.

That particular result was probably not unwelcome for Stalin, but it is a reminder that wars can cause countries to shift alignments in unforeseen ways. Earthshaking geopolitical shocks have follow-on tremors and aftershocks. Stalin's 1939 agreement with Adolf Hitler to carve up Poland following Britain's betrayal of Czechoslovakia at Munich illustrates how large those aftershocks can sometimes be. In the case of a PRC attack on Taiwan, one obvious concern would be that Japan or even South Korea might reconsider its nuclear nonproliferation commitments and reliance on the US to provide nuclear deterrence.

For the past few years, Beijing has been conducting increasingly provocative demonstrations of military power in the vicinity of Taiwan. It has even released footage of "real combat" conducted in Taiwanese airspace.[13] Whether these threatening actions are meant to intimidate the Taiwanese people or dull the sensitivity of Taiwan's warning systems, these threats of force violate the PRC's past promises to pursue a peaceful resolution of the Taiwan issue. These include particularly the PRC's commitment—as part of the 1979 normalization of US-PRC relations—to a peaceful resolution of its disputes with Taiwan, in return for the US renouncing its diplomatic recognition of Taiwan, abrogating the military treaty with the ROC, and removing US troops from the island.[14]

A Chinese invasion would present the greatest threat to global peace in a generation. The US would confront an agonizing dilemma: risk an armed clash between two nuclear superpowers or abandon a free people to Communist tyranny. But there's an alternative—deter the threat by committing to oppose it, by force if necessary.[15]

Deterrence rests on a paradox: The best way to prevent war is to threaten war. The history of the 20th century illustrates what successful deterrence can accomplish. It enabled West Berlin to survive as a free city despite a political status even more ambiguous than Taiwan's and a truly indefensible military position. Cold War history also illustrates a corollary: A failure of resolve can invite catastrophe. The Korean War was preventable, if only the US had made clear beforehand that it would forcefully oppose North Korean aggression.

The Korean War Could Have Been Prevented

Throughout the Cold War, many historians of the "revisionist" school sought to portray the Korean War as a product of a canny plot by the US or its South Korean "puppet" Syngman Rhee to provoke a North Korean attack. It was a thesis that flew in the face of the many statements by senior US officials that the US had no strategic interest in Korea and the evident lack of US armed forces' preparedness for a war on the Korean Peninsula. Soviet documents released in 1995, after the end of the Cold War, should have ended that line of argument. They reveal that Kim—North Korea's first dictator and the grandfather of Kim Jong Un, the current despot— visited Stalin in Moscow in March 1949.[16] The elder Kim spent the better part of that month trying to persuade the Soviet dictator to support an invasion of the South. Stalin, concerned that American troops would "interfere in case of hostilities," rejected the idea.[17]

But Stalin's thinking changed after China fell to the Communist Party in October 1949. According to the documents, the lack of a serious American response to that cataclysmic event demonstrated to the Soviets the "weakness of Asian reactionaries" and their American "mentors," who "left China" without daring "to challenge the new Chinese authorities."[18]

By 1950, US combat forces had left Korea based on the Joint Chiefs of Staff's stated belief that "Korea is of little strategic value" and a commitment to use military force in Korea would be "ill-advised and impracticable."[19] Gen. Douglas MacArthur endorsed that view publicly in a March 1949 interview, as did Secretary of State Acheson in a January 1950 speech.[20]

At that point, citing the "changed international environment,"[21] Stalin invited Kim and his deputy premier and foreign minister, Pak Hon-yong,[22] the founder of the North Korean Communist Party, to visit Moscow, where the pair spent March 30 to April 25 discussing in detail with their Soviet counterparts the strategy and tactics for their planned conquest of South Korea. A lengthy summary of those discussions prepared by the Soviet foreign ministry, which historian Kathryn Weathersby calls the clearest expression of "Stalin's reasoning about the war," explains what Stalin meant by the "changed international situation" that made it possible to support a North Korean invasion.[23] That account also makes clear why Stalin insisted that Kim first obtain Mao Zedong's approval.

Although Secretary Acheson's speech has drawn deserved criticism and is often blamed for inviting the North Korean invasion, that conclusion is at odds with the Soviet summary and reflects a distinct partisan bias by failing to mention MacArthur's earlier interview. Neither Acheson's speech nor MacArthur's interview are mentioned in that Soviet summary of Stalin's monthlong talks with the North Koreans. What the summary emphasized was that the Chinese Communist Party's victory meant that China could devote its attention and energy to the assistance of Korea. Moreover, that victory had "proved the strength of Asian revolutionaries, and shown the weakness of Asian reactionaries and their mentors in the West, in America. Americans left China and did not dare to challenge the new Chinese authorities militarily."[24]

If we were to rewrite those quoted sentences as "Afghanistan proved the strength of Asian extremists and showed the weakness of American puppets and their mentors in the West, in America," and "the Americans left Afghanistan and did not dare to challenge the new Taliban authorities militarily," then the disturbing parallels between Stalin's reasoning about South Korea and Putin's possible reasoning about Ukraine are cause for reflection. Afghanistan and Ukraine are both distant and different from Taiwan, but judgments about American will and resolve formed from those distant places could lead Xi into dangerous miscalculations about the dangers of an attack on Taiwan.

Stalin also referred to "information coming from the United States" showing that "the prevailing mood is not to interfere."[25] Weathersby speculates this may be a reference to knowledge Stalin might have obtained from his British spy in Washington, Donald McLean, who would have been in a position to know about an official White House document labeled NSC-48, which drew the US defense perimeter west of Japan and the Philippines, excluding Korea and the Asian mainland.

Yet even despite these reassuring signs and even after American troops had withdrawn from the peninsula, Stalin remained concerned that an attack might prompt a US intervention and drag the Soviets into a direct conflict with the world's first nuclear power. Since "the USSR was not ready to get involved in Korean affairs directly," in the event that the US did "venture to send troops to Korea," and if Kim were to need reinforcements, he would have to get them from China. Accordingly, Stalin insisted that Kim travel to Beijing to get Mao's approval, which Mao was in no position to refuse since he was heavily dependent on the Soviet Union for both economic and military support.[26] With Mao's approval in hand, Stalin unleashed Kim on South Korea and started a horrible war.

Oddly enough, Stalin approved of a last-minute tactical change from a planned small-scale incursion on the Ongjin peninsula, with the aim of provoking the South Koreans to respond and make them appear responsible for starting the war. Instead, Stalin agreed to an initial overall attack along the whole front line.

As Weathersby notes, while this decision may have been

> sensible from a strictly military point of view, it reflected a disastrous misapprehension of how a World War II–style invasion across the South Korean border would be perceived in the West. Since Stalin had shared with his Western counterparts the trauma of a sudden, massive German attack, his failure to foresee the forebodings such an attack in Korea would immediately evoke in the minds of many of the world's political leaders is all the more striking.[27]

Stalin's spies weren't wrong in their assessment of the American mood. Before the invasion, US political and military leaders considered an invasion of South Korea unlikely and didn't want to defend it in the event of one. But a surprise attack by seven well-equipped North Korean divisions advancing rapidly down the peninsula changed both the strategic and political calculus.

A War over Taiwan Must Be Prevented by Deterrence

Since 1979, when the US normalized relations with Beijing and Congress enacted the Taiwan Relations Act, Washington's relations with Taipei have been ambiguous. Yet an unambiguous deterrence commitment would be fully consistent with the long-standing US position that differences between Taiwan and the mainland need to be resolved peacefully, without the use or threat of force and with no unilateral declaration of Taiwanese independence. Painful though it may be for the Taiwanese to live with their ambiguous international status, preserving peace in the Taiwan Strait and freedom for the Taiwanese people is much more important.

A peaceful resolution seems like a remote prospect today. But the world—and the Chinese people—should be reminded that Xi has made it more remote by eviscerating the concept of "one country, two systems," which Deng Xiaoping originally intended for Taiwan and not just for Hong Kong.

The Taiwan Relations Act provides that "any effort to determine the future of Taiwan by other than peaceful means" will be considered a threat "of grave concern to the United States."[28] To make that part of the law meaningful, the US and Taiwanese militaries need to coordinate planning so that an attack wouldn't overwhelm Taiwan's defenses before help can arrive. It will also require what has been called "thinking more creatively" about nonnuclear options that might cause Xi to recalculate the costs of an attack.[29]

Unfortunately, the threat of economic sanctions and diplomatic pressure will unlikely be sufficient in forcing such a recalculation, given how little impact such measures have had on Chinese actions in Xinjiang and Hong Kong. While the world should do more to compel Xi to honor China's promise of autonomy for Hong Kong and halt the forced detention of Uyghurs in Xinjiang, if the US stands aside and allows Taiwan's autonomy to be crushed by force, the repercussions would be far more severe. It would shake the foundations of security and stability in East Asia.

We can't know how Xi would react to a credible redline (or the failure to draw one). Historical analogies are always imprecise; the Korean scenario was complex, and the situation of Taiwan differs from both Korea and Berlin. And there's no denying that creating redlines entails significant risks. But so can the failure to do so, as the Korean example shows. Continued ambiguity in the face of Xi's escalating rhetoric and provocative movements by his armed forces in the Taiwan Strait presents the greater risk of a confrontation that could be as dangerous as the Cuban missile crisis. That leaves us with the credible threat of military force as the best hope of avoiding war.

Xi must decide whether there will be a war over Taiwan. But as the PRC elevates its military threat to Taiwan, both in word and deed, the US needs to take corresponding steps to elevate and clarify its defense relationship with Taiwan. And deeds may be more important than words.

Much of what is needed flows from ideas laid out in an excellent essay by Dan Blumenthal titled "The U.S.-Taiwan Relationship Needs Alliance Management."[30] Central to his argument is that the US needs a political and strategic framework for its defense relationship with Taiwan and not merely a tactical one built out of individual decisions, mostly about arms sales. The key points that emerge from that essay are as follows.

That political framework would begin with recognition that the PRC has departed fundamentally from the commitment to seek a peaceful resolution of the differences between Taiwan and the mainland, which it made in the three communiqués that provide the foundation of the US-China relationship. To the contrary, the PRC has been going backward, even shredding the promises it made to the people of Hong Kong and the UK concerning the fundamental rights of Hong Kong citizens after Hong Kong's return to China.

In addition to a political framework based on continuing insistence that peaceful resolution is the core principle of the US approach to the Taiwan issue, there needs to be a better framework for managing what is effectively an alliance relationship, although not so designated officially. There appears to be a complacency, bordering on smugness, among government officials and many commentators—here and in Europe—that Putin's "failure" in Ukraine presents a warning to Xi of the dangers he could encounter with an invasion of Taiwan. That is a dangerous illusion and rather premature given that Putin has not yet lost this war, and, unfortunately, it is by no means clear that he will.

Moreover, as Hal Brands points out, the lessons that Xi takes from Ukraine might not be about the hazards Putin's army blundered into. They might be about how to avoid those blunders by attacking successfully by moving quickly with shock and surprise before either the Taiwanese or their American and Japanese friends can even begin to think about coming to Taiwan's aid.[31] Ukraine's heroic President Volodymyr Zelenskyy has frequently criticized the Western failure to provide his country with the weapons they need in a timely fashion.

The delays in providing Ukraine with weapons deemed to be "escalatory" have been costly,[32] and the restrictions on fighter aircraft and ground-based air defenses continue to cause avoidable Ukrainian deaths. As one congressional source told Josh Rogin of the *Washington Post*, more than a month after the start of Putin's invasion,

> The transfer of any system is being closely scrutinized by the White House and National Security Council as to whether or not it meets their test of what's escalatory and what's not. . . . That's causing the system to be constipated.[33]

Fortunately, however, the heroic Ukrainian resistance has bought that country time for the US and Ukraine's other friends to come to their senses about that country's defense needs—much more time than Taiwan could count on having.

Whatever lessons Xi may be drawing from Ukraine, US officials appear to have learned nothing from the costly delays imposed by that vague escalatory standard that delayed or blocked needed weapons for Ukraine. A similar disagreement obstructing the responses to Taiwan's weapons requests is a US demand that Taiwan obtain only what are vaguely defined as "asymmetric capabilities," as though US officials have a better idea than the Taiwanese do about the scenarios they need to prepare for and what their requirements might be to face them.

If Taiwan ends up—six or 12 months from now—facing a situation comparable to what Ukraine faced in February 2022, we will be wishing that we had decided today to enable Taiwan to acquire the weaponry that might deter a future PRC attack. Now is the time to begin addressing Taiwan's defense needs with a sense of urgency. If we wait until after an attack, as we did with Ukraine, it will probably be too late.

There is no other situation comparable to the one with Taiwan, in which the US contemplates possible cooperation with another military with so little interaction among senior decision makers undergirding the planning and procurement process. A better framework is needed to engage strategic and operational thinking at the highest levels among the US and Taiwanese officials who would make some of the most fateful decisions in the event of a crisis. Doing so requires an understanding among the highest levels of government, something that cannot be achieved simply through occasional and often virtual staff talks at lower levels.

There needs to be a better understanding of what Taiwan's real defense needs are. That also entails stockpiling the necessary weapons systems and munitions on the island for Taiwanese use—or American use, in the event that this or some future president decides it is necessary—to intervene before a conflict, deter one, or help defeat one in its early stages.

Instead, it increasingly appears as though the US-Taiwan relationship is fraught with disagreements not unlike those that seem to get in the way of providing Ukraine with weapons that could help it inflict a serious defeat on the Russians—weapons that US bureaucrats have apparently classified as escalatory.

Having summarized the main points in Blumenthal's essay, perhaps it would be appropriate to close this chapter with the following words from a famous American:

> The issues are global and so interlocked that to consider the problems of one sector, oblivious to those of another, is but to court disaster for the whole. While Asia is commonly referred to as the Gateway to Europe, it is no less true that Europe is the Gateway to Asia, and the broad influence of the one cannot fail to have its impact upon the other. There are those who claim our strength is inadequate to protect on both fronts, that we

cannot divide our effort. I can think of no greater expression of defeatism. If a potential enemy can divide his strength on two fronts, it is for us to counter his effort.[34]

No, the above quote is not from the head of the Trilateral Commission or the Council on Foreign Relations. It's from Gen. MacArthur's famous farewell address to a joint session of Congress on April 19, 1951.

Notes

1. Chris Buckley, "Bristling Against the West, China Rallies Domestic Sympathy for Russia," *New York Times*, April 4, 2022, https://www.nytimes.com/2022/04/04/world/asia/china-russia-ukraine.html.

2. US Department of Defense, "Freedom Is Not Free: Take a Look Inside the Korean War Veterans Memorial," https://www.defense.gov/Experience/Korean-War-Memorial.

3. Defense Casualty Analysis System, "U.S. Military Casualties—Korean War Casualty Summary," April 7, 2022, https://dcas.dmdc.osd.mil/dcas/pages/report_korea_sum.xhtml; Alan R. Millett, "Korean War," *Encyclopedia Britannica*, https://www.britannica.com/event/Korean-War; and Guenter Lewy, *America in Vietnam* (Oxford, UK: Oxford University Press, 1980), 450.

4. *China Daily*, "China Holds Burial Ceremony for Soldier Remains Returned from ROK," April 2, 2016, https://www.chinadaily.com.cn/china/2016-04/02/content_24248911.htm; Xinhua News Agency, "Silent Tribute Paid to Martyrs in War to Resist U.S. Aggression and Aid Korea," October 23, 2020, http://www.news.cn/english/2020-10/23/c_139460878.htm; and Xu Yang, "kang mei yuan chao lie shi xin que ren wei 197653 ren Fu jun zhang er zi dao ching" [The Newly Confirmed Number of Martyrs Sacrificed in the War to Resist US Aggression and Aid Korea is 197653. The Son of the Deputy Commander Was Present], People's Daily Online, October 30, 2014, http://world.people.com.cn/n/2014/1030/c1002-25939560.html. Title and quotation translated by Cindy Chen.

5. Lewy, *America in Vietnam*.

6. North Atlantic Treaty Organization, "NATO Leaders: Dwight D. Eisenhower," November 23, 2016, https://www.nato.int/cps/en/natohq/declassified_137961.htm.

7. Helga Haftendorn, "Germany's Accession to NATO: 50 Years On," North Atlantic Treaty Organization, June 1, 2005, https://www.nato.int/docu/review/articles/2005/06/01/germanys-accession-to-nato-50-years-on/index.html.

8. Office of the Secretary of Defense, Historical Office, "Louis A. Johnson," https://history.defense.gov/Multimedia/Biographies/Article-View/Article/571265/louis-a-johnson.

9. US Department of State, Office of the Historian, "NSC-68, 1950," https://history.state.gov/milestones/1945-1952/NSC68.

10. Martin Calhoun, "U.S. Military Spending, 1945–1996," Center for Defense Information, July 9, 1996, http://academic.brooklyn.cuny.edu/history/johnson/milspend.htm.

11. PBS, "The Korean War," https://www.pbs.org/wgbh/americanexperience/features/bomb-korean-war.

12. Yale Law School, Lillian Goldman Law Library, Avalon Project, "Mutual Defense Treaty Between the United States and the Republic of China; December 2, 1954," https://avalon.law.yale.edu/20th_century/chin001.asp.

13. *Daily Mail*, "China Releases Footage of Its Troops Conducting Live-Fire Drill near Taiwan After President Xi Ordered His Soldiers to Be Prepared for War 'at All Times,'" January 14, 2021, https://www.dailymail.co.uk/news/article-9147009/China-releases-footage-troops-conducting-live-fire-drill-near-Taiwan.html.

14. Dan Blumenthal, "The U.S.-Taiwan Relationship Needs Alliance Management," *National Interest*, December 18, 2021, https://nationalinterest.org/feature/us-taiwan-relationship-needs-alliance-management-198147.

15. This paragraph and some other portions of the present chapter were taken from an earlier article by the author. See Paul Wolfowitz, "The Korean War's Lesson for Taiwan," *Wall Street Journal*, October 13, 2020, https://www.wsj.com/articles/the-korean-wars-lesson-for-taiwan-11602628554.

16. Wilson Center, Digital Archive, "March 05, 1949 Notes of the Conversation Between Comrade I.V. Stalin and a Governmental Delegation from the Democratic People's Republic of Korea Headed by Kim Il Sung," https://digitalarchive.wilsoncenter.org/document/112127.pdf.

17. Wolfowitz, "The Korean War's Lesson for Taiwan."

18. Wolfowitz, "The Korean War's Lesson for Taiwan."

19. Daniel C. Sneider, "The United States and Northeast Asia: The Cold War Legacy," in *Cross Currents: Regionalism and Nationalism in Northeast Asia* (Stanford, CA: Shorenstein Asia-Pacific Research Center, 2007), 259, https://fsi-live.s3.us-west-1.amazonaws.com/s3fs-public/11_Sneider_FINAL_CC2007.pdf.

20. Wolfowitz, "The Korean War's Lesson for Taiwan."

21. Kathryn Weathersby, "'Should We Fear This?' Stalin and the Danger of War with America" (working paper, Wilson Center, Washington, DC, July 2002), 11, https://www.wilsoncenter.org/sites/default/files/media/documents/publication/ACFAEF.pdf.

22. That trip proved fatal for Pak Hon-yong, since Kim Il Sung blamed him in 1953 for the failure of the North Korean invasion and accused him of being a spy for the United States and Japan. That earned Pak the dubious distinction of becoming victim to the last show trial in North Korean history. (That regime subsequently decided it is better for its victims to disappear without a trace.) Pak was sentenced to death and subsequently executed, despite appeals for clemency from China and the Soviet Union. Andrei Lankov, *The Real North Korea: Life and Politics in the Failed Stalinist Utopia* (Oxford, UK: Oxford University Press, 2014), 45–46.

23. Weathersby, "'Should We Fear This?,'" 16.

24. Quoted in Weathersby, "'Should We Fear This?,'" 9.

25. Weathersby, "'Should We Fear This?'"

26. Weathersby, "'Should We Fear This?'"

27. Weathersby, "'Should We Fear This?,'" 15.

28. Taiwan Relations Act, 22 USC § 3301 et seq. (1979), https://www.ait.org.tw/our-relationship/policy-history/key-u-s-foreign-policy-documents-region/taiwan-relations-act.

29. Michèle A. Flournoy, "How to Prevent a War in Asia," *Foreign Affairs*, June 18, 2020, https://www.foreignaffairs.com/articles/united-states/2020-06-18/how-prevent-war-asia.

30. Blumenthal, "The U.S.-Taiwan Relationship Needs Alliance Management."

31. Hal Brands, "Putin's Struggles in Ukraine May Embolden Xi on Taiwan," Bloomberg Opinion, April 21, 2022, https://www.bloomberg.com/opinion/articles/2022-04-21/russia-ukraine-war-putin-s-struggles-may-embolden-xi-s-china-on-taiwan.

32. Josh Rogin, "Ukraine Needs Better Air Defense Systems, Not More Excuses," *Washington Post*, March 31, 2022, https://www.washingtonpost.com/opinions/2022/03/31/us-nato-slovakia-ukraine-s300-air-missile-defense-russia.

33. Rogin, "Ukraine Needs Better Air Defense Systems, Not More Excuses."

34. American Rhetoric, "General Douglas MacArthur Farwell Speech to Congress," April 19, 1951, https://www.americanrhetoric.com/speeches/douglasmacarthur farewelladdress.htm.

About the Authors

Michael Beckley is a nonresident senior fellow at the American Enterprise Institute, where his research focuses on US-China competition, long-term trends in the US-China power balance, US alliances and grand strategy, and US economic and defense policy in East Asia. Concurrently, he is an associate professor at Tufts University.

Dan Blumenthal is a senior fellow at AEI and author of *The China Nightmare: The Grand Ambitions of a Decaying State* (AEI Press, 2020).

Hal Brands is a senior fellow at the American Enterprise Institute, where he studies US foreign policy and defense strategy. Concurrently, Brands is the Henry A. Kissinger Distinguished Professor of Global Affairs at the Johns Hopkins School of Advanced International Studies. He is also a columnist for Bloomberg Opinion.

Elisabeth Braw is a senior fellow at the American Enterprise Institute, where she focuses on defense against emerging national security challenges, such as hybrid and gray-zone threats. Concurrently, she is a columnist with *Foreign Policy*, where she writes on national security and the globalized economy, and a member of the UK National Preparedness Commission.

Emily Coletta was a project manager and research associate at the American Enterprise Institute, where her work focused on defense budgeting and strategy. She led the Defense Futures Simulator project.

Zack Cooper is a senior fellow at the American Enterprise Institute where he studies US strategy and alliances in Asia. He also teaches at Princeton University, codirects the Alliance for Securing Democracy, and cohosted the *Net Assessment* podcast. He previously served in the Pentagon and White House.

Giselle Donnelly is a senior fellow in defense and national security at the American Enterprise Institute, where she focuses on national security and military strategy, operations, programs, and defense budgets.

Mackenzie Eaglen is a senior fellow at the American Enterprise Institute, where she works on defense strategy, defense budgets, and military readiness.

John G. Ferrari is a nonresident senior fellow at the American Enterprise Institute and the former director of program analysis and evaluation for the US Army. He is a retired US Army major general.

Olivia Garard was a research contributor for the American Enterprise Institute. She served as an active duty officer in the US Marine Corps from 2014 to 2020 and holds a master's degree in war studies from King's College London and an undergraduate degree in philosophy from Princeton University. She attended St. John's College Graduate Institute. She recently published her first book, *An Annotated Guide to Tactics: Carl von Clausewitz's Theory of the Combat* (Marine Corps University Press, 2021), and tweets at @teaandtactics.

Sheena Chestnut Greitens is a Jeane Kirkpatrick Visiting Fellow at the American Enterprise Institute, where she focuses on China and East Asia, Indo-Pacific security, and authoritarianism and democracy in Asia. Concurrently, she is a tenured associate professor at the Lyndon B. Johnson School of Public Affairs at the University of Texas at Austin and director of the Asia Policy Program at the Clements Center for National Security and the Strauss Center for International Security and Law. She is currently writing a book on how internal security considerations shape Chinese grand strategy.

Blake Herzinger was a nonresident fellow at the American Enterprise Institute and is a research fellow at the United States Studies Centre in Sydney, Australia. He served as an intelligence officer in the US Navy, before transitioning to the Navy Reserves, where he continues to serve. Herzinger spent 11 years living in East and Southeast Asia working on security assistance and regional strategy. All opinions are his own and do not reflect those of the US government or Department of Defense.

Frederick W. Kagan is a senior fellow and the director of the Critical Threats Project at AEI. He was previously an associate professor of military history at West Point. He holds a PhD in Russian and Soviet military history from Yale University.

Klon Kitchen is a senior nonresident fellow at the American Enterprise Institute, where he focuses on the intersection of national security and defense technologies and innovation. Through his research, he works to understand and explain how emerging technologies are shaping modern statecraft, intelligence, and warfighting while focusing on cybersecurity, artificial intelligence, robotics, and quantum sciences.

Elaine McCusker is a senior fellow at the American Enterprise Institute (AEI), where she focuses on defense strategy, budget, and innovation; the US military; and national security. Before joining AEI, she served as deputy and then acting undersecretary of defense (comptroller) from August 2017 to June 2020.

Michael Rubin is a senior fellow at the American Enterprise Institute.

Kori Schake is a senior fellow and the director of Foreign and Defense Policy studies at the American Enterprise Institute.

Allison Schwartz was a research and communications associate at the American Enterprise Institute. She received her master's degree from Georgetown's Security Studies Program.

Paul Wolfowitz was a senior fellow at the American Enterprise Institute, where he worked on development and national security issues, and a distinguished visiting fellow at the Hoover Institution.

RESEARCH STAFF

SAMUEL J. ABRAMS
Nonresident Senior Fellow

BETH AKERS
Senior Fellow

J. JOEL ALICEA
Nonresident Fellow

JOSEPH ANTOS
*Senior Fellow; Wilson H. Taylor
Scholar in Health Care and
Retirement Policy*

LEON ARON
Senior Fellow

KIRSTEN AXELSEN
Nonresident Fellow

JOHN P. BAILEY
Nonresident Senior Fellow

CLAUDE BARFIELD
Senior Fellow

MICHAEL BARONE
Senior Fellow Emeritus

ROBERT J. BARRO
Nonresident Senior Fellow

MICHAEL BECKLEY
Nonresident Senior Fellow

ERIC J. BELASCO
Nonresident Senior Fellow

ANDREW G. BIGGS
Senior Fellow

MASON M. BISHOP
Nonresident Fellow

JASON BLESSING
*Jeane Kirkpatrick Visiting
Research Fellow*

DAN BLUMENTHAL
Senior Fellow

KARLYN BOWMAN
*Distinguished Senior
Fellow Emeritus*

HAL BRANDS
Senior Fellow

ELISABETH BRAW
Senior Fellow

ALEX BRILL
Senior Fellow

ARTHUR C. BROOKS
President Emeritus

RICHARD BURKHAUSER
Nonresident Senior Fellow

JAMES C. CAPRETTA
Senior Fellow; Milton Friedman Chair

TIMOTHY P. CARNEY
Senior Fellow

AMITABH CHANDRA
Nonresident Fellow

LYNNE V. CHENEY
Distinguished Senior Fellow

JAMES W. COLEMAN
Nonresident Senior Fellow

MATTHEW CONTINETTI
*Senior Fellow; Patrick and
Charlene Neal Chair in
American Prosperity*

ZACK COOPER
Senior Fellow

JAY COST
*Gerald R. Ford Nonresident
Senior Fellow*

DANIEL A. COX
Senior Fellow

SADANAND DHUME
Senior Fellow

GISELLE DONNELLY
Senior Fellow

MICHAEL BRENDAN
DOUGHERTY
Nonresident Fellow

ROSS DOUTHAT
Nonresident Fellow

COLIN DUECK
Nonresident Senior Fellow

MACKENZIE EAGLEN
Senior Fellow

NICHOLAS EBERSTADT
*Henry Wendt Chair in
Political Economy*

MAX EDEN
Research Fellow

JEFFREY EISENACH
Nonresident Senior Fellow

EMILY ESTELLE
Research Fellow

ANDREW FERGUSON
Nonresident Fellow

JESÚS FERNÁNDEZ-
VILLAVERDE
John H. Makin Visiting Scholar

JOHN G. FERRARI
Nonresident Senior Fellow

JOHN C. FORTIER
Senior Fellow

AARON FRIEDBERG
Nonresident Senior Fellow

JOSEPH B. FULLER
Nonresident Senior Fellow

SCOTT GANZ
Research Fellow

R. RICHARD GEDDES
Nonresident Senior Fellow

ROBERT P. GEORGE
Nonresident Senior Fellow

JOSEPH W. GLAUBER
Nonresident Senior Fellow

JONAH GOLDBERG
*Senior Fellow; Asness Chair
in Applied Liberty*

BARRY K. GOODWIN
Nonresident Senior Fellow

SCOTT GOTTLIEB, MD
Senior Fellow

PHIL GRAMM
Nonresident Senior Fellow

WILLIAM C. GREENWALT
Nonresident Senior Fellow

SHEENA CHESTNUT
GREITENS
Jeane Kirkpatrick Visiting Fellow

JIM HARPER
Nonresident Senior Fellow

WILLIAM HAUN
Nonresident Fellow

BLAKE HERZINGER
Nonresident Fellow

FREDERICK M. HESS
*Senior Fellow; Director,
Education Policy Studies*

BRONWYN HOWELL
Nonresident Senior Fellow

R. GLENN HUBBARD
Nonresident Senior Fellow

HOWARD HUSOCK
Senior Fellow

BENEDIC N. IPPOLITO
Senior Fellow

TAMAR JACOBY
Nonresident Fellow

MARK JAMISON
Nonresident Senior Fellow

FREDERICK W. KAGAN
*Senior Fellow; Director,
Critical Threats Project*

STEVEN B. KAMIN
Senior Fellow

LEON R. KASS, MD
Senior Fellow Emeritus

JOSHUA T. KATZ
Senior Fellow

KLON KITCHEN
Nonresident Senior Fellow

KEVIN R. KOSAR
Senior Fellow

ROBERT KULICK
Visiting Fellow

PAUL H. KUPIEC
Senior Fellow

DESMOND LACHMAN
Senior Fellow

DANIEL LYONS
Nonresident Senior Fellow

Printed in the USA
CPSIA information can be obtained
at www.ICGtesting.com
JSHW020037270224
58096JS00004B/189